Forging Peace in Southeast Asia

Peace and Security in the 21st Century Series

Until recently, security was defined mostly in geopolitical terms with the assumption that it could only be achieved through at least the threat of military force. Today, however, people from as different backgrounds as planners in the Pentagon and veteran peace activists think in terms of human or global security, where no one is secure unless everyone is secure in all areas of their lives. This means that it is impossible nowadays to separate issues of war and peace, the environment, sustainability, identity, global health, and the like.

The books in the series aim to make sense of this changing world of peace and security by investigating security issues and peace efforts that involve cooperation at several levels. By looking at how security and peace interrelate at various stages of conflict, the series explore new ideas for a fast changing world and seeks to redefine and rethink what peace and security mean in the first decades of the new century.

Multidisciplinary in approach and authorship, the books cover a variety of topics, focusing on the overarching theme that students, scholars, practitioners, and policymakers have to find new models and theories to account for, diagnose, and respond to the difficulties of a more complex world. Authors are established scholars and practitioners in their fields of expertise.

In addition, it is hoped that the series will contribute to bringing together authors and readers in concrete, applied projects, and thus help create, under the sponsorship of Alliance for Peacebuilding (AfP), a community of practice.

The series is sponsored by the Alliance for Peacebuilding:

http://www.allianceforpeacebuilding.org/ and edited by Charles Hauss, Government Liaison.

Forging Peace in Southeast Asia

Insurgencies, Peace Processes, and Reconciliation

Zachary Abuza

ROWMAN & LITTLEFIELD
Lanham • Boulder • New York • London

Published by Rowman & Littlefield
A wholly owned subsidiary of The Rowman & Littlefield Publishing Group, Inc.
4501 Forbes Boulevard, Suite 200, Lanham, Maryland 20706
www.rowman.com

Unit A, Whitacre Mews, 26-34 Stannary Street, London SE11 4AB

British Library Cataloguing in Publication Information Available

Library of Congress Cataloging-in-Publication Data

Names: Abuza, Zachary, author.
Title: Forging peace in Southeast Asia : insurgencies, peace processes, and reconciliation / Zachary
    Abuza.
Description: Lanham, Maryland : Rowman & Littlefield, 2016. | Includes bibliographical references
    and index.
Identifiers: LCCN 2016027417 (print) | LCCN 2016038651 (ebook) | ISBN 9781442257559 (cloth :
    alk. paper) | ISBN 9781442257566 (pbk. : alk. paper) | ISBN 9781442257573 (electronic)
Subjects: LCSH: Peace-building--Southeast Asia--Case studies. | Insurgency--Southeast Asia--Case
    studies. | Reconciliation--Southeast Asia--Case studies. | Gerakan Aceh Merdeka. | Moro Nation-
    al Liberation Front. | Moro Islamic Liberation Front. | Barisan Revolusi Nasional Coordinate.
Classification: LCC JZ5584.A785 A38 2016 (print) | LCC JZ5584.A785 (ebook) | DDC 303.6/
    60959--dc23

Printed in the United States of America

Contents

Acknowledgments

There is nothing harder than a peace process. But writing about them sometimes feels like a close second. There are so many narratives, contradictory facts, dissonant information, and deep-seated beliefs and passions. Trying to step back and write a balanced approach that takes the perspectives of all sides into consideration is a hard task, and I could not have done it without the support and help of many people. Over the years I have conducted hundreds of interviews with activists, separatists, government officials, lawyers, negotiators, journalists, and victims. I am truly grateful to all those who sat down and talked with me.

In particular, I need to thank a handful of people who played formative roles in this research. I am indebted to the support and mentorship of Eugene Martin, who headed the Philippine Facilitation Project at the US Institute of Peace before passing away in 2011. My friend and colleague Dean Benedicto "Benny" Baccani is the most passionate peace activist I know. His Institute of Autonomy and Governance has been a forward-leaning NGO, and his wise counsel to me over the years was invaluable. I would also like to thank Abhoud Sayed Lingga of the Institute of Bangsamoro Studies. W. Scott Thompson has been a loyal friend and supporter of this and other projects in the Philippines.

In Thailand, I need to single out two friends and colleagues, Noi Thammarat and Don Pathan, who have served in turn as journalists trying to expose the injustices in the south, mentors and civil society conveyors, and human rights and peace advocates. Their assistance has been invaluable over the years. I would also like to thank friends Rungrawee Chalermsripinyorat, Matt Wheeler of the International Crisis Group, and Tony Davis of Jane's for their thoughts and wise counsel.

The USIP supported early portions of this research during my 2004–2005 fellowship. I would also like to thank Allan Song of the Smith Richardson Foundation for supporting early rounds of research that went into this book project. Dr. Stephen Metz of the US Army War College's Security Studies Institute supported spinoff projects and has been a staunch supporter of my work over the years. Dr. Maria Rasmussen of the Naval Postgraduate School invited me to work on a Minerva Project that allowed me to gain further insights into the peace process in southern Thailand. Ms. Susan Stipanovich of the Institute of National Security Studies Project on Irregular Warfare at the National Defense University also helped to support fieldwork in southern Thailand.

At the National War College, I would like to thank the Commandant Brigadier General Darren Hartford, Dr. David Tretler, and Colonel Troy Perry for giving me the time to finish this important project. Dr. Desaix "Terry" Myers shared lots of recollections of his experiences in East Timor and Aceh, which were invaluable in helping my understanding. Most of all, I would like to thank Dr. Cynthia Watson for her untiring support, counsel, and feedback on the manuscript. She has been a friend and mentor to whom I am deeply grateful.

I would like to thank Marie-Claire Antoine of Rowman & Littlefield for all of her encouragement, support, and firm prodding in getting this project from inception to completion. It was an absolute pleasure working with her.

Bits and pieces of the book have appeared in various publications. I would like to thank James Giggacher and Mish Khan at New Mandala, the Coral Bell School of Asia Pacific Affairs, Australian National University; Phuong Nguyen at the Center for Strategic and International Studies, Southeast Asia Program; Alec Forrs at the Institute of Defense and Policy Studies in Sweden; Sanitsuda Ekachai of the *Bangkok Post*; and Prashanth Parameswaran at *The Diplomat*.

One person deserves special mention, my dear friend Dr. Bridget Welsh, the most accomplished Southeast Asianist that I know; a true friend, who has kept me focused and helped me hone my research. I could not have done it without her unwavering support.

Finally, I need to thank my family, wife Junko and children Taeko and Charley for their support and understanding. In a way, I have been working on this book their entire lifetime. I was often away for long periods of time, but I was never not thinking of you. I've loved being able to talk to you about war, peace, politics, justice and rights, and I know that you will build on these lessons. It's a hard row to hoe, but it is the right row.

Chapter One

Introduction

Forging Peace in Southeast Asia

Nothing is harder than a peace process. After a protracted conflict that has created thousands of casualties, often one that has been a multigenerational fight, that has seen egregious human rights abuses by all sides, far from the media or diplomatic attention, and that has inflamed passions, reinforced zero-sum worldviews, and embedded beliefs and historical narratives, making concessions is not easy. Negotiations leave constituents feeling betrayed, feeling that their sacrifices have been for nought, and having grieving widows and parents to explain to. Vested interests in continued conflict may threaten, and hard-line rivals wait in the wings, hoping to spoil the peace process and garner support in their bid for power and more resources. A multigenerational conflict has created its own historical narrative and realities, often reinforced by large-scale displacement. Conflicts legitimize the current power structure and often gut the traditional social fabric.

Peace processes require enormous political commitments, the right political environments, the right external security and diplomatic environments, certain social conditions, and a massive amount of luck. That peace processes happen at all is almost a miracle. And that some succeed takes an amazing confluence of events. The stars truly have to align.

While the potential for a peace process is enormous in terms of ending fighting that is costly in both blood and treasure and delivering an equitable peace and the hope for reconciliation and development, both sides are subject to enormous risks.

RISKS AND COSTS TO THE STATE

A state faces numerous risks in entering a peace process. It is often said that an insurgent group does not have to win—it's enough for them not to lose. By surviving they can deny the government a clear-cut military victory, provide it with no easy off-ramp, and compel it to make concessions.

The greatest threat, of course, is the potential for secession: the loss of sovereign territory. Regardless of regime type, the loss of sovereign territory would pose an enormous challenge to any government. Patriots always warn that the loss of any territory represents an existential threat to the state.

One way to think of this is that the government is already past a certain threshold. This is a rebellion that, on a scale needed for civil war, is simply not feasible in most cases. But here it is, and strong enough that it cannot be militarily defeated and must be negotiated with. This is well beyond the Webberean notion of the state, that which has a monopoly of coercive force.

While a negotiated settlement may potentially preclude a region from breaking away, that is far from certain. Peace processes in East Timor and South Sudan both led to the eventual formation of independent states. In both cases, the governments negotiated with secessionist rebels, agreeing to a popular referendum on independence.

Even with no process in place for a referendum, if a rebel group successfully negotiates autonomy, that could lead to the de facto breakup of the state. While some autonomy agreements are on paper only, others are very successful. Small regions that are bound by a shared ethnicity, language, history, and religion may prove to be more comfortable than a larger multiethnic state. Geography, too, can be a factor; some regions are simply more governable than others. They might have a strategic port or waterway or other geographical feature that gives them some sort of strength. And it's quite possible that they receive more resources to set up governing institutions from the international community that is trying to support the peace process. Even if rebel groups are unable to win independence, by negotiating an autonomy agreement, they may be sowing the seeds of future independence. And that certainly is going to weigh heavily on the minds of those in government, the military, and parliament who oppose any negotiated settlement.

Obviously, the potential exists for the loss of natural resources and revenue for the state. One of the major grievances that propel rebel groups into fighting is the lack of shared wealth from natural resources extracted from their homeland. Every rebel group believes, often with more than sufficient grounds, that its constituents have been exploited by the central government, that a process of internal colonialism is in place through which the group is sure resources have been exploited by the voracious central government. Paul Collier and his World Bank team found that the single greatest cause of insurgency or rebellion against a central government was control over natural resources.[1] Thus, any negotiated settlement will be partly about the sharing of resources if not the total loss of them and other revenue streams.

But the real risk for any government is that a peace process with one ethnic group or inhabitants of one particular region will lead to others demanding the same treatment. Why them and not us? In the case of Indonesia, East Timor's successful negotiation for a referendum empowered the rebels in Aceh and fuels separatists in the Free Papua Movement in the resource-rich province of Irian Jaya. A peace process creates an incredibly dangerous precedent and, in the eyes of some, inevitable centrifugal forces that will lead to the weakening of central government authority at the least or the breakup of the state at the extreme.

A government also shoulders other risks. Insurgencies tend to take place in the developing world, where government and political institutions are relatively weak. The government may have to contend with challenges from political opponents, including those using extralegal means. In some countries, the military or security service may present the constant threat of a coup d'état and justify its actions in the name of defending the territorial integrity of the state.

For political leaders, a peace process entails great personal risk. They will make enemies, plenty of them. A peace process could simply mean the end of their careers. The risk of a revolt by hard-liners from their own government or of a coup d'état is a sword of Damocles. Or worse. No one wants to be the next Anwar Sadat or Yitzhak Rabin. Making peace requires enormous political courage, something that most political leaders do not have an excess of.

RISKS AND COSTS TO THE REBELS

The decision by a rebel group to enter into a peace process poses a far greater risk than it does to the government. A peace process potentially poses an existential threat to an insurgent movement. At the end of the peace process, a government will still be a government, though it may relinquish some powers to autonomous government. But the state will continue to exist and in many ways emerges stronger because of it. The state is no longer draining resources on an intractable conflict, it garners diplomatic goodwill, and accommodating an aggrieved minority makes the government stronger and more accountable. By contrast, a peace process will fundamentally transform an insurgent group. Even the decision to enter a peace process is likely to be an extremely contentious decision. Hard-liners will always be there to reject any negotiated settlement as a betrayal of their cause, and although hard-liners on the government's side reject any compromise with a rebel group as a threat to national sovereignty or the constitution, the reality is that they lose a political challenge to the state but not an existential one. If a hard-line faction from a rebel movement defects, it could take with it a critical mass of the movement's capabilities, whether it be men, arms, or external support. Indeed, no other issue is more likely to cause internal dissension within a rebel group than the decision to start a peace process.

A peace process transforms an insurgency in many other ways. The *raison d'être* of a militant movement is to fight. Most guerrilla movements have few other capabilities or resources. With a cease-fire comes the loss of control over their constituency. Cease-fires invariably lead to trade, commerce, and the flow of people across what had been front lines. Control over the flow of information gives way, but more importantly, the rebel constituents begin to see how far behind they have fallen because of the conflict. Materially, they are less well off and seek to improve their livelihoods. Their willingness to support a rebel movement through taxes or conscription declines. And while the social services provided by a government may be wanting, they remain far better than anything the rebels have ever provided. The expectations for a peace dividend are very high; the rebel movement would alienate the population if the peace process broke down and hostilities renewed. The insurgent movement must fundamentally transform itself from a fighting force into a political movement that must now govern and provide basic social services. Of course, all insurgencies are political in nature, and most have dedicated political arms and cadres. But the reality is that the political arms of most insurgencies are woefully underdeveloped and resourced; they serve the armed wing, not the other way around, in a classic Maoist sense. Some movements are able to make the transition to peacefully contested politics and governance. But most do not, for making such a transition requires a completely different skill set. What is needed to be a successful guerrilla is very different from reaching compromise, the pacific settlement of disputes, rule by law, and civil administration. Or even if a rebel group is largely able to make that transition, many guerrilla leaders will not, and they stand to lose significant political and economic power.

As part of most peace processes, insurgents have to demobilize and disarm. Some former combatants are then integrated into the national military or police force. Invariably, these are the best-trained and disciplined men. Most insurgencies have to either surrender their weapons or put them beyond use. This fundamentally weakens an insurgency. They have taken the ability to resort to armed hostilities, should the peace process break down, off the table. Even a protracted peace process fundamentally weakens an insurgent group's operational capacity. Insurgents do not have the luxury of having the time or the resources for the training of their combatants; they learn by fighting. Thus, any peace process weakens their military effectiveness and the imperative to maintain discipline, a steady flow of funds, and black market sources of weapons and ammunition.

Beyond a peace dividend, the leaders of an insurgency have to manage expectations. This is almost an impossible task. Their former combatants and veterans will expect to be given jobs or be provided for as a reward for their service and sacrifice, but while governments may induct some into their security services, it is a relatively small number. In the case of East Timor, former Revolutionary Front for an Independent East Timor (FRETILIN) resistance fighters mutinied against the newly independent Timorese government when they were not given jobs in the security forces. The populace will expect that a cease-fire will rapidly improve the livelihoods and welfare of the people. And when former insurgent leaders are unable to deliver on these, the people will question the leaders' legitimacy. Few insurgents successfully transition into political leaders and competent administrators.

Both governments and peacemakers (domestic or third party) must recognize that the peace process in itself poses an existential threat to a rebel group. They will emerge from a peace process fundamentally different and in most cases militarily and politically weaker. While this might seem appealing to those on the government side, if the rebels are too weak, it could pose a threat to the implementation of the peace process and lead to further insecurity.

RISKS AND COSTS OF NOT NEGOTIATING

While both rebels and governments incur risks and costs for negotiating, they also face, of course, risks and costs for not seeking a negotiated settlement. The most obvious is blood and treasure. War is costly. As the old saying goes, an expensive peace is cheaper than a cheap war. Indeed, there is no greater cost on a society than war. People die, those who are wounded cause undue burdens on fragile health-care systems, and refugees and displaced peoples tax limited resources.

War inevitably leads to high opportunity costs. War takes people out of the workforce through conscription or voluntary military service, adversely affects agriculture and business, and destroys infrastructure while governments fail to invest in critical infrastructure during hostilities. Taxes rise during wartime, but they go to the sector of the economy that not only generates no economic return but indeed gives a negative return on investment. Bullets and bombs cannot be reused. The public investment in a school, a road, or a power plant will generate a virtuous cycle of growth. Yet during war, governments and rebels alike dedicate their limited resources to the military effort. All other sectors, in particular health and human services, education, and physical infrastructure, all of which are the foundations for economic growth and development, are ignored. By every measure of human development, war-torn regions or those subject to endemic insecurity are the poorest parts of what are frequently poor countries to start with.

But conflict also has other costs. Thucydides noted that war fundamentally transformed societies. Most societies emerge from conflict, in particular protracted conflict, weaker. The social contract between citizen and state erodes, and the ideals and values on which the state is founded are corrupted. As Stewart Patrick puts it, states that don't reach settlements are likely to be less inclusive, and "regimes that institutionalize policies of exclusion, discrimination, and repression against particular communal groups are likewise vulnerable."[2]

And unlike a breakup after a failed romance, time does not make it easier. Indeed, as a conflict drags on and becomes a multigenerational struggle, both the emotional stakes and the vested interests in prolonging the conflict only seem to grow. Time does not heal all wounds.

And the risks and costs of not negotiating are real. When you go to war, you are rolling the dice. The decision to continue a conflict could potentially lead to the end of the state or the rebel movement.

A protracted conflict and battlefield stalemate, with the knowledge that resources are scarce and running out, very often leads one side to take undue military risks to achieve a crippling defeat of the adversary. The French had ample opportunities to negotiate with Ho Chi Minh but refused. They gambled everything on the battle of Dien Bien Phu in 1954. They not only lost the battle, they lost their colonies in Southeast Asia and, ultimately, their colonial empire.

While it's highly unlikely that a state would cease to exist, it does run the risk of losing territory with all the political baggage that entails. Short of state collapse is the palpable risk of regime collapse. And seeing that too many governments in the world equate regime survival with national survival, the decision to go to war or continue armed conflict should weigh heavily on national leaders.

The risk to an insurgent group is much greater. The group is limited in size, scope, and resources. The state that it is fighting is invariably stronger with far more resources at its command. If a state is short of resources, it can go to allies or even capital markets to raise the requisite funds. States have a steady supply of weaponry and ammunition. Even if the security forces of a state are incompetent, poorly disciplined, and third rate, over time they can wear down a rebel movement through attrition.

And of course, the greatest risk to not negotiating for a rebel movement is military defeat. While governments do not often thoroughly defeat rebel movements, it does happen. In Sri Lanka, the Tamil Tigers' hard-line position over post-tsunami aid and development funds in 2005 led to not just a resumption of war but ultimately the group's complete annihilation by 2009.

But at the very least, the continuation of armed conflict can lead to the systematic degradation of the movement.

Of course, both rebel movements and governments face the risk of losing the support of their constituency by prolonging the conflict. Wars are costly. But it can be worse for rebel movements, as they always represent themselves as a vanguard of society and overestimate their degree of popular support. Governments, too, may overestimate their degree of popular support, but at the end of the day, they have more resources to use in buying off the population with social services and other goods and programs.

Rebels might have an ability to seize territory, but they rarely have the ability to hold it, let alone effectively administer it. In many ways, the best that they can do is to make a region ungovernable for the state. But the gradual erosion of territory by state forces does delegitimize rebel movements in the eyes of their population. This was clearly the case in Sri Lanka, where the Tamil Tigers protostate was not just a source of legitimacy for the movement but, once the Mahinda Rajapakse government came to office, the primary target of the military despite high civilian casualties.

RISKS AND COSTS OF PEACE

Counterintuitively, a negotiated settlement also has risks and costs. Obviously, the state has the palpable fear that a negotiated settlement with one ethnic group or region will lead to demands from other minorities or regions for similar political rights, economic privileges, and control over resources. But decentralization is not always a bad thing; most states are overcentralized to start with.

The greatest risk, of course, is not that a peace process succeeds and creates a contagion effect but that it will fail. Even successfully negotiated peace processes are incredibly fragile. Indeed, the empirical evidence suggests that it will. Postconflict situations are extremely fragile, and a large percentage revert to violence within a decade. Paul Collier estimates the reversion rate to be 40 percent. Stewart Patrick's data set suggests 44 percent.[3] Despite a large-scale intervention by the United Nations, including the holding of a referendum on independence, East Timor quickly reverted to violence. Countries that have had a civil war are more susceptible to having another one.

Peace agreements can be poorly implemented, leading one side or another to quit the peace process. We saw this in the Philippines. Or a critical mass of spoilers can opt out and continue the conflict. This is what happened in Cambodia in 1992–1993 when the Khmer Rouge quit the peace process and continued their civil war. Although they eventually imploded, the civil war dragged on for another five to six years.

And it's important to note that peace processes can break down not because of spoilers but simply because of weak government institutions. Peace processes must be implemented across a spectrum of bureaucratic institutions, from the military, to the police, to the health and education ministries, the legislature, the tax collection agencies and the judiciaries, to name just a few. A peace process is a whole-of-government enterprise.

While Collier found that the rate of reversion to violence or the complete failure of the peace process decreased dramatically with the inclusion of a third-party peacekeeping force, these are rarely employed and, if they are, not deployed for sufficiently long enough periods to consolidate the peace.[4]

Even elections held as part of the peace process are no guarantee of a lasting peace. Indeed, what really concerned Collier and his team was that an election held as part of the peace process did not only *not* diminish the potential for violence but actually increased it. As he put it, "A post-conflict election shifts the risk of conflict reversion," especially in the year after the election. "In the run-up to an election there is a strong incentive for the parties to participate: after all, this is the route to power. And so energies get diverted into campaigning and so risks fall. But then comes the election result. Someone has won and someone has lost."[5]

One of the hardest things for me to quantify is this: war not only destroys the social fabric of society, it destroys or at the very least degrades political institutions. But because the rule of law breaks down, there is little trust in formal, legal institutions of the state; people know only the power of the gun. They do not have trust in nonviolent means to adjudicate disputes. Conflicts are not resolved on the basis of principles or loss; they are resolved through hard power. Compromise holds no incentive. People view any interaction through stark zero-sum terms. And until people stop viewing the world in such a zero-sum framework, no development of democracy and rule of law can occur, which only perpetuates political violence.

Moving away from zero-sum thinking takes a long time. And in its absence, the willingness of former combatants to disarm is negligible. Demobilization is already difficult, as it takes away the insurgents' recourse to resume armed conflict should the peace process fail. Getting former combatants to surrender their weapons in the absence of the rule of law or any culture (or recent memory) of peaceful settlement of disputes is next to impossible and requires a leap of faith and change in political culture.

Peace dividends might not be forthcoming or might be insufficient. While economic development may be a key ingredient to a peace process, when resources are scarce, absorptive capacity is low, and the rule of law and oversight are nearly nonexistent, the likelihood of corruption is very high. Moreover, expectations of a postconflict prosperity are usually too high and quickly dashed as people see the fruits of peace go to small groups of former combatant leaders rather than toward any broad based development.

Finally, there are actual costs to a peace process that are not insignificant. The UN Transitional Authority in Cambodia (UNTAC) from 1991 to 1993 was a two-billion-dollar endeavor that fundamentally altered peace processes, with large-scale civilian intervention alongside peacekeeping forces. UNTAC administered the government during the peace process, engaged in voter education, conducted an election, and oversaw the return and reintegration of some four hundred thousand refugees. While not all peace processes are that complex, they often require peacekeepers or at least peace monitors, refugee or IDP resettlement, postconflict justice mechanisms, and large-scale development projects. These are beyond the means of the government and require the goodwill and support of the bi- and multilateral donor community over many years. But an expensive peace is still cheaper than a cheap war.

WHAT MAKES A PEACE PROCESS GEL?

Despite all the inherent risks and costs, the potential for failure, and the reversion to war, some peace processes defy the odds and succeed. What makes a successful peace process possible? I have identified twenty factors that are essential to any peace process between a government and a substate insurgent group, whether they be an ethnic-based secessionist movement or an ideological force.

1. Elites from both the government and rebels must realize that nothing more can be gained through fighting. A battlefield stalemate must occur along with a declining marginal utility of additional casualties. As long as one side believes that it can gain something from continued combat, a peace process is impossible. Cease-fires might be reached and talks begun, but they are only tactical lulls if one side still believes it can improve its negotiating position through gains or by weakening its adversary's position on the battlefield. Sometimes you just have to give war a chance. You cannot rush or force a peace process. In some cases, patrons to the warring parties compel their clients to get to the negotiating table. But the stars aligning at the international level does not happen often.

2. Insurgent groups invariably view themselves as vanguards and the natural leaders of their constituents. But they always overestimate their popular support, especially in protracted conflicts, and discount the war wariness of the population. There must be a realistic assessment by the insurgents of their popular support. This is both harder and rarer than it would seem.

3. The two sides must build trust. This is a long-term process and one that is so hard to achieve. Cease-fires are broken, and deals are under-

mined by politicians or thwarted by hard-liners in the military or government. Often these actions are perceived to be an intentional and calculated ploy, when all too often negotiators are hung out to dry by their political leaders or opponents to the peace process. You need to be able to overcome these setbacks, and that is possible only through high degrees of personal trust. And trust is different from co-option or trying to buy off your adversary, which is a common tactic but one that fails to secure a lasting peace.

4. Peace processes require bold and courageous leadership on the part of both the rebels and the government. And not mere leadership. Genuine statesmanship is required. Both parties need to look beyond their short-term political horizon. Usually peace processes are nearly as protracted as the conflict. They have failed or been set back on multiple occasions, and they have outlasted political leaders on both sides. Leaders have to be bold and creative, willing to reject old and failed paradigms. Successful peace processes require leaders who can empathize with their adversary and convey that empathy to their own supporters. They have to have enough political capital and be willing to spend it to achieve long-term goals of peace and reconciliation. And leaders have to be willing to take personal risks: they will be challenged by hard-liners, from political challenges to attempts on their lives. Successful peace processes take more than simply political courage. But that is important and includes members of the legislature who are willing to do something for the greater national good rather than their short-term political interests.

5. All parties must acknowledge the concept of *bellum se ipsum alet*, "war feeds itself." Leaders must demonstrate an ability and willingness to take on vested interests within their own constituency, including the will and capability to neutralize hard-line spoilers. Stephen Stedman presents a framework for three types of spoiler management: inducement, socialization, and coercion.[6] Leaders usually need to employ all three. Negotiators must assuage military commanders who fear that the peace process will lead to cuts in budgets, giving them new roles and missions with new hardware and requisite funding.

6. Negotiators must create new mechanisms and institutions. These institutions must be durable and outlive the people who negotiated them, and they have to be transparent to win the trust of the local community. These include cease-fire organizations, transitional justice mechanisms, development agencies, internally displaced person (IDP) and refugee resettlement bodies, and organizations to resolve land ownership and other compensation.

7. The peace process and its agreements and annexes have to be fair and equitable. Both sides have to acknowledge the other's right to exist,

that their core grievances are legitimate, and that historical wrongs were committed and must be addressed. Many times, simple acknowledgment of injustices and the taking of land satisfies many. The acknowledgment that an ethnic minority is a "first nation" goes a long way in recognizing that it has historical claims to the land. Not everyone expects historical wrongs to be reversed (although that is an ideal), but they have to at least be acknowledged. It's amazing how far formal apologies and/or official acknowledgments of misdeeds, abusive policies, and internal colonial practices go in winning over popular support.

8. Some sort of transitional justice mechanisms must exist. These can range from a South African–style truth and reconciliation commission to a formal war crimes tribunal. But the justice mechanism has to be something, even if it is merely symbolic. Lasting peace cannot happen without some form of justice. Yet there are limits. No government will agree to its security forces being scapegoated, and if security forces believe that they are being sacrificed for the sake of peace, then they will act as spoilers. It's important to address wrongs by all sides, as insurgents who operated in the shadows were often abusive and terrorized the local population into supporting their struggle, and some of the civilian population is responsible for battlefield losses through their active or passive support for the government.

9. Related to this are general amnesties. POWs and political prisoners must be released. But in most insurgencies, the government doesn't give insurgents belligerent status for fear that doing so might legitimize their struggle. Most governments treat captured insurgents as terrorists, murderers, and other common criminals. And governments have difficulty putting in place the legal mechanisms to free these individuals and even more in selling their release to the public, especially outraged victims groups and the politicians who cynically champion them. A general amnesty does undermine the government's wartime narrative, but it is absolutely essential for a lasting peace.

10. International support must be at an adequate degree, including postconflict rehabilitation and development. The international community can serve as facilitators, host back-channel meetings, deploy peacekeepers or simply monitors, engage in training and capacity building, and coordinate postconflict aid and human capital development. External partners can turn off the supply of arms, funding, and diplomatic support. Most importantly, the presence of the international community is a type of guarantor that makes reneging, backsliding, and other violations more costly. But we should not overstate the power and influence of external actors. A peace process can only be facilitated or supported by the international community. It cannot be imposed,

no matter how much leverage, political, financial, or economic, they might wield over their clients. For example, in 1989 the Cambodian peace process got started with the Jakarta Informal Meeting process, whereby the client states—the United States, the Soviet Union, China, and France, all permanent members of the UN Security Council—wanted an end to the civil war and compelled their clients to attend. Though a peace agreement was signed in 1991 and UNTAC was stood up and conducted an election, the civil war continued another six years.

11. The peace process is unlikely to be successful on its own. It has to be part of a broader political transformation, including the devolution of political and economic powers. For example, in Cambodia, peace meant not only the end of a Cold War proxy conflict but the end of one-party communist rule. Now Cambodia remains a one-party-dominated state, though there are opposition parties and a relatively free press, and the ruling party jettisoned socialist policies in favor of market reforms. Myanmar's ongoing insurgencies with ethnic militias would have little chance of being resolved under military rule. But the political reforms put in place since 2010, including gradual democratization that led to the 2015 opposition victory in the polls, press liberalization, and a constitution that enshrined regional assemblies makes any negotiated settlement far more likely and durable. In the case of Northern Ireland, the peace process was made possible by the membership of both the Republic of Ireland and the United Kingdom in the European Union, which eliminated internal borders. Without EU membership and commitment to the European project, the peace process may not have been possible, which is why the June 2016 "Brexit" referendum has undermined the peace accord.

12. Wealth must be shared between the central government and the post-conflict region. While most conflicts were never completely about resources or inequitable distributions of wealth, they are often major contributors to the conflict and central in the narrative of resistance. So a peace process must include mechanisms to allow for greater wealth sharing and/or control over natural resources. This could be in the form of keeping more tax revenue local, declining transfer payments, or issuing larger block grants from the central government. Or it could be wealth sharing of subterranean resources, including minerals and hydrocarbons. This is more than what is often described as a "peace dividend." The regions really need a degree of fiscal and economic autonomy in order to right the wrongs of internal colonialism that so often fueled the conflict. But it is also important for former insurgents to demonstrate to their constituents that the armed struggle

did result in control over local resources. This is the most tangible proof of a meaningful autonomy.

13. The peace process must develop and engage civil society. No civil society, no peace. Independent civil society is often weak, especially in conflict zones. But it plays a key role in the peace process. Civil society is essential in pushing the warring parties to the table, keeping them honest through investigations and reporting, and mobilizing popular support for the peace process. Women's groups, trade unions, clergy, youth and student organizations, environmental groups, human rights organizations, the legal establishment or bar association, and even business groups or chambers of commerce must be behind the peace process. If a peace process is simply negotiated by political elites without mass buy-in, it will never have traction. A broad societal buy in is necessary, and it is civil society, not the government or substate combatants, that is best able to mobilize popular support before, during, and after the peace process. Most importantly, at its core, an insurgency is about social justice, and the best guarantors and groups committed to expending social justice are noncombatant civil society organizations. But civil society plays one other critical role. By their nature, insurgencies are violent. And one of the most important things in a peace process is a broad societal rejection of violence as a means to settle disputes. After protracted conflicts, violence is so ingrained in the social fabric that this is arguably the greatest challenge. Civil society is responsible for altering the thinking, creating moral pressure to sanction offenders, socializing people in nonviolent dispute resolution, and establishing effective mechanisms to make that possible.

14. A well-thought-out and funded disarmament, demobilization, and rehabilitation (DDR) program must be in place for former combatants. The region cannot be awash in both weapons and young men with no livelihoods or career prospects. A process of disarmament of at least a critical mass of weaponry must occur. While a surrender of weapons may be politically untenable, combatants can put weapons under third-party or technical guard or put beyond use entirely. Disarmament is a highly emotional issue for insurgents, who often went through enormous hurdles to acquire their weaponry, which they see as the manifestation of their struggle and without which they never could have advanced the cause of their population. In regions with endemic crime in which such crime often went hand in hand with or under the cover of insurgency, with weak rule of law, and with a culture of violence, getting people to relinquish their weapons is very hard. As Mao Zedong quipped, "Political power grows out of the barrel of a gun," and in postconflict environments, weapons remain an insurance policy.

But not disarming simply leads to insecurity and crime. Any peace process must give a lot of thought and resources to giving something for the insurgents to return to, that is, job or vocational training, land allocation, livelihood projects, and/or integration into the security forces or new government. Governments must handle this well. Not every former guerrilla is going to be given a job, so managing expectations is a serious challenge. The failure to do so led to a mutiny and a potential coup in East Timor when FRETILIN rebels revolted after not being hired as local police. A peace dividend, something more appealing than continued combat, must be available. This is an inherently difficult task, not only logistically but also socially.

15.   Insurgents must find a way to transform themselves into effective political parties that are capable of governing. This, again, is not an easy task. Retail politics requires a very different skill set from guerrilla warfare. Insurgents have to develop platforms, establish party organizations, mobilize the electorate, appeal to the population without threat of coercion, and compete in an open process. And they have to be prepared to lose and cede power, a bitter pill to swallow. Most insurgents feel a sense of entitlement to rule because of the sacrifices they made under armed conflict. Most importantly, they have to effectively administer and provide social services, a responsibility for which they have very little experience. All insurgent groups claim to have shadow governments and provide basic social services, but these are really quite rudimentary. No group provides the degree of social services that they claim to, as most resources are marshaled into the war effort. Even the Tamil Tigers, who were arguably the most effective administrators, still relied on the Sri Lankan government to provide electricity and other utilities in their "liberated zone." But more than developing a political organization and administrative capabilities, former insurgents have to change their leadership styles. Insurgencies are not as top-down or disciplined as the government militaries that they aspire to, yet they are disciplined enough to have "command mentalities." They are not democratic, they are not used to compromise, and they are not given to building up popular support or mobilizing the community over low political issues. Insurgents are romantics and often poorly suited for the task of day-to-day administration. The leadership traits that can inspire people to engage in combat, take incredible risks, and make enormous personal sacrifices are rarely suited for the mundane task of administration. Yet most guerrilla leaders see themselves as the inheritors of political power borne of their military leadership. Insurgent leaders have stepped aside and handed over power to technocrats and administrators who did not struggle in the *maquis*, or "underground," in only a few cases. Most

insurgent leaders have proven to be woefully incompetent administrators whose misrule has done much to undermine fragile peace accords.

16. Insurgents really need to have good independent and external council. While they may have proved themselves adept (or at least sufficiently adequate) guerrillas, complex legal negotiations again require a completely different skill set. They are facing off with skilled negotiators and legal teams that have years of training and practice. Governments do not send their B teams to these negotiations. They have teams of technical experts on issues ranging from mineral rights to the law, transitional justice, and tax collection. No rebel group can match that experience. Moreover, having spent years in the jungle, they are insular and secretive by nature. They need expert advice on the law and other technical issues, which they might be very resistant to or untrusting of. And governments, if they are serious about the durability of a peace process, should encourage rebel groups to seek outside counsel. Again, it may seem counterintuitive for governments to encourage their adversary to have better counsel and advisers at the negotiating table, but if an agreement is not deemed equitable or is seen as having too many loopholes, it will not be durable.

17. The peace process must be a formal mechanism, not an *ad hoc* or informal process. The absence of violence is not peace. It is important that the peace process have a strong sense of formality, legality, and finality. This is an issue of "face." The state needs to make the insurgents feel they are equal partners despite the asymmetry in the relationship. But an agreement is also based on the principle of sovereign equality. Any government that thinks it can simply cut side deals or buy off some of the insurgent leaders without making meaningful concessions or addressing core grievances and forging a durable political peace process is sowing the seeds of future conflicts.

18. The best and most equitable agreements can be negotiated, but they still have to be ratified by legislatures, which must also pass implementing legislation. This is truly the weak link in any peace process. Understanding the role of the legislature is key. Once a deal is reached between the negotiating teams representing their various executives, legislatures make a dangerous assumption about the prospects for peace. They invariably water down peace agreements that they see as affecting their purview and power or that set what they consider to be dangerous precedents in other parts of the country. Some members will support the peace process; some will not. Most will be somewhere in the middle, swayed by political expediency: whether they'll be subject to future vote trading, whether support for the agreement impacts their own chances at reelection, or whether a stance, one way or another, can be exploited for political gain or used as a springboard to

higher office. The legislature cannot be expected to work for the common good but instead will be pulled in as many ways as it has legislators. A lot of political grandstanding will invariably occur. The executive branch must work assiduously to build up a solid coalition in parliament and be willing to use all political capital and cudgels at the ruler's disposal to prevent the peace process from being sufficiently watered down to the point where dissatisfaction reaches a level at which the rebels quit the peace process *en masse* or *in toto*. The greatest threat to a peace process invariably comes from politicians. Once the agreement is signed, it becomes a political tussle that is very hard for the government to control.

19. The process must protect cultural and minority rights, including language rights. This has to be a cornerstone of any peace process, the agreements, and the postconflict political order. A group's identity must have genuine protections. And what is critical, though so often lacking, is that identity become not merely protected but embraced by the country as a whole. Group members have to feel that they are part of a national narrative. For example, my friend often talks about how American Indian symbols are celebrated in the United States as symbols of warriors, bravery, and resoluteness: Tomahawk missiles and Apache attack helicopters are core components of the US arsenal.

20. Finally, a formal process must exist to resolve disputes over implementation (or nonimplementation) after the parties have concluded the agreement. This can include third-party adjudicators or internal/bilateral mechanisms. But disputes will invariably arise, so pre-agreed mechanisms for resolution are imperative.

ACEH, MINDANAO, AND SOUTHERN THAILAND

Until recently, Southeast Asia was plagued by separatist insurgencies that had simmered for several decades. These conflicts were in part the result of colonialism but were exacerbated by internal colonial and repressive policies, overcentralization, an unwillingness to share natural resource wealth, policies that excluded or denied the rights of minorities, and egregious human rights abuses perpetrated by governments and their security forces. Ongoing insurgencies in Myanmar continue this trend. But elsewhere in Southeast Asia, insurgencies have gradually been brought to heel.

Some insurgencies have simply been defeated (Malay Communist Party), withered away (Thai Communist Party), imploded (Khmer Rouge), or maintained such a low level of operations that they are little more than a criminal nuisance (New People's Army of Philippines). No peace processes have finalized or addressed the original grievances that led to the insurgencies.

The governments took advantage of the various groups' inability to continue sustained armed conflict. But, as is often said, the absence of war is not peace. A peace process or some formal legal mechanism to address core grievances is an important way to prevent a relapse into violence.

But in three cases, formal peace processes have succeeded between governments in Southeast Asia and rebel movements that have been fighting for an independent homeland over the past decade, legal mechanisms to end hostilities and address core grievances of a persecuted minority. Indeed, the peace processes in Aceh, Indonesia, and the Mindanao, Philippines, have been some of the most innovative and successful in the world.

Since the 1970s, Indonesia, the Philippines, and Thailand have all wrestled with secessionist insurgent groups who have sought to establish their own homeland. This book analyzes three recent peace processes in Aceh, Mindanao, and southern Thailand. Collectively, well over one hundred thousand people were killed, with some estimates closer to two hundred thousand. Each has been described as an intractable conflict at some point in time. Each government entered into peace talks with rebels in the 1970s, though without any sincerity or willingness to make significant concessions. As a result, the insurgencies in all three countries continued through the 1990s, creating large tracts of relatively ungoverned space and hampering socioeconomic development.

By the turn of the millennium, the governments of Indonesia and the Philippines began to reevaluate their strategies, while the insurgents came to a conclusion that the changed global environment and waning capabilities made victory unlikely. In Indonesia, the psychological impact of the 2004 tsunami, in which over 120,000 people were killed in Aceh alone, provided both another impetus and the involvement of the donor community. Peace processes began in both countries. In Thailand, all parties recognize the need for a peace process, but they are simply not there yet; the domestic context makes any political settlement unlikely.

The three case studies have been chosen for nine key reasons.

First, each insurgency has reached a critical mass and had a large degree of military success, at least at critical junctures. Each has controlled territory or at least made large swaths of territory ungovernable for the various states. Although none of these groups ever came close to achieving their goal of winning an independent homeland, each tied down the security forces of an infinitely more resourced state for decades and fought to a battlefield stalemate. None of the three governments was able to militarily defeat these rebel groups. Though each insurgency had some degree of external support, it was never enough to give them the capabilities to win independence.

Second, each of these movements viewed itself as a vanguard organization for its specific population. While each overstated the degree of its popular support, each does have significant degrees of popular legitimacy. Each has been able to articulate the interests of its respective constituency and negotiate on its behalf.

Third, these are apples to apples comparisons. These are three conflicts within the broader Malay world. Although the Philippines is a predominantly Catholic country, Thailand a majority Buddhist country, and Indonesia a majority Muslim country, all three rebel groups studied are Muslim. Although each rebel group is primarily ethno-nationalist, all of them have strains of Islamist ideology.

Fourth, the time frames are similar. Each conflict has its antecedents in colonialism but really erupted in the 1970s. Given this, the international context, both global and regional, remained very similar. Despite differences, the Philippines, Indonesia, and Thailand were founding members of the Association of Southeast Asian Nations (ASEAN) in 1967, anticommunist in their nature and allied with (in the cases of the Philippines and Thailand) or closely tied to (in the case of Indonesia) the United States. The end of the Cold War had little bearing on any of these conflicts, yet the post-9/11 world did have a significant and similar impact on each, inasmuch as insurgencies had a much harder time operating transnationally with greater scrutiny on the flows of resources (weapons and money) to substate actors. Likewise, states were under far more pressure to deal with the issue of ungoverned space.

Fifth, each conflict has several key commonalities, including the protection of national identity, the quest for an independent homeland; the protection of linguistic, religious, or cultural rights; anger at internal colonialism and the unwillingness of governments to share rents from natural resource wealth; and political cultures that were racist and condescending toward the minorities. No groups felt that their national narrative had any space for them.

Sixth, the state side also had similarities: the governments were overly centralized and had ruled over the festering insurgencies for long periods via autocratic regimes, which imposed policies inimical, if not completely prejudicial, to the interests of the minority communities. Each of the three has transitioned from authoritarianism to democratic rule, though in the case of Thailand, it has backslid following the 2014 coup d'état. Each government maintained policies of internal colonialism, which economically disenfranchised the regions, fueling the insurgencies. Their militaries were largely centered on internal stability operations and counterinsurgency operations due to these threats. The militaries operated with near total impunity and engaged in serious human rights abuses, unaccountable to the public as well as political elites.

Seventh, these three are contemporary cases in which we can look at the process of implementation or nonimplementation. These are not historical cases. Even in the case of Aceh, which has been relatively well implemented, a process of postconflict reconciliation and implementation is still working. Aceh's peace remains fragile and is sometimes in flux.

Eighth, each has been a protracted process, lasting in all cases more than forty years. Early attempts to negotiate peace or at least end the armed insurrection failed. Each government and rebel group has built on a history of broken promises, weak implementation, and betrayal. None has been a fast or easy settlement but something that required a generational struggle, changes in leadership, and changes in political structure.

Finally, these are excellent case studies with lessons to be learned for peacemakers from other parts of the world. These are thorough studies that include the history of the conflict, the growth of the insurgent movement, rationales by both sides to negotiate, an analysis of the negotiation process, the agreements reached, and the pitfalls of implementation.

The peace agreements in Aceh and Mindanao (at least what was negotiated and on paper but has not been implemented) are among the most progressive agreements in the world. They were equitable, balancing the interests of the central government and insurgents, they provided for significant autonomy, creatively regarding postconflict governance and displaying a willingness to protect "ancestral domain" at least as a concept, they recognized historical wrongs against the minority group, and they provided transitional justice mechanisms, equitable wealth sharing, and effective DDR programs. Indonesia and the Philippines successfully implemented their peace processes for a number of key reasons: first, all sides came to the conclusion that they could gain nothing more from fighting, indeed, that armed conflict was starting to be counterproductive. Second, the peace processes were part of an overall move toward greater decentralization of politics and economic decision making. Third, both the Philippines and Indonesia were willing to share significant amounts of natural resource wealth with the new autonomous governments. Fourth, the countries protected cultural/minority rights. Fifth, they enshrined democratic rule. Sixth, both countries and insurgent groups had bold and creative leaders who were willing to reject old and failed paradigms and dogma. They were creative and willing to take great personal risks. They were truly statesmen. Eighth, both sides did a good job at neutralizing spoilers. In particular, the governments did a very good job in convincing the militaries that they had more to gain by accepting autonomy arrangements and that their budgets would not only not decrease but would instead increase as they began to focus on external threats. Ninth, the emergence of civil society played an important role, pressuring both the state and the armed combatants. The tenth factor is the ability of the GAM (Gerakan Aceh Merdeka, or "Free Aceh Movement") and now the MILF (Moro Islamic Liberation Front) to transition themselves into effective governing parties. Finally, in both cases, neutral third-party mediators and or facilitators played a key and important role.

This is not to say that everything has gone well. Despite huge hopes and high expectations, the peace process in Mindanao has, at the time of writing, completely stalled. Yet that too is a teaching moment. We can draw key lessons regarding the issue of implementation and the role of the national legislature in implementing any peace agreement. Successful devolution of political and economic powers that have protected the cultural rights of the minority population along with substantial wealth sharing brought an end to seemingly intractable conflicts. They serve as both a model and counterpoint for Thailand, which is in the throes of its own insurgency.

The Thai government, in particular following the May 2014 coup d'état, is totally unwilling to make any meaningful concessions to come to a political resolution. Its goal is to degrade the insurgency to the point that it can ascribe the violence to routine and low-level criminality without any devolution of power. In short, these three case studies provide important lessons for the fields of counterinsurgency and peacemaking and will add to the literature on peacemaking. They provide not only detailed histories of the peace processes but, more importantly, analysis of what made them successes or failures.

Each of the case studies begins with a history of the insurgency and an analysis of the insurgent group's organization, operations, tactics, and capabilities before delving into the history of the peace processes and an analysis of the factors that made them successful. As stated earlier, nothing is harder than a peace process. But the lessons of Southeast Asia show that peace processes are possible as part of a national devaluation of power, with bold and creative statesmanship, the successful neutralization of spoilers, and the role of neutral third-party facilitators.

The chapter on Aceh, Indonesia, begins with a historical overview of the conflict, reviewing the Dutch colonial legacy and Aceh's role during the formation of the Republic of Indonesia. It analyzes the failed attempts to negotiate/establish autonomy in the 1950s and 1960s, the reasons for the eruption of armed separatism in 1976, and the insincere efforts to negotiate autonomy under Suharto's "New Order" regime. The second section of the chapter focuses on the emergence of GAM and the armed uprising. The third section analyzes the growth, tactics, capabilities, and resources of GAM as a fighting force. The fourth section analyzes the peace process, starting with the failed attempts under President Megawati Sukarnoputri but then under President Susilo Bambang Yudhoyono, even before the 2004 Boxing Day tsunami. The chapter also looks at the impact that natural disaster had on the peace process. The final section analyzes the factors that have made the Acehnese peace process the most recently successful in the world, bar none.

The Philippine case study also begins with a broad historical overview of the conflict, including an analysis of the role of the Spanish and later the American colonists. The section analyzes the first insurgency, fought by the

Moro National Liberation Front (MNLF), until the conclusion of an autonomy agreement with the government in 1996. The third section focuses on the MILF's split from the MNLF in 1978 and its rise from a fringe group to the dominant force in the region. The fourth section focuses on MILF's tactics, capabilities, organization, and resources. It also assesses the group's relationship with the regional terrorist organization Jemaah Islamiyah. The fifth section analyzes the peace process that began in 2003 under President Gloria Macapagal Arroyo through the present time. The final section—which is tentative, because the agreement is still being implemented and much could go wrong—analyzes what has made the agreement successful to date. It has involved some highly creative decisions on governance and political structures.

The Thai case study is the counterpoint. Thailand effectively quelled its insurgency by the late 1990s, though there was no peace process (section 1). The insurgency erupted again in 2004 and is now in its thirteenth year (section 2). Section 3 analyzes the tactics, modus operandi, and capabilities of the various insurgent groups and includes very good data on the violence. The fourth section discusses the various attempts to negotiate an end to the insurgency, something that every government since Thaksin Shinawatra has attempted to do with little effect. Section 5 analyzes the political situation in Thailand since the coup and explains why, despite the government's attempts to go through the motions and forge a peace, it has no willingness to devolve power or make any concessions to the insurgents.

The conclusion ties together the commonalities of what made the peace processes more or less successful and offers lessons to practitioners and analysts who work on other conflicts. As discussed earlier, I suggest twenty key factors that make a peace process successful or not. Not all twenty have to be present, but the absence of many will never lead to a durable peace.

NOTES

1. Paul Collier and Anke Hoeffler, "Greed and Grievance in Civil War" (Policy Research Working Paper 2355, World Bank Development Research Group, May 2000), https://openknowledge.worldbank.org/bitstream/handle/10986/18853/multi_page.pdf?sequence=1.

2. Stewart Patrick, "Left Behind: Understanding State Fragility," in *Weak Links: Fragile States, Global Threats, and International Security* (New York: Oxford University Press, 2011), 38.

3. Collier, "Greed and Grievance," 129; Patrick, "Left Behind," 38.

4. Collier, 83.

5. Paul Collier, *War, Guns, and Votes: Democracy in Dangerous Places* (New York: HarperCollins, 2009), 81.

6. Stephen John Stedman, "Spoiler Problems in Peace Processes," *International Security* 22, no. 2 (Fall 1997): 5–53.

Chapter Two

Case Study 1—The Gerakan Aceh Merdeka (GAM)

Aceh, Indonesia

1. BACKGROUND TO THE CONFLICT

Aceh is the most northwestern province of Indonesia, on the island of Sumatra, covering just under fifty-nine thousand square kilometers. It straddles the western side of the strategic waterway the Strait of Malacca, through which nearly 25 percent of the world's maritime trade passes. Today, the population of Aceh is slightly over five million people.

Islam came to Aceh in the early thirteenth century. And while it spread to other parts of the seventeen thousand islands that make up the Indonesian archipelago, it grafted onto very rich Hindu and other indigenous cultures, making Islam highly syncretic. By the fifteenth century, Islam had reached all of the coast of Aceh and continued down the eastern bank of Sumatra. But Islam really did not spread to all of Sumatra and Java until the seventeenth and eighteenth centuries. While Aceh shows some evidence of early (pre-fourteenth-century) Hindu culture, including a few Sanskrit words in the language, the rich Hindu and Buddhist culture that one sees in Java is not evident in Aceh. (For example, the main cultural form in Java is the *wayang* shadow puppets, based on the Hindu Ramayana, the most important historical relics are all Hindu temples, the national airline is named after the vehicle for Vishnu, and Javanese rites are steeped in Hinduism.) Islam grafted on to Hinduism in most of Indonesia. In Aceh, it totally supplanted Hinduism. Moreover, Islam in Aceh was always more entrenched in the political culture as the sultanate imposed *sharia* law. In Java and Sumatra, the political elites through the early twentieth century relied on *adat*, an indigenous customary law, and to a much lesser extent *sharia*. This is coupled with a very strong sense of ethnic chauvinism by the Acehnese, who always bristled that Indonesia, from the time of Dutch colonial rule, was Java-centric. Java has always dominated political and cultural life.

Bahasa-Indonesian, the national language, is a relatively new phenomenon. It was established in the early twentieth century based on Malayu, the common language of neighboring Malaysia. Every region of Indonesia has its own dialect, which is indecipherable to someone from another region. As Java is home to 50 percent of the population, Javanese has always been the most prevalent dialect. But the Island of Sumatra has many dialects, roughly twenty on a linguistic map, including Acehnese.

Aceh has a long history of rebellion. Indeed, this might be considered one of the longest continual rebellions in the world. For more than four and a half centuries, the Sultanate of Aceh and its successors have resisted external domination (Dutch, British, Japanese, Indonesian), which means very few periods of prolonged peace. The Acehnese pride themselves on the fact that they were the last part of Indonesia to be colonized by the Dutch.

Dutch colonizers established Batavia (Jakarta) on the island of Java in 1596 and gradually expanded their holdings in the Dutch East Indies following wars with the Portuguese (1605) and British (1810–1811). The 1824 Anglo-Dutch agreement resulted in territorial swaps and established the border between British Malaya and the Dutch East Indies. Under that agreement, Aceh remained autonomous, technically a protectorate of the Ottoman Empire. Yet Aceh's importance in the mid-nineteenth century grew with the spice trade, and the Dutch tried to exert more control. The British preferred to see Aceh as an independent sultanate for fear that the Dutch could use Aceh to block the strategic Strait of Malacca. Anglo-Dutch competition grew following the 1869 opening of the Suez Canal, which catalyzed trade with Asia. The British recognized Dutch control over the entire island of Sumatra, including Aceh, in return for Dutch holdings in West Africa in the 1871 Anglo-Dutch agreement.

The Acehnese fiercely resisted Dutch conquest. The Aceh Sultanate fended off the first Dutch assault in 1873 and fought continually for the next forty years, ultimately succumbing in 1914. It was the last territory in Indonesia that the Dutch colonized. The war, however, was exceptionally costly in both blood and treasure for the Dutch colonial regime, which had to alter its socioeconomic policies in the rest of the Dutch East Indies to help finance the war. The war was exceptionally violent; some thirty-seven thousand Dutch and an estimated seventy thousand Acehnese were killed in the protracted conflict. Following the war, rather than imposing direct colonial administration as they did in the rest of the country starting in 1830, the Dutch ruled indirectly through what was left of the Acehnese aristocracy. Yet the province remained restive. A low-level anti-Dutch rebellion resumed in the mid-1920s. In short, the Dutch were never able to pacify Aceh.

Following the Japanese invasion of Indonesia in 1941–1942, Acehnese rebelled against them, too. Following the Japanese surrender on August 14, 1945, the Dutch returned to reclaim their colonial territory in Indonesia, ignoring the August 9, 1945, declaration of independence by self-proclaimed president Sukarno (sometimes spelled Soekarno). Sukarno was a nationalist leader arrested by the Dutch in 1924 and later freed and used as a figurehead leader by the Japanese in 1942. War quickly broke out, and it was a very violent conflict. The Dutch, however, never reentered Aceh. Most of the war was fought in Java or in more economically important regions in central Sumatra. The Indonesian war for independence raged from 1945 to 1949, when the Dutch recognized Indonesian independence. During this period of time, Aceh was governed by Tungku Daud Beureu'eh, a religious and military leader.

Aceh proved to be a strong base of support for Sukarno in the post–World War II era. While many Acehnese participated in the anticolonial struggle against the Dutch, clearly many hoped for significant autonomy upon independence.[1] Following independence, the Acehnese were angered by both the ethnic Javanese domination of the Indonesian government and the overly centralized nature of the state.

The country was at first governed by the 1945 constitution, written and passed at the end of Japan's rule before the Dutch returned *en masse*. The 1945 constitution gave the president concentrated power and weakened the power of the legislature; in short, strong and centralized decision making was necessary in order to fight the Dutch. Following independence, a new constitution was promulgated in 1950. This charter weakened the power of the presidency to almost a ceremonial position and strengthened the position of the 232-member People's Representative Council. This was a tumultuous period in Indonesia's history, although it culminated with the 1955 election.

Aceh was at first folded into the Christian-dominated province of Batak, and the government dropped its initial promise to Aceh that *sharia* law could be implemented. Unrest began to grow, but it was only one of many challenges for the new republic.

Indonesia was immediately beset by a number of rebellions, including a separatist rebellion in North Sulawesi and the Maluku Islands (Christian majority regions) and a lingering rebellion by an Islamist movement, Darul Islam, that had also fought the Dutch but had done so to establish Indonesia as an independent Islamic state. Many in Aceh, which is much more culturally and religiously conservative than the rest of the archipelago, supported Darul Islam, whose stronghold was in western Java and Sumatra. But under Tungku Daud Beureu'eh, Aceh itself revolted against central government control from 1953 to 1959 in an attempt to become an independent Islamic state. Daud's forces were small and were never able to gain mass support for their movement. They were hampered by shortages of weapons and other resources. Their attacks, which focused on police stations and remote army outposts to seize weapons, were predictable, and they experienced heavy losses. The Indonesian National Armed Forces (TNI) engaged in large-scale counterinsurgency operations in Aceh through 1957, when a cease-fire was signed. Low-level fighting continued through 1959, pushing many of the remaining Darul Islam and Acehnese rebels into the mountains of Aceh. Darul Islam's own leader, S. M. Kartosuwiryo, was captured and executed in 1962, which effectively ended the armed rebellion. Remnants of both insurgent groups would go on to form the nucleus of the Free Aceh Movement (GAM) in 1976.

In an attempt to end both the Darul Islam and Acehnese uprisings, the central government awarded Aceh "special status" in 1959. In 1963 Tungku Daud Beureu'eh signed a formal peace agreement ending the conflict. Yet this autonomy pact was short-lived.

The government had neither the will nor the capability to actually fulfill its commitment. Sukarno had suspended democracy in 1960 and proclaimed himself president for life in 1963. Aceh's autonomy at this time was more the result of the fact that the central government in Jakarta was reeling from disastrous economic policies, a 1963 border war with Malaysia (Konfrontasi), and the specter of civil war. Sukarno's ostensible political allies, the Communist Party of Indonesia (PKI), were poised to seize power due to the economic collapse. From 1949 to 1965, economic growth was stagnant. Following the 1957–1958 nationalization of Dutch assets, the economy not only contracted but also lost much of its Western aid and assistance. In 1959 Sukarno revived the 1945 constitution, stating the need for "guided democracy." In March 1960 Sukarno dissolved the elected assembly and replaced it with an appointed assembly. In July 1963 Sukarno proclaimed himself "president for life."

In 1965, a group of military officers staged a coup, ostensibly to preempt a communist putsch. Some three hundred thousand PKI members and their supporters were liquidated following the coup.

Acehnese had every reason to believe that the fall of Sukarno would be good for them. His government was too weak and mired in economic and political crises to ever negotiate an autonomy agreement. Moreover, the military relied on the landed Islamic clergy to help it root out the PKI. Though intense crackdowns occurred in Medan and other parts of western Sumatra, the PKI actually had little foothold in the religious province of Aceh. Thus only a fraction of the bloodshed following the September 30, 1965, coup took place in Aceh. Yet Acehnese felt that they were owed something by the New Order regime.

The New Order regime of Suharto did restore political order and bring the country back from the economic brink, restoring ties with the West, rejoining the United Nations, and strongly cracking down on the PKI. But in the process, the New Order highly centralized political and economic control. The military dominated the government in a system known as *Dwi Fungsi*, or "dual function": military commanders governed down to the village level. In areas that had histories of rebellion, such as West Papua or Aceh, the military presence was even more onerous. The military held block representation in the parliament, accounting for 13 percent of the seats, while most ministries and state-owned corporations were controlled by uniformed officers. In spite of—or maybe because of—"dual function," the central government paid roughly only one-third of the TNI's annual budget. The TNI was left to raise its own funds, which it did through legitimate and illegitimate businesses, collection of taxes, and control over natural resources. This policy coupled with increased transfer payments to the central government, including all rents from natural resource extraction, increased Acehnese resentment.

Suharto reversed Sukarno's 1957 policy of nationalization of foreign-owned enterprises and encouraged foreign direct investment. The American oil giant Mobil began exploration in Aceh in 1971, and it became a highly lucrative field. Aceh's share of Indonesia's natural gas is often overestimated; it is only four trillion of ninety-four trillion cubic feet of natural gas per year, but little of the four billion dollars in revenue stayed in the province. Indonesia, a member of OPEC, was a key beneficiary of the global spike in oil prices in 1973 and 1976, though the province of Aceh received almost no benefit. Indeed, it began to lag behind Java and the other regions of the country despite the fact that the government's share of the Mobil fields was an estimated fifteen billion dollars per year. Aceh's per capita GDP was among the highest in the country on paper, but per capita income and consumption were among the lowest in national rankings.

The Acehnese were also angered at the New Order regime's assault on Islamists. Following the highly secular Sukarno, who was politically dependent on the PKI, the country's Islamists had high expectations that Suharto would allow the application of *sharia* law. They were disappointed, as Suharto proved adroit at using the Islamists to ferret out members of the PKI and then politically emasculate them. Indonesia remained a highly secular and centralized state.

More Javanese migration followed the 1965 coup that brought General Suharto to power because of the highly centralized nature of the state. Suharto implemented a program of forced migration, known as Transmigrasi, to relocate landless peasants from Java to less populated regions of the country. Many were sent to parts of Sumatra (an estimated 60 percent of the population of one region, Lampung, were transmigrants). Popular anger toward the government grew with the large influx of Javanese in the late 1970s. According to the 2010 census, 15 million transmigrants and their progeny lived in Sumatra alone, including 4.3 million in North Sumatra Province, which abuts Aceh. Less evidence exists that they were sent to Aceh in significant numbers. Acehnese were vociferous in their resistance to accepting transmigrants.[2]

Aceh is rich in natural resources, especially oil and natural gas, and also in agriculture. And unlike the island of Java—the most densely populated piece of real estate on the planet (over 100 million of Indonesia's 240 million people live on Java)—Sumatra in general and Aceh in particular are sparsely populated and are net exporters of food. The conflict in Aceh is a classic case of center-periphery relations: overcentralized politics and economics, inequitable sharing of proceeds of natural resource extraction, and unwillingness to protect local religious and cultural traditions.

2. THE RISE OF ARMED INSURRECTION

Acehnese began armed rebellion under the leadership of the newly formed Free Aceh Movement (GAM) in 1976. GAM was founded on December 4, 1976, by Hasan di Tiro, a descendant of the last sultan of Aceh. The movement was very small, with no more than several hundred guerrilla fighters at the time. GAM was the outgrowth of a small rebellion that was put down by Indonesia in 1963.

GAM was never a large organization and was able to win over the hearts and minds of the broader population for only brief periods. It was geographically contained in the mountainous hinterland. And while some militant groups are able to bolster their ranks following periods of success, GAM never really gained military traction. GAM was an irritant that could never achieve its goals militarily. It did have more success when it received external support, but even then, it could never leverage that support into sustained victories on the battlefield. The conflict in Aceh was very low level. Only an estimated ten thousand people were killed between 1976 and 2004. GAM was an irritant but never a threat to the territorial integrity of the Republic of Indonesia.

GAM's goal was always independence, and it never seriously considered autonomy as an acceptable solution until 2004–2005. While Islam is deeply rooted in the territory and the *sharia* has been part of the legal code in different periods, GAM never stated that it wanted to be an Islamic state, though it did hark back to the Acehnese sultanate. It is important that GAM's founder was a descendant of the last sultan.

GAM has has gone through four distinct phases, 1976–1979, 1979–1989, 1989–1998, and 1998–2005, as a result of external security force operations against it.[3]

From 1976 to 1979, GAM was an extremely small organization. Estimates are that it had only between 150 and 200 guerrilla fighters at the time, all poorly armed and with no formal training. Their weapons were all those that they had captured on the battlefield or had had since the Darul Islam rebellion in the 1950s. Indeed, many of their weapons dated from the 1950s and 1960s. GAM decided to focus its meager resources on attacks that would quickly pressure Jakarta. GAM focused its attacks on quick assaults on Mobil's oil fields, hoping that it could quickly prove the government's economic vulnerability and highlight the asymmetric center-periphery relationship. In 1977 GAM rebels killed an American petroleum engineer working for Mobil, one of the few foreigners to have been killed in the conflict.

From 1979 to 1989, GAM atrophied, both militarily and politically. Hasan di Tiro's inner circle comprised younger urban members of the middle class who had no combat experience and the field commanders who, although they had combat experience in the 1950s, were no longer young men. The government simply overwhelmed GAM with a greater deployment around the oil and gas fields and, ultimately, an even greater military presence in the region. Its attacks on government security forces took very heavy casualties and were so costly that they could not be sustained.

Much of the leadership, including Hasan di Tiro, fled to Europe, where they received political asylum in the 1980s. In this phase, they began to use diplomacy and public international pressure on Indonesia's human rights abuses. Here they were able to tap into a growing chorus of critics of the Suharto regime following Suharto's 1975 invasion and 1976 annexation of the former Portuguese colony of East Timor. So while GAM was not a military threat in the 1980s, it became a diplomatic irritant.

During this second period, GAM was never able to win broad public support. Indeed, in 1987, the ruling Golkar Party won its first majority in the province. While the public was unhappy that the province's vast natural resource wealth was not trickling down to it in any way, it still offered no broad support for armed rebellion. The security force presence, though large, was not oppressive, and the human rights abuses were not endemic, certainly no worse than in other parts of the country. GAM was isolated, living in very remote parts of the interior, in a province with few roads. Its entire strategy during this period of time was based on rural guerrilla ambushes. Much of GAM's manpower was either killed or arrested in this period, and from 1979 to 1989, few operations took place. Indeed, the insurgency seemed broadly quelled. By the 1980s, most of the leadership, including Hasan di Tiro, were in exile in Europe, removed from their supporters and troops, though able to increase diplomatic pressure on Indonesia. The GAM government-in-exile, as it was, was very small and included Hasan di Tiro's small inner circle.

Tensions continued to rise, and in 1989, the civil war resumed. Attempts to negotiate a settlement with the Scandinavian-based exiled leadership were halfhearted at best. The war was bloody and very costly for GAM, with several thousand members killed.[4] The TNI increased its presence in the province throughout the 1990s, reaching a peak of thirty thousand troops (the police were part of the army until 1999). The TNI was accused of using scorched-earth tactics, destroying entire villages suspected of supporting or giving sanctuary to rebels. The government engaged in torture, extrajudicial killings, and unlawful detentions under the vague "Anti-Subversion Law." An estimated one thousand Acehnese are thought to have been killed while in detention, and the state-controlled media could offer no oversight or independent reporting.[5] GAM countered with its own brutality.

When GAM resumed hostilities in 1989, it was an altogether different organization, much larger, better trained, and better armed. Starting in 1985, GAM was able to capitalize on Libyan president Muammar Gaddafi's willingness to train anticolonial groups—especially Muslim movements. Libya had provided such assistance to the Moro National Liberation Front of the Philippines. Libya provided training and arms for an estimated five hundred to six hundred Acehnese during the decade, though GAM claimed one thousand to two thousand.[6] Even the lower estimate represents a significant increase in the number of trained and armed combatants. This cadre was able to lead and train GAM as it grew into a broader-based movement in the late 1980s to 1990s.

In addition, GAM benefited from the end of the Cambodian civil war in 1991. The western Cambodian border region was absolutely awash in small arms and ammunition (primarily Chinese manufactured) that had been trans-shipped to the Khmer Rouge via Thailand. As the civil war came to an end with a large UN-sponsored peace process from 1991 to 1993, large illegal arms markets emerged, attracting buyers from ethnic conflicts in Myanmar, the Tamil Tigers, and arms runners for the Acehnese.[7] Large numbers of weapons were shipped overland through southern Thailand and supported by Acehnese exiles in Malaysia.

With a cadre of foreign-trained members and a steadier supply of weapons, GAM's ranks did grow to just over a thousand guerrillas. But they were still short of resources as Libyan support was not open ended and diaspora communities were not that large. Their tactics expanded to include arson, sabotage, and targeted assassinations. Coordinated attacks on security forces improved.

But despite bolstered ranks and new capabilities, GAM was confronted with a massive influx of government forces, to some thirty thousand, including Kopasus (a special forces group), who had spent the 1980s engaged in counterinsurgency in East Timor. GAM could not begin to match the increased resources and manpower of the TNI.

The government used several very small outbreaks of violence in the mid-1990s to justify a stepped-up security force presence, and the TNI was broadly implicated in widespread human rights abuses.[8] Popular antipathy for the government grew as a result of the human rights abuses and the culture of impunity that permeated the security forces.

The TNI was absolutely brutal during this period of time, engaging in scorched-earth tactics and collective punishment, which did make many Acehnese at least sympathetic to GAM, though it never became a mass-based movement. It remained contained in the mountainous interior, unable to operate in the population centers, although it did increase propaganda and recruitment in the towns and cities.

The government offensive clearly weakened GAM. And this had an interesting impact on GAM's operations. The militants became much more predatory on the local population. They engaged in massive extortion, demanded revolutionary taxes, and began to be abusive toward the parts of the population that were not overt in their support. GAM suspected that large numbers of Acehnese were government informants and began to target people it deemed as traitors. GAM also began to target schools and other government-provided social services.

GAM's fourth phase began in 1999 with a renewed offensive to take advantage of the collapse of the Suharto regime/military-backed government. The system of civilian administration by the military ended, though civil administration was initially very weak. The military was on the defensive for human rights abuses and its role in keeping Suharto in power, so GAM seized the initiative and launched a wave of attacks. GAM truly believed that Indonesia was on the cusp of being a failed state and that independence was inevitable. GAM was a much larger organization in this period, with a high estimate of fifteen thousand to twenty thousand fighters. GAM was clearly able to recruit a large group of younger militants, especially following the government's failure to implement its own 2001 autonomy law. GAM had the broadest base of popular support in its history and enough armed militants to control vast swaths of the countryside (up to 65 percent).[9] GAM actively recruited from the enormous pool of unemployed youth, exacerbated by the Asian Economic Crisis (1997–2000). GAM also benefited from a growing chorus for independence. In November 1999, over a half-million people demonstrated for independence.

Yet little changed for GAM. Its base area remained isolated from population centers. GAM itself could be very predatory, unpopular, and far more hard-line than the majority of the population, which was eager for more autonomy and peace. GAM was also surprised by the emergence of Acehnese civil society. In November 2000, a major conference that was run by civil society, academics, and religious leaders supported enhanced autonomy; GAM was left out of the conference and was clearly alarmed that it was not in charge.

Moreover, the situation on the battlefield began to turn against it again. By this time, the black arms markets in Cambodia had dried up; the ability to acquire arms and ammunitions was based on the limited domestic black market. GAM's tactics and target remained the same: security forces when the militants had high probability of success, informants or government supporters, oil and gas facilities when they could, and government-provided social services. Because GAM was so much larger at this period, it had to extort more money from the local population. A lot more young men began walking around with arms. GAM, to many people, was looking more like a thuggish protection racket. And militarily it was thwarted by a huge influx of government troops in May 2003, from thirty thousand to fifty thousand. GAM's movements were severely hampered, and it lost over four thousand combatants in this period. In 2002, the TNI estimated that GAM had under four thousand combatants.

Although the TNI controlled only 30 percent of the villages in 2001, GAM was increasingly hindered in its operations and being driven further into the mountainous interior. By 2004, it had lost nearly 25 percent of its manpower and was operating almost exclusively from the hinterland.

After 2001, the international environment had changed greatly for GAM, making arms imports, remittances, and overseas fund-raising all the more difficult. International condemnation toward governments with insurgencies disappeared as the West feared the emergence of more ungoverned space. Significantly more regional security cooperation further dented the cross-border flow of people, money, and weapons. Stepped-up maritime patrols diminished local piracy, a lucrative source of funds for GAM.

GAM did engage in some terrorist operations in Jakarta. In 2000, it bombed the Jakarta Stock Exchange, which killed fifteen people. Then, in April 2003, following the collapse of peace talks and a resumption of hostilities, GAM bombed the Soekarno-Hatta Airport, the country's main gateway, injuring eleven.[10] The international community and Indonesian government were already nervous following the October 2002 terrorist attack in Bali conducted by Jemaah Islamiyah, a regional al-Qaeda affiliate. These attacks neither put additional pressure on the government nor garnered GAM support or international media attention. Such attacks were unusual for GAM, which tended to conduct only in-area operations and low-level guerrilla ambushes. More importantly, the international community pressured the group not to use such tactics. Though the US or EU governments never designated GAM as a terrorist organization, the threat of prescription loomed.

As an insurgent group, GAM had many weaknesses. First, it was never able to become a broad-based social movement. Though many Acehnese were sympathetic, most were driven to that sympathy by government repression and human rights abuses than attraction to GAM's goals. Few saw GAM's goals as ever being attainable, and many more were horrified by the degree to which the Indonesian government would go to quell secessionist aspirations. Most Acehnese were more than happy to have greater autonomy and renounce any claim for independence in return for peace. GAM's appeal and strength did grow, but only after the fall of the New Order regime, when other parts of the country benefited from democratization and other freedoms, including press and association. Second, GAM had limited state sponsorship, and its pool of overseas diaspora support was not that large. This forced GAM to garner resources from its own constituency. GAM extorted a lot of money and food from the local population. Third, although GAM took advantage of the cascade of weapons from Cambodia's civil war in the early 1990s, those markets soon dried up. GAM's arsenal comprised small arms only, and its military capabilities never got beyond simple guerrilla ambushes. GAM's insurgents were not creative military innovators in tactics the way the Tamil Tigers were. Fourth, GAM remained largely confined to the mountainous hinterlands, with only a limited ability to recruit and operate in urban population centers during brief periods when it was stronger. Fifth, while Indonesia received condemnation for its human rights abuses in Aceh, a large degree of international support for Acehnese independence never materialized; this is in contrast to East Timor. GAM had very limited success in propaganda. Both GAM and FRETILIN (the East Timorese liberation movement) had offices and representatives overseas. But FRETILIN did a much better job than GAM in lobbying governments, especially in Europe, to keep up pressure on the Indonesian government.

For example, in 1996, the exiled "foreign minister" of East Timor, José Ramos-Horta, shared the Nobel Peace Prize with Bishop Ximenes Belo. While Ramos-Horta was exiled, Bishop Belo lived in East Timor and represented a nonviolent path for East Timor. FRETILIN was a guerrilla force, but it worked with civil society and actively searched for diplomatic and nonviolent ways to end the conflict. Guerrilla war was simply a tool to get the Indonesian government to negotiate. The Acehnese government-in-exile never was able to lobby as effectively. Its leaders did not win Nobel Prizes, they did a poor job in lobbying Western governments to pressure Indonesia, and they never seemed to be really willing to negotiate in earnest. In part, I think the fact that East Timorese are largely Catholic and FRETILIN's leaders were Portuguese speakers helped in East Timor's success. Until 1971, East Timor was a Portuguese colony.

Another weakness was that the exiled leadership was far removed from the field commanders, who had considerable autonomy. GAM was a highly cellular organization. But it was not Maoist in the sense that the cells saw their primary mission as ideological and political indoctrination. GAM did not subscribe to any notion of "armed propaganda." In my estimate, it did a very poor job in ideological education and political work.

Yet GAM had some strengths. If nothing else, the TNI could never fully eradicate it. GAM could always benefit from the brutal counterinsurgent operations of the TNI to bolster its ranks. Though not military innovators, the insurgents were competent at simple rural-based guerrilla tactics. And GAM itself was an extremely difficult organization for the security forces to penetrate and take apart. GAM was built on tight kinship networks, and the organization comprised highly autonomous cells, which proved to be especially resilient.

Second, GAM was always able to capitalize on Acehnese resentment that 80–90 percent of the natural resource wealth from the province went to Jakarta.

3. THE PEACE PROCESS

The conflict resolution process was long. The broad contours of an agreement became discernable back in 1959, when the province was first given autonomy. Autonomy was either agreed to or being negotiated in 1959, 1963, 1979, 2000, and 2002. In each case, the agreement failed or was not concluded because of one of two things: government unwillingness to implement meaningful autonomy, cede full political control, and allow the province to have economic and fiscal control (especially over its natural resource) or rebels' refusal to formally renounce their demand for independence, accept autonomy, or disarm.

The 1959–1963 process was the result of the first Acehnese rebellion as well as the campaign against Darul Islam. Acehnese leader Tungku Daud Beureu'eh was able to negotiate "special status" for Aceh in 1959. By that, what I really mean is some degree of cultural and religious autonomy (i.e., the application of *sharia* law). Aceh had *de facto* political autonomy, but only because the government was in shambles. Economic autonomy and revenue sharing was not an issue at the time because oil and gas production was years away from going online. For the most part, Acehnese were engaged in subsistence farming or fishing. In 1963, Daud signed a formal agreement in which he renounced the goal of independence. These agreements had little traction or institutional support. Daud's side had at least broad-based support for autonomy. On the government side, parliament had been suspended. Sukarno had implemented what he called "guided democracy" and established himself as president for life. There was no broad governmental or parliamentary support for the agreement. The military, for its part, opposed the agreement. And the military-backed regime that came to power in the 1965 coup all but ignored the agreement.

The 1979 autonomy agreement came after a three-year war against a new and very small organization, GAM. The government clearly hoped that it

could buy off GAM with promises of political and cultural/religious autonomy before GAM became a larger, broader-based movement. The rebel leader, Hasan di Tiro, was little known with a very limited base of support, no
international support, few resources, and by this time exiled in Malaysia.
Many other of his cabinet members had been killed or arrested. In short,
GAM did not have a chance of achieving its goals, so the government assumed that the Acehnese would gladly accept the autonomy plan that the
government put on the table, similar to the 1959 proposal but with some
provisions for revenue sharing from natural resource exploration. But again,
the New Order government was highly centralized and unwilling to actually
implement the agreement that it signed. Although the war resumed in 1998
and was bolstered by more and better armed forces, the Indonesians had only
a military response to the insurgency. While the government made some
attempts to reach out to the exiled Acehnese leadership, it still made no
serious attempts at negotiation.

Not until the fall of Suharto and the end of Dwi Fungsi in May 1998 was
any traction gained toward peace. The transition to democracy was not easy
or completely peaceful, but it was essential for dealing with Indonesia's
separatist rebellions.

Each of the successive four presidents following the fall of Suharto made
attempts to negotiate with the rebels. It is not that any were insincere. The
failure of the peace process through the Habibie, Wahid, and Sukarnoputri
regimes had much more to do with the chaotic transition to democracy and
the political weaknesses of each leader. Each wanted to resolve the crisis, but
they simply didn't know how far they could go to get it, how much they
could resist military pressure, or how much of their limited political capital
they could spend amid a host of other and greater economic and political
problems. Indonesia had four separate presidents between 1998 and 2001.
None had a clear mandate, and all were concerned about the military's re-
intervention into politics.

In late 1998, president Habibie (r. 1998–1999) ordered the withdrawal of
most of Indonesia's forces from the province as a show of goodwill. Some
estimates put the number of troops down to a low of two thousand. In 1999,
the government held a nonbinding plebiscite in which the population largely
demanded greater autonomy. This is an important distinction, because that
same year, President Habibie allowed a binding referendum, conducted by
the UN, in East Timor, a former Portuguese colony occupied and annexed by
Indonesia in 1975 and 1976, respectively. There, people had the option of
voting for either independence or greater autonomy; they overwhelmingly
(78.5 percent) voted for independence.

For the Acehnese, this was an important precedent, but one that went
unfulfilled in Aceh. The government was unwilling to hold a binding interna-
tionally monitored referendum in Aceh, which it had little confidence in

winning. Most Acehnese viewed the plebiscite as a sham, and only a half-million of the four million population took part in it. GAM wanted independence and saw the political weakness of the state and significantly increased insurgent attacks. By this time, GAM had won significant popular support. Acehnese watched the fall of the New Order government and felt vindicated in their demands for autonomy if not independence. Rather than negotiate, GAM significantly increased its attacks, and the government had to rapidly reintroduce security forces. Habibie was under attack from the military and pressured to not even run for president in the October 1999 election. Many of the troops that had withdrawn from the province in 1998 to early 1999 returned to Aceh as violence rekindled.

In May 2000, newly elected president Abdurrahman Wahid (Gus Dur) implemented a cease-fire, the Joint Understanding on a Humanitarian Pause, intended to open up the war-torn province to humanitarian assistance.

Wahid wanted to build on the 1999 plebiscite in which the voters indicated they wanted greater autonomy. Wahid thought he could capitalize on five points: first, as a cleric and former head of the Nahdlatul Ulama (NU), a mass-based Islamic organization, Wahid clearly tried to capitalize on his own Islamic (though very moderate) credentials, appealing to the Acehnese. Second, he had broad popular support nationally, and his status as someone persecuted by the Suharto regime allowed him to empathize with the Aceh-nese. Third, he was a committed democrat who began implementing massive political and economic decentralization, Indonesia's "Big Bang," which was accommodating to Acehnese public sentiment for greater autonomy. Fourth, he was committed to weakening the TNI's hold on politics and policymaking, which ended the policy of Dwi Fungsi and brought the TNI largely under civilian control. Fifth, unlike his predecessors who were completely unwilling to allow any role for outsiders, he had no insecurities over the loss of Indonesian sovereignty. In 2000 he allowed the Henri Dunant Center, a Swiss NGO, to begin playing a role in mediation.

All of this paved the way for a draft agreement on revenue sharing and the implementation of *sharia* law starting in 2001.

Despite progress, the agreements did little to end the war. By early 2001, GAM stepped up attacks, including on Exxon-Mobil facilities, forcing them to close for the first time in the thirty-year war. Under pressure from the military, which was angered at his political reforms and attempts to neutralize them, Wahid had to accede to their demands to respond militarily. In April 2001, Wahid authorized all-out operations against GAM to recommence.

To be fair, blame should be shared by GAM. Wahid was a very sympathetic negotiating partner for GAM. But GAM was really in no mood to compromise. It was pushing for maximalist goals, while the Acehnese population was interested in Wahid's reforms and offers. It was the hard-line and exiled GAM leadership that was out of step, not Jakarta, for a change.

All hopes at an agreement came to naught with the impeachment of President Wahid in July 2001. The provincial government, moreover, never passed the implementing legislation for revenue sharing and *sharia*. As Indonesia became more insistent that any negotiation had to be in the context of the 2001 Special Autonomy Law, that is, there could be no quest for independence, the cease-fire started to break down. As the security situation became worse, the government began to quietly reintroduce security forces.

President Megawati Sukarnoputri (2001–2004), the daughter of the country's founder and first president Sukarno, did little to address Aceh during her first years in office. Parliament did pass the autonomy law submitted by impeached president Wahid. This included limited *sharia*, revenue sharing, and limited autonomy, but it failed to stem the violence. GAM rejected the unilateral autonomy law and never worked with the government to implement it. At the core, the issue came down to this: the government "saw the already-passed autonomy law as their maximum offer, not an opening gambit, while GAM reiterated that special autonomy was not the end of their independence struggle."[11]

In August 2002, Sukarnoputri's government issued a seven-point policy on Aceh that was hard-line and nonconciliatory. The points included a restoration of security "by crushing the separatist movement," negotiations only if GAM accepted the special autonomy law, and an ultimatum that "the government will intensify security operations" if GAM did not meet the conditions or the December 2002 deadline to cease military operations.[12] And that is what happened: the TNI stepped up its offensive in the latter half of 2002, compelling GAM back to the table.

Negotiations between GAM and the government took place in late 2002. In December 2002, the two sides signed the "Cessation of Hostilities Agreement" and began formal peace talks under the support of the Henry Dunant Center.[13] The government had made significant concessions in the draft autonomy agreement. Under the plan, Jakarta allowed Aceh to have free elections and a partially autonomous government that would be allowed to keep 70 percent of oil revenue. In return, GAM had to formally abandon its claims for complete independence and completely disarm.

But GAM was unwilling to formally renounce independence and disarm, and talks stalled in May 2003. The exiled leadership was out of touch with its constituency and unwilling to make the needed concessions. GAM was intransigent in principle, but for the first time it also had broader popular support and enough armed rebels to control vast swaths of the countryside (up to 65 percent). While many criticized GAM's hard-line stance, the reality is that President Sukarnoputri was truly in a weak position, and I am not certain that she could have pushed through the implementation of the agreement past either the military or parliament.

GAM had already severely challenged the cease-fire on the ground. An ambush in January 2003 was the *casus belli* for government forces to resume their offensive.

President Sukarnoputri immediately authorized a resumption of military operations in the province. The number of security forces increased from thirty thousand to fifty thousand, and on May 18, President Sukarnoputri placed the province under martial law as the rest of the country was moving toward greater democracy, rule of law, and political and economic decentralization.

The TNI was determined to wipe out GAM once and for all, and their operations through mid-2004 significantly degraded GAM's capabilities. The TNI claimed that by mid-2004, nearly 2,000 GAM combatants had been killed, while some 2,100 were arrested and 1,300 had voluntarily surrendered. In May 2004, the government replaced martial law with a lesser status of "civil emergency." But clearly GAM was on the ropes. By its own account, by 2004 it had lost more than 25 percent of its manpower and had been driven into the mountainous interior. As a senior commander recounted: "Not only were we no longer able to support from the outside, but unit after unit of our people lost contact."[14]

War resumed in 2003 for several reasons, and both GAM and the government were to blame. GAM was always suspicious of autonomy agreements and the government's outreach to more moderate leaders of the Acehnese who were willing to negotiate with the government. These talks invariably did not include GAM, whose position at the time was intransigent. As the armed resistance, GAM saw itself as the vanguard for all Acehnese. Importantly, GAM became highly predatory on the local population. On the government side, the transition to democracy was messy, and the state was quite weak during this period.

It's important to remember that Indonesia had five presidents in a seven-year span between 1998 and 2004. President Sukarnoputri, for her part, was politically very weak and was under intense pressure from the military to act following the loss of East Timor in 2000. For the TNI at that time, autonomy was a first step toward independence. This return to war also helped to shore up Sukarnoputri's nationalist credentials in the 2004 presidential election, which by then was evident that she was losing. She was also trying to shore up political support from the military, which was indicating that it would back former general Susilo Bambang Yudhoyono, the president's coordinating minister for politics and security affairs.

In June 2004, the Indonesian government tried to further pressure and weaken GAM by requesting the Swedish government to arrest three exiled members for terrorism.[15] This failed as the three were soon released, and ultimately the plan backfired: it made them popular heroes in Aceh, even among people who were not traditionally supporters of GAM.

As a result of human rights abuses by government security forces, the provinces became closed to all foreigners, including journalists and aid workers. This, of course, led to suspicion and allegations of even greater violations of human rights. But clearly the offensive had netted some results. GAM was rooted out from the towns and cities (though never from their stronghold), their communications and supply lines were decimated, and the influx of troops made movement, even in the countryside, perilous. The TNI claims that over 9,500 members of GAM were killed or captured or had surrendered between May 2003 and May 2004. GAM ordered its forces to withdraw back into the mountains. GAM was significantly weaker, and by May 2004 martial law ended, replaced by a "civil emergency" status. Counterinsurgency operations continued, but GAM was never able to regain any battlefield initiative. It was on the run.

The election of Susilo Bambang Yudhoyono—SBY as he was commonly referred to—as president in mid-2004 set the stage for a new round of talks. SBY was the first popularly elected president, and he had a popular mandate, including to resolve the Acehnese insurgency. As a cabinet minster, SBY always advocated an "integrated approach": enough military pressure to set the stage for talks.

But he remained cognizant that the insurgency could never be eliminated through military means alone and that the costs of continued conflict, estimated to be $130 million per year, were unsustainable. SBY was committed from the outset of his tenure in September 2004 to reach a durable political solution. Importantly, his vice president, Jusuf Kalla, who hailed from another political party, the Suharto-era Golkar, had also been in President Sukarnoputri's cabinet and had long advocated the resumption of talks. Even before the election, he had secretly approached former Finnish president Martti Ahtisaari to serve as a back channel and mediator. This process was immediately endorsed when SBY and Kalla were inaugurated in October 2004.

SBY clearly used his influence as a retired general to sway the military. As Indonesia's top mediator recounted, people were pessimistic that the military would ever support peace talks. "People believed that the armed forces would be an obstacle to peace, because they would lose the economic benefits they had derived from the war."[16] Yet he claims to have had "full support" from the commander in chief of the armed forces, General Endriartono, who also was convinced that a military victory was beyond reach. The hardliners within the TNI and government were neutralized. Most significantly, SBY ousted Rizamizard Ryucudu, the hard-line TNI chief, who was vehemently opposed to a negotiated settlement and continued to push for the military defeat of GAM.

The government immediately restarted peace talks with the rebels in October 2004. The talks were two-track: Vice President Kalla led the more public talks with the GAM leadership in Europe. [17]

But this is not where the real effort lay. The government's negotiating team all but ignored the hard-line leaders who were removed from the ground, exiled in Europe. It was this group of aging leaders, out of touch with the local population and not living under the intense military and security operations in the province, who refused to make significant concessions in early 2003. The government team gambled that Hasan di Tiro's legitimacy and leadership were in decline and that the exiles could be compelled to make concessions if they were outflanked. So while talking to Hasan di Tiro in Europe, SBY's negotiators and interlocutors from the security forces began to secretly meet with GAM's field commanders, in particular Muzakir Manaf, who were increasingly ready to accept autonomy. Would the field commanders ignore the leaders and cut their own deal with the government?

By October 2004, GAM field commanders had accepted the fact that they had nothing more to gain on the battlefield. If anything, further military operations would lead to greater losses. A negotiated settlement was the best way to preserve what they had. Even those who did not share this dire assessment, such as GAM prime minister Malik Mahmud, acknowledged, "The existing strategies applied by both parties had caused a costly stalemate." [18]

Other commanders looked to the inherent weakness of the Indonesian state. Democracy was weak, support for democracy in the country was low at the time, government institutions were underperforming, and government legitimacy was low. The hope was that Indonesia would not break up but instead break into highly autonomous regions. One GAM leader explained, "We in GAM understood very well that it was not possible to fight militarily to win. But we were waiting, although the term came later, for the Balkanization of Indonesia." [19]

When the contours of an agreement started to leak out, the GAM leadership-in-exile denounced it. But by early December the exiles had come to the conclusion that the peace process was happening without them and that to protect their own interests and prestige, they had to get on board. [20]

Everything changed on December 26, 2004, when a massive tsunami caused by an undersea earthquake ravaged the province. Roughly 177,000 people out of the population of 4.3 million were killed in Aceh alone. Eight hundred thousand people were made homeless and destitute. Some 350,000 buildings, 499 bridges, 120 of 240 health clinics, and 1,200 of 3,400 schools were destroyed. Forty thousand hectares of farmland were wiped out. Eighty percent of the electrical infrastructure and 70 percent of the fishing fleet were destroyed. While it impacted 2.2 percent of Indonesia's GDP, the tsunami impacted 90 percent of Aceh's. This was the largest humanitarian catastrophe in modern times.

Many in the media drew a direct line between the tsunami and the peace process. That is simplistic. For example, the media assumed that GAM's ranks were devastated by the catastrophe. It was not the case, as GAM's heartland was in the mountainous interior. The media's assessment also overlooked the fact that the peace process had been underway for several months and was bearing fruit. If anything, the TNI's casualty rates were far higher: an estimated two-thirds of its thirty thousand troops were killed.

The tsunami was a catalyst, not a cause. The tsunami did not make the peace process happen—it was in place—but it did expedite it. Although limited hostilities resumed, the large international presence and commitment to Aceh led to expedited peace talks under international mediation.

Yet the tsunami did play a positive role in several ways. First, the two sides quickly agreed to a cease-fire to help aid distribution. This was an important confidence-building measure. This was a very fragile cease-fire and it was broken, though no one honestly knows which side was truly responsible. The government accused GAM of stealing aid supplies to support the insurgency (either by diverting the relief supplies and food to its own ranks or as a tool to win hearts and minds). The TNI asserts that it killed 120 GAM members for raiding aid convoys. GAM denied these raids: "Our main concern right now is the relief operation in Aceh," said the rebel's spokesman at the time.[21] GAM asserted that the military was using the opportunity of the cease-fire when GAM rebels were out in the open to launch attacks on them. GAM claims that the TNI killed twenty members and over one thousand civilians in these attacks.

GAM was also very concerned that the military really was not that involved in relief efforts. The TNI was providing some but was clearly being overshadowed by the military relief programs of the United States, Australia, and even Singapore. GAM thought that the TNI was using the relief efforts as a justification for the deployment of some fifteen thousand more soldiers. Though the TNI asserted that two-thirds of its troops deployed in Aceh were solely involved in relief work, the influx of new troops allowed them to maintain a high degree of operational readiness. But the government's pledge of $542 million in aid was significant.

The cease-fire could have unraveled at this point, as it did at the same juncture in Sri Lanka, but for the international community. This was the largest international relief mission in history. The large international presence, including 1,700 foreign troops and 2,500 international aid workers, and an intense media presence in a region that heretofore had been closed to them put intense pressure on the Indonesian military not to resume hostilities. The Indonesian government in many ways was very embarrassed that it needed so much international assistance. It may also have not liked being under such international scrutiny. For issues of sovereignty and security, Indonesia announced a timetable for all foreign militaries to withdraw by April 2005. This represented a huge threat to GAM. Although international aid workers and the media were not being forced out, the withdrawal of foreign troops threatened the cease-fire. Both GAM and Acehnese provincial officials appealed for the international community to stay on, both to forestall the offensive as well as to deliver aid. To its credit, the TNI did not resume hostilities (at least no major counterinsurgency operations).

The most important impact of the tsunami was that the international community's commitment to relief efforts could not be decoupled from its commitment to seeking a durable peace process. Out of tragedy came a historic opportunity. The international community, under the leadership of former Finnish president Martti Ahtisaari, stepped in, mediated the conflict, and committed itself to overseeing the implementation of the peace. Formal talks began in Helsinki on February 25, 2005.

The international community collectively provided several billion dollars in relief assistance and long-term development aid following the tsunami, which was essential. But the access accorded to the international community due to the overwhelming economic and humanitarian needs allowed the international community to inject itself into the peace process, something the Indonesian government had never really allowed.

But what was also sobering for GAM was the fact that despite the commitment by the international community to Aceh's rehabilitation and a nego tiated settlement, it offered no public support for Acehnese independence and remained steadfast in its commitment to maintaining Indonesia's territorial integrity. As GAM prime minister Malik acknowledged: "We saw also that the world kept silent about our move for independence, so we thought during the process [of negotiations] that that [autonomy and self-government] was the best solution that was in front of us."[22]

By this time, the exiled leadership had become cognizant that a parallel process of negotiation was transpiring between the government and the field commanders, who were reeling from the devastation caused by the tsunami. The exiled leaders realized that the train was pulling out of the station, with them or without them. They jumped on board.[23]

With war wariness and psychological trauma on the part of GAM (militants' families were the ones killed; an estimated four times the number of women as men died)[24] and international pressure on Indonesia, hostilities never really resumed.

A formal autonomy agreement was concluded by all parties in August 2005, bringing an end to the conflict that had claimed an estimated ten thousand people since 1976. It was not the first time that Aceh has been promised autonomy, but it is the first time that the government has implemented the agreement and ensured meaningful political, economic and fiscal, and religious and cultural autonomy. This has happened only because of changes within the Indonesian polity: a successful transition to democracy, decentralization of political and economic decision making, a greater commitment to the rule of law, the professionalization of the military, and the understanding that this was essentially a political conflict, not a military one, which required a political solution. The agreement has proved remarkably durable, and I would argue that it is the most successful peace process I have witnessed in Southeast Asia.

4. THE COSTS OF THE CONFLICT

The war in Aceh lasted some thirty years. An estimated fifteen thousand people were killed, and some estimates put the figure at thirty thousand.[25] More than 3.5 million were displaced at some point during the conflict.[26] The insurgency decimated the provision of social services. More than 1,040 schools were destroyed or badly damaged, including 900 from 1990 to 2004, as were 22 percent of all health clinics. The social fabric was destroyed.

In part, the failure to provide social services was a derivative of GAM's military success. By 2001, over 70 percent of all villages were under GAM's control or sway. "Across most of the province the Indonesian government had ceased to function and many local politicians and civil servants were either co-opted by GAM or killed."

Insurgent recruitment decreased agricultural production and productivity while tax collection, cash or in kind, by both GAM and the government created an undue burden on the farmers. The destruction of 11–20 percent of all roads further hampered economic development.

The economic costs of the insurgency are incalculable. By one measure, in 1990 Aceh accounted for 3.6 percent of national GDP. By the end of the conflict, that had fallen to 2.2 percent.[27] And that had grave impacts on poverty.

In 1996, "The poverty rate in Aceh was 12.7 percent, very close to the national average." By 2002, it peaked at 30 percent; only four other provinces were poorer. Yet Aceh enjoyed vast wealth from natural resources. As the World Bank summed up, "Poverty in Aceh pre-tsunami, at 28.4 percent of the population in 2004, was substantially higher than in the rest of Indonesia, at 16.7 percent."[28] This was no surprise as "Aceh has experienced very low or negative growth rates for most of the past three decades, lagging behind Indonesia and North Sumatra in most years" due to the war. Aceh experienced four years of negative growth following the 1997–1998 Asian financial crisis but then underperformed the rest of the country for the following years. By 2004, Aceh's poverty rate was twice the national average.

In terms of human development indicators, Aceh "slipped from 9th in national rankings in 1996 to 15th in 2002" and twenty-ninth in 2008.[29] The costs of protracted war were clear: Aceh was a poor province in a poor country.

And because of structural issues and central government rents, "High GDP per capita in Aceh, primarily the result of the large gas and oil reserves on Aceh's east coast, has not translated into lower poverty levels."[30] Aceh experienced lower levels of growth not only due to the insurgency but also from the structure of its resource-extractive-based economy. In essence, it experienced Dutch Disease:

> Before the exploitation of gas started in the late 1970s, Aceh had one of the lowest poverty rates in the country and better socio-economic indicators than most other provinces. By the end of the conflict, Aceh had one of the highest poverty levels in Indonesia.[31]

Finally, the war and economic underdevelopment led to a substantial brain drain from the province.

5. THE PEACE AGREEMENT

Five rounds of tough negotiations between January and July 2005, aided by Finnish mediation, led to the signing of the Helsinki Memorandum of Understanding (MoU) on August 15, 2005.[32] A critical concession came in February 2005, when GAM renounced its quest for independence and said it would accept self-government. GAM was no longer an illegal separatist organization.

The Helsinki MoU was divided into six sections, including governance, human rights, amnesty and reintegration, security, postconflict monitoring, and dispute resolution. It is a model peace agreement. Yet it is, certainly in contrast to the Philippine agreements, a model of brevity, a mere eight pages. It is elegant in its simplicity, built on broad principles and trust.

The section on governance is divided into four sections: the Basic Law, political participation, economics, and the rule of law.

Basic Law for the Governance of Aceh

The first part was the government's commitment for passage of the implementing legislation, the Basic Law for the Governance of Aceh (BLGA), within a year of the signing of the MoU. The BLGA legally enshrined Aceh's autonomy. Aceh would have full autonomy over civil and judicial affairs, the provision of social services except defense, foreign affairs, and monetary and fiscal matters. Any national laws, decisions, or regulations that impacted

Aceh would have to be made in consultation with Aceh's parliament, Kanun Aceh. But importantly, the BLGA respected rites, symbols, institutions, and customs of Aceh, manifestations of its autonomy.

Political Participation

The MoU established full democratic powers and processes to the autonomous region. Free elections in which Acehnese-based parties could run were to be held within a year of the signing of the agreement. The autonomous government of Aceh would include its own executive and legislature, the Majelis Nasional.

Section 1.2.1 required that the government "create, within one year or at the latest 18 months from the signing of this MoU, the political and legal conditions for the establishment of local political parties in Aceh in consultation with Parliament." Section 1.2.2 stated, "Upon the signature of this MoU, the people of Aceh will have the right to nominate candidates for the positions of all elected officials to contest the elections in Aceh in April 2006 and thereafter."

But this was enormously controversial and the one provision that nearly broke the Helsinki process, according to Edward Aspinall, a GAM adviser. Fearful that locally based parties might create centrifugal forces potentially breaking up the country, the post–Suharto era Law on Political Parties stipulated that "only parties with a demonstrable presence in half the districts in half the provinces of the country can register with the government."[33] As such, the establishment of a local party in Aceh set a dangerous precedent, whereby individuals at the local level, not national parties, nominated candidates. Thus the parties agreed to the compromise language "in consultation with Parliament."

Outside monitors would be allowed during all elections and transparency over campaign funding was called for, though without being spelled out how to accomplish it. Acehnese would be given their own identification cards rather than national ID cards, and they would still be allowed to participate in national-level elections.

Economics

The MoU gave Aceh considerable economic autonomy. The autonomous government had the right to set and raise taxes, set its own interest rate, and borrow money, including from abroad. Aceh had the authority over all natural resource (including offshore) exploitation, and would keep 70 percent of revenue from all current and future natural resources, including offshore hydrocarbons. Taxes and revenue shared with the central government were to be independently monitored. Aceh had the right to open and administer ports and airports for the sake of commerce, including international.

Rule of Law

The autonomous government would have a full separation of powers between the executive, legislative, and judicial branches according to the MoU. An independent judiciary, including a court of appeals, was to be established. Recruitment of the police would be local (organic), and the head of the police in the province would have to be approved by the Acehnese parliament. Any crimes committed by military personnel in Aceh would be tried in civilian, not military, courts, an enormous concession by the government.

The second part of the MoU focused on human rights. And again, it was very sparse in detail. On the one hand, it committed the Indonesian government to adhering to the United Nations International Covenants on Civil and Political Rights and on Economic, Social and Cultural Rights. It committed the Acehnese government to establishing a separate and independent human rights court. Moreover, it bound the autonomous government to international human rights covenants. Finally, a truth and reconciliation commission would be established "with the task of formulating and determining reconciliation measures."

The third section was on amnesty and reintegration. In it, the government granted full amnesty to all GAM members and pledged to release all detainees and political prisoners within fifteen days of the signing of the agreement. Any disputed cases would be resolved by the Aceh Monitoring Mission (see the discussion below), and the use of weapons by GAM members hereafter would be a crime for which they were ineligible for amnesty. The government pledged to restore all citizenship rights and privileges to GAM members, including those living in exile.

The government agreed to support reintegration of former combatants, including the allocation of farmland to all GAM members, or financial assistance to those unable to farm. The allocation of farmland extended to former detainees/political prisoners as well as civilians who could prove "demonstrable loss" from the war. The two governments would establish a joint Claims Settlement Commission to deal with unmet claims.

The government set up and endowed the Reintegration Fund administered by the autonomous government to support reintegration of former combatants. And the government pledged to allocate funds (the amount was never determined) "for the rehabilitation of public and private property destroyed or damaged as a consequence of the conflict," which would be administered by the Acehnese government.

Finally, former GAM combatants were eligible for employment in the organic police and other security forces without prejudice to their background, though they still had to meet national police and army standards for education, health, and so on.

The section on security was, in many ways, the most detailed. It called for a total cessation of hostilities. GAM committed itself to the demobilization of its three thousand insurgents and decommissioning of their arms, ammunition, and explosives. GAM pledged to surrender 840 arms between September 15 and December 31, 2005.[34]

In return and in parallel, the government pledged to withdraw all nonorganic security forces (police and military) from the province. A set number of "organic" police (9,100) and soldiers (14,700) was established. What is meant by "organic" is that although the Indonesian police and military are national forces, within the province of Aceh, all members of the police and military had to be locally recruited from Aceh; the government could not transfer in non-Acehnese. And the organic forces could include former GAM combatants. Only the organic forces were authorized to "uphold internal law and order in Aceh." And even external defense of Aceh was the responsibility of organic forces.

As crime and lawlessness often run parallel to insurgencies, the government was responsible for seizing weapons and other arms from non-GAM members and criminal syndicates beyond GAM's control.

As the transition from rebels to police is a rough one, the agreement called for special training, including overseas and from the donor community, for the organic police force "with emphasis on respect for human rights."

The fourth section established the international Aceh Monitoring Mission (AMM),[35] funded and staffed by members from the European Union and Association of Southeast Asian Nations (ASEAN). The civilian agency was headed by Pieter Feith to "monitor the implementation of the commitments taken by the parties in this Memorandum of Understanding." Its responsibilities included:

a. monitor the demobilization of GAM and decommissioning of its armaments,
b. monitor the relocation of nonorganic military forces and nonorganic police troops,
c. monitor the reintegration of active GAM members,
d. monitor the human rights situation and provide assistance in this field,
e. monitor the process of legislation change,
f. rule on disputed amnesty cases,
g. investigate and rule on complaints and alleged violations of the MoU, and
h. establish and maintain liaison and good cooperation with the parties.

Indonesia, which is highly defensive of its sovereignty, an indication of its national insecurity, agreed to give the AMM full autonomy and support for the AMM in carrying out its mandate. Both sides agreed to cooperate and provide the AMM with a safe operating environment. The AMM's decisions/ findings for the investigation and adjudication of disputes were binding.

The AMM's mandate was originally for only six months, clearly insufficient. It was extended three times and finally expired in December 2006, so it was incredibly short-lived. Many Acehnese insisted that it needed a longer mandate to ensure full implementation, but Indonesia fiercely guards its sovereignty and would not allow it. But even in that time, the AMM oversaw the decommissioning of more than 840 GAM weapons and the withdrawal of nonorganic security forces.[36]

The AMM was also quite small, including 125 EU and 93 ASEAN monitors and personnel, who were gradually withdrawn. By the end of the mission there were only twenty-nine EU and seven ASEAN personnel remaining.[37]

An important provision in this section was that the government of Indonesia had to allow "full access for the representatives of national and international media to Aceh" in order to facilitate transparency. This was absolutely critical and completely new: for decades Indonesia had the province on lockdown and had routinely banned foreign journalists, which allowed its security forces to operate with total impunity.

The final section of the Helsinki MoU was on dispute resolution. Until its mandate expired, the arbiter of all disputes was the head of the AMM. If the leader was unable to resolve the dispute, then it became a more complex political issue, involving the government's coordinating minister for political, law and security affairs, the political leadership of GAM, and the chair of the board of directors of the Crisis Management Initiative, with the latter's ruling binding on the parties. But what the agreement did not include was a dispute resolution mechanism for use after the AMM's mandate expired.

6. IMPLEMENTATION AND AFTERMATH

While the Helsinki MoU was signed and, in parts, quickly implemented with enormous goodwill and political commitment, many problems and issues emerged as the more complex components were implemented. While the overall agreement was never really in doubt, or at least the return to armed hostilities was unlikely, the peace process was not to be taken for granted. There was considerable inconsistency in the implementation of all aspects of the peace agreement. Some parts of the MoU were implemented well and quickly, and both sides shared a lot of goodwill along with the tight deadlines. But other provisions were poorly conceived and executed, deadlines were pushed back, and the implementing legislation began to undermine the core principles of the Helsinki MoU.

The Indonesian parliament passed the implementing legislation, the Law on the Governance of Aceh (LoGA), in July 2006, but only after significant delay—four months beyond the deadline set in the MoU—and several re-drafts.

Also many potential spoilers who were against the peace process sat in parliament. Vice President Kalla was the head of Golkar, the largest single party in parliament, which held 128 of 545 seats (24.5 percent). The president's Democrat Party held fifty-seven seats (10.5 percent), so together they easily commanded over one-third of parliament and were able to easily cobble together enough votes from the other parties, but not without important concessions.

And those concessions came through the minutiae of the law. The LoGA was an enormously complex piece of legislation, according to the German adviser to the Acehnese government, as it was

> not limited to the core issues of "autonomous" regional governance, but covers numerous aspects that are usually regulated in sectoral laws. It includes, for example, regulations on public health and education, natural resources management, including fisheries and mining, economic development and investment, human rights, the armed forces, the police and the judiciary. This wide scope of rather superficial regulations, which necessitate many references to the more detailed sectoral laws, distracts from focusing on the basic principles of "special autonomy."[38]

The breadth of the law led to "the direct involvement of an unusually large number of stakeholders with a vast scope of varying interests in all stages of the drafting process," which led to "many compromises . . . at the cost of clarity and consistency of the law."[39]

The problem with the law was that it undermined the core purpose: to give the Acehnese autonomy in governance. The minutiae included in the law to reconcile it with national laws actually served to restrict Acehnese autonomy. As May put it, "The four main legal principles that GAM had negotiated in Helsinki promised a fundamentally revised relationship between Aceh and the central government. The way they have been translated into the law does not do justice to this promise."[40]

While many provisions were contentious, the greatest concern was one provision: "The central government sets norms, standards and procedures and conducts the supervision over the implementation of government functions by the Government of Aceh and District/City governments," interpreted by many as Jakarta's continued exercise of control over local administration.

And note that in the time it took to pass the LoGA, much of the implementation of other components had already been started and implemented in good faith. The LoGA actually undermined many of the principles of the MoU.

Other parts of the agreement were implemented well, but even those were not without some controversy. For example, the amnesty provision was relatively successful. Indonesia released the first 298 prisoners within two days of signing the agreement. It released 1,424 more by August 30, 2005. For a government such as Indonesia, with its notoriously plodding bureaucracy, that is light speed. But some disputes arose, as Kirsten Schulze notes. These centered on the charges by which people were jailed, that is, the government did not release GAM members who had been arrested on ordinary criminal charges, for example, murder, rape, assault, hostage taking, or extortion.[41] Only those incarcerated for their direct involvement in the insurgency were released.[42]

Disarmament was another relatively successful provision that also had some controversy. GAM turned over 341 and 291 weapons to Indonesian authorities in the first two rounds of decommissioning, respectively. But some weapons were rejected for being too old and unserviceable, leading authorities to believe that the rebels were trying to stockpile their arms, Things almost fell apart during the third round when GAM's representatives declared that there were no more weapons to be turned in. It was only under AMM pressure that they turned in 286 weapons in November and 162 in December 2005. Despite the fact that they turned in more weapons than originally agreed upon, the number of "rejected" weapons left Indonesian officials never fully convinced that GAM had completely disarmed.

The mistrust went both ways. In that same time frame, Indonesia withdrew 25,890 TNI and 5,791 BRIMOB forces from the province. While AMM was confident that the nonorganic security forces had been removed, GAM regularly raised concerns that a number of undercover TNI intelligence units remained and was actually growing in number over time.[43]

More importantly, Article 202 of the LoGA clearly violated the MoU's provision for having only locally based security forces: "The Indonesian Armed Forces (TNI) are responsible for maintaining the security of the state and for other duties in Aceh in accordance with laws and regulations." As May notes, the reference to "laws and regulations" is geared specifically to Law 34/2004 on the Indonesian Armed Forces that gives the TNI the same duties and responsibilities throughout the country, including internal security.[44]

A number of anti-GAM paramilitaries that arose during the conflict have not gone away. Most operate under the umbrella association Pembela Tanah Air, meaning "homeland defenders," or PETA. Under the Helsinki MoU, they were not obligated to disband or disarm.

But if one looks at the actual number of violent incidents, the peace process was inordinately successful. Violence did build during 2005 as peace talks were ongoing, reflecting frustration at slowdowns or unwillingness of the other side to make concessions. Sometimes the violence was simply a signal of the costs of failing to reach a conclusion. Violence spiked in June 2005, with forty-five armed clashes between GAM and government security forces. But the number fell to thirty in July and by half in August, the month of signing. There were fewer than five clashes in September, and throughout 2008, no month saw more than two or three clashes between GAM and government security forces.[45]

That's not to say there was an absence of violence. Indeed in the years after the peace accord was signed, actual violence steadily increased. The region was still awash in weapons and there were large numbers of unemployed and under-employed young men; an estimated 15-25,000. Political competition was seen in zero sum terms and control over both tsunami and post conflict funding was intense. And finally, there really was no rule of law. Thirty years of war, has meant that violence remained the default conflict resolution mechanism.

Other components of the security provisions were also unevenly implemented. In 2006, the government established the Aceh Peace Reintegration Agency (BRA), to help ex combatants and prisoners to find jobs, allocate farmland, and ensure access to social benefits for three distinct groups: ex-combatants and their supporters, amnestied political prisoners, and civilians affected by the conflict.[46]

GAM members have been very critical of the government's failure to hire them into the organic police or army units.[47]

The government insisted that GAM provide them with a list of members to facilitate the disbursement of rehabilitation funds. GAM refused to turn over its membership rolls, fearing that it could be used as a hit list—a legitimate concern. In the end, the government agreed to allocate funds to field commanders, who were expected to disburse funds equitably. Invariably they were not, causing dissension.[48] But herein lay a problem. During the peace negotiations, GAM claimed to have some three thousand armed combatants. The Indonesian government allocated sixty-eight million euros for their reintegration, and that in itself didn't include the two thousand political prisoners released from Indonesian prisons. In the end, more than twenty-five thousand people, including dependents, applied for funds, completely overwhelming the system.[49]

And it was not easy to integrate these combatants, especially those recruited in the final phase of the war, 1999–2004, who had spent their entire teenage/adult lives fighting and knew nothing else. Other issues emerged, such as: Should victims of the conflict be compensated? What constituted victims? What was meant by "affected by conflict"?

As the scope of the program grew, the BRA was simply incapable of coping. It was further hobbled in long-term planning by the annual budgeting process, which prevented it from establishing clear long-term goals. [50]

Economically, Aceh has benefited. It has kept 70 percent of revenue from rents on natural resources. But still concerns arose that the provincial government's ability to attract foreign investment and award concessions was undermined by the central government's ability to set rules and standards under the LoGA. [51]

The World Bank and United Nations Development Programme (UNDP) both make clear that there were peace dividends; that the overall economy grew, instances of poverty fell, and Human Development Index (HDI) indicators improved in the aftermath of the civil war. But overall, the gains of peace were disturbingly small, inequitably shared, and in some ways caused social dissension and a breakdown in political unity enjoyed during the conflict.

By 2009, the rate of poverty in Aceh had declined to 22 percent, though it was still significantly above the national average of 14 percent. HDI indicators also improved. Still, incredible inequalities remained, caused in part by uneven distribution of aid. Unemployment rates improved, but only gradually. Fifteen thousand to twenty-five thousand former combatants and supporters were still searching for work.

Part of the problem was that the amount of post-tsunami aid—some $8 billion—completely dwarfed the amount of funds for postconflict reconstruction, a mere $230 million. This was an unprecedented outpouring of aid. Of the nine billion dollars in total tsunami relief, eight billion dollars went to Indonesia. This was not merely an issue of the Indonesian government that saw giving aid and rehabilitation funds to those stricken by natural disaster to be more palatable than giving funds to former enemies of the state. The donor community pledged $5.3 billion of the $8 billion in post-tsunami aid.

And it's important to understand that "aid is not aid." The regions most impacted by war and conflict were on the northeast coast, while the most damaged regions from the tsunami were the west and northern coasts. While the interpretation of tsunami recovery was stretched to include postconflict projects and communities, it caused real inequalities.

Another issue was that due to the high levels of poverty and the fact that the vast majority of the population lived in the countryside, the donor community really wanted to see agriculture and poverty alleviation at the core of any development strategies. And they were no doubt disappointed in the results. Declines in agricultural employment led to increases in overall unemployment.

The World Bank and UNDP both found that after 2006, villages destroyed by the tsunami grew at much faster rates than conflict-affected villages.[52] The rates were simply staggering and caused huge amounts of resentment.

The autonomous government now keeps 70 percent of revenue from rents on natural resources. But people have real concerns about how well and equitably these proceeds are being shared within the province. More importantly, the government has failed utterly to diversify the economy beyond natural resource extraction, which proved catastrophic in 2004–2005 when that sector contracted by 9.6 and 10.1 percent, respectively. It remains at roughly 24 percent, the same as at the end of the war.

Aceh, like every other province, receives a block grant annually from the central government. After 2008, Aceh received an additional 2 percent for a fifteen-year period, and 1 percent for five additional years.[53] This was seen as both a form of concession and a realization that the oil and gas rents would decline as the fields entered the period of post-peak production.

While more students are in school, educational spending as a percentage of total government spending is actually twice the national average. Yet per capita health-care spending remained unchanged between 2002 and 2008, at roughly 6 percent. But despite these improvements, access to both education and health care are very uneven.

Local accountability has risen. Pre-Helsinki, the central government allocated most development funds. By 2008, nearly 70 percent were administered and allocated by the provincial government.

Perhaps the most maligned aspect of the peace process was the failings of the BRA. It did not know how to disburse money for development funds, constantly shifting between community-designated projects, individual applications, and World Bank–led projects. The BRA was inconsistent, poorly run, and bureaucratic. It clearly did not meet the expectations of the Acehnese in general and GAM members in particular.

Politically it was a mixed bag as well. As noted earlier, the LoGA actually undermined political autonomy as the central government retained its purview over "national norms," yet GAM established a political party, Partai Aceh, and former imprisoned GAM leader and intelligence chief Irwandi Yusuf was elected governor of Aceh in the first direct gubernatorial elections in December 2006.

But this was not an easy or linear process. Inter-GAM competition over the peace dividend was real, and democratic political competition was seen in postconflict zero-sum terms.

As mentioned earlier, the establishment of local parties was nearly a deal breaker in the Helsinki process due to Indonesian concerns about the recent practice of legalizing locally based parties. GAM did not become a registered political party until May 2008. Though the parties reached a compromise, the LoGA further watered down autonomy by stipulating that any local Acehnese party had to be loyal to the founding ideology of Pancasila, which is based on the concept of national unity.[54]

In the 2006 election, national parties, including the Islamist National Mandate Party (PAN), the Ikhwan-linked Prosperous Justice Party (PKS), and the Suharto-era umbrella United Development Party (PPP) all fielded or endorsed local candidates and hoped to capitalize on their political machine and party coffers.

GAM was immediately beset by a lack of unity over whom to field as their candidate. The leadership of GAM, comprising the returned exiles, backed one candidate, who came in second in an internal poll. The winner of that poll actually took himself out of the running, which allowed Yusuf Irwandi to see a political opening. Irwandi and his running mate, Muhammad Nazar, garnered the support of key commanders and ran as independents. They were effectively able to cast the GAM-sponsored candidates as too quick to get in bed with national-level political parties, a blow to regional independence but also tying Irwandi and Nazar to the corruption of Jakarta that fueled the insurgency. A schism within GAM, in particular a generational one, emerged.[55]

Yet Irwandi won 38 percent of the vote, over two times that of his nearest competitor, and won a plurality in fifteen of the twenty-one districts.

GAM has fared well in all elections since the peace accord was signed. In the 2009 Majelis Nasional elections, Partai Aceh won 49 percent of the vote, becoming the largest parliamentary block. Outside monitors found the elections to be relatively free and fair despite some preelection political violence.

For the most part they have been able to maintain their very effective network throughout the countryside. Their grassroots network was coupled with their decades of experience in mass mobilization and organizational skills. They have also been able to differentiate themselves from national parties' candidates. More importantly, people view them as the most likely to safeguard the autonomy gained in the Helsinki process. Acehnese have watched parliament and national-level politicians constantly try to dilute the Helsinki MoU, and locally based politicians, untainted by Jakarta, are seen as the last line of defense. Finally, they have done a fairly good job improving their performance-based legitimacy.

"The decision to establish a political party shows that former GAM members have the aspiration and intention to participate in a normalized, democratic political process."[56] Yet there are plenty of concerns. First, the capacity of administrative units remains very low, especially at the district level. Most revenue and transfer payments are kept by the provincial government, leaving district-level governments quite weak with no provision of social services. Second, anti-GAM paramilitaries that have neither gone away nor disarmed, such as PETA, have not shown any propensity toward entering democratic politics. Third, a move to split the province in two has arisen.

Proponents of the establishment of Aceh Leuser Antara have been pushing the issue in the Indonesian parliament, further undermining popular confidence of the province's autonomy.

Fourth, because the 2006 elections were held before local political parties could be established (to wit, GAM only formally transformed into a political party in May 2008), the LoGA allowed independent candidates to run for office in the 2006 election only.[57] As Edward Aspinall rightly notes, the legislators in Jakarta that drafted the LoGA were all nominated by political parties and themselves feared political challenges from independents.[58] This precedent had to be quashed. In 2010, the Indonesian Supreme Court ruled Article 256 invalid. But Partai Aceh, by then the largest party in the province and one that sought to challenge the independent governor with its own candidate (the brother of the man Irwandi defeated in 2006), refused to be bound by the ruling, saying that the court's failure to "consult" with the Acehnese parliament was a violation of the LoGA.[59] In June 2011, the Acehnese parliament passed its own law banning independents. The governor refused to be bound by the new law, and the Supreme Court invalidated it by upholding its original ruling. Partai Aceh threatened to boycott the polls.

> On this central point, what was essentially an internal conflict between former GAM supporters had escalated into a full-blown political and legal crisis. Partai Aceh spokespeople claim their position is a defence of the principles of self-government embodied in the Helsinki MoU.[60]

Yet what Partai Aceh presented as a fierce defense of the region's autonomy and principles of Helsinki was seen by many Acehnese as a bald-faced grab for power against a very popular and successful governor. But others within the Partai Aceh saw Irwandi Yusuf as someone who dispensed wealth and benefits only to his supporters.

In the end, Partai Aceh did not boycott the 2012 gubernatorial election, and its candidate, Zaini Abdullah, won 55.6 percent of the vote to Irwandi's 29.2 percent.[61] Some political violence surrounded the election but less than had been feared, and for the most part, former combatants have remained committed to the democratic process. The next gubernatorial election is scheduled for 2017.

In addition to Partai Aceh, a number of other local parties have sprung up, including the Aceh People's Independent Voice Party (Partai Suara Independen Rakyat Aceh—PSIRA); the Aceh People's Party (Partai Rakyat Aceh—PRA); the Sovereign Aceh Party (Partai Daulat Aceh—PDA); the United Aceh Party (Partai Bersatu Aceh—PBA); and the Safe and Prosperous Aceh Party (Partai Aceh Aman dan Sejahtera—PAAS).

Of all the provisions of the Helsinki MoU, the human rights component has probably been the most controversial. As Amnesty International summed up, "Hardly any of those responsible for serious human rights abuses have been brought to justice, while attempts to provide reparation to victims have been inadequate."

In December 2013, after years of delay, the Acehnese parliament passed the Aceh Truth and Reconciliation bylaw, which called on the government to establish a full truth and reconciliation commission.[62] To date, the commission still has not been established.

A similar bill at the national level, which would include other conflicts, has also made no progress. In 2006, the Indonesian Supreme Court struck down a law establishing a truth and reconciliation commission.[63] Parliament has shown no political will to take up the measure again.

But the real issue of human rights has centered on the establishment of *sharia* law, including sections of the *hukum hudud* and stringent restrictions for women.

The government had pledged the right to establish *sharia* courts in the province at several junctures in the peace process. And indeed, starting six years before the peace process, Aceh's provincial legislature passed a series of bylaws governing the implementation of *sharia* law. The 2009 law that implemented Aceh's "special status" (Law No. 44/1999) offered limited *sharia*, giving the local government the right to set up policies on religion, education, and custom. The Special Autonomy Law (Law No.18/2001), enacted in 2001 under President Wahid, gave the province the right to establish *sharia* courts and included an extended mandate that covered family law and religion and now included criminal law.[64] In 2002, the parliament passed laws on Islamic dress, which effectively forced Muslim women to cover their heads. The following year it passed laws banning a host of morality issues, including the consumption of alcohol, pre- and extramarital sex, and gambling. Syiar Islam, a broad category related to the promotion of an Islamic environment, was codified, broadening the *sharia* court's mandate. Public canings were prescribed as punishments. In 2005, for example, at least thirty-five people were publicly caned.[65]

While the Helsinki MoU states that Aceh could draft its own legal code and establish its own judiciary, it did not explicitly state that this would be an Islamic law system. The 2006 LoGA codified *sharia* legally, expanding the application of *sharia* to include criminal law as well as family law and religious issues. A provincial religious affairs bureau, the Dinas Shari'ah, was established with its own morality/religious police force, the *wiliyatul hisbah*, who are incredibly abusive and operate despite their lack of legal power to make arrests.[66]

This has been controversial both within Aceh and in the donor community.

In 2009, the Acehnese parliament passed the Aceh Criminal Code (Qanun Hukum Jinayat), which broadens the application of *hukum hudud* and provides for stoning to death (*rajam*) for adultery and caning of up to one hundred lashes for homosexuality. Yet due to a public and diplomatic backlash, Governor Irwandi refused to sign the Criminal Code into law.[67] Some provisions, including those for adultery, consumption of alcohol, unmarried adult couples who are alone in close proximity (*khalwat*), gambling, and any Muslim found eating, drinking, or selling food during sunlight hours in the fasting month of Ramadan, were still in place under the 2001 bylaws, and Amnesty International reported that at least sixteen men and women were caned in 2010.[68] The number of public canings soared in 2011, including twenty-two in a ten-day period.

A newly elected provincial parliament took up the Criminal Code again, and Governor Zaini Abdullah signed it into law in December 2013. By this point the law had been expanded far beyond the scope of the 2009 bill. The Qanun Jinayat (behavior-governing bylaw) obliges not only every Muslim but also every non-Muslim in Aceh to follow *sharia*. Key provisions of the law include the following:

1. The *sharia* authorities, the *wiliyatul hisbah*, have the power to arrest suspected violators, conduct raids on private property, and confiscate evidence, based on only preliminary evidence.
2. The authorities have the power to detain any violator for up to thirty days prior to trial. *Sharia* courts can extend the detention by another thirty days.
3. A suspect has the right to be defended by a lawyer.
4. Non-Muslim or military suspects will be tried in a *sharia* court unless the violation is covered by the Criminal Code or the Military Code, respectively.
5. Even if the *sharia* court acquits a defendant, he or she will be required to undergo rehabilitation administered by the Dinas Shari'ah.
6. Defendants have the right of only one appeal in the *sharia* court.
7. Sentences include prison terms up to forty months, caning, and fines up to a maximum of eight hundred grams of gold.[69]

Since passage of that law, the extension and application of *sharia* has dramatically expanded. In September 2014, the government passed a law criminalizing extramarital sex and homosexuality, the latter punishable by one hundred lashes, one hundred months in jail, or a fine of one thousand grams of pure gold.[70]

In May 2015, one regency passed legislation requiring schools to teach boys and girls separately from kindergarten through university. That same regency was drafting regulations to prohibit the two sexes from riding motorcycles together. Other draft regulations include compulsory Koranic study sessions, bans on school-age children being outside their family home after dark, prohibitions on all businesses during the five daily prayer times, and banning of mannequins as well as any clothing that does not comply with *sharia* guidelines on "modesty." While these are in only one regency, they suggest how the law will continue to be applied at the provincial level.[71]

On the one hand, the implementation of *sharia* law, including *hukum hudud*, is but a clear sign of the successful implementation of Aceh's political autonomy. But it is clearly an enormous setback for human rights and universal norms.

While some argue that the *sharia* courts have helped protect women's rights regarding inheritance and property, restrictions on women's clothing and on times that they can work and the shifting burdens of proof in domestic violence and rape have been enormous setbacks for women.[72] Women and human rights groups have argued that the new *sharia* laws have codified domestic and sexual violence and deterred women from going to the police or seeking legal redress. Regulations banning women from being out at night after 11:00 p.m. without their husband or a male family member have struck women's rights to work and feed themselves.[73]

One shocking case demonstrates the horrific abuse of the *sharia* system. In May 2014, a group of *sharia* policemen—or was it *sharia* vigilantes?— broke into a house, where they found a twenty-five-year old woman alone with a married man. The "policemen" accused the two of adultery, beat the man, and gang-raped the woman. Yet it was the woman who was publicly caned for her violation of public morality. None of the assailants was ever punished.[74]

Other critics find that the application of *sharia* has gone too far and fails to conform both to the "judicial system of the Republic of Indonesia" as well as "the universal principles of human rights as provided for in the United Nations International Covenants on Civil and Political Rights and on Economic, Social and Cultural Rights," as stipulated in the Helsinki MoU. Caning is a form of torture and thus a violation of Indonesian law and international treaty obligations, which cannot be superseded by local law protecting a region's autonomy.

Yet *sharia* courts receive high plaudits from the general population for delivering fast, corruption-free, and fair justice.

7. CONCLUSION

Despite problems in implementation and some public dissatisfaction, the Acehnese peace process is the most successful peace process that I can think of, and not only in Southeast Asia. Not only has it held for over ten years, but Aceh's autonomy is now deeply entrenched. This is not to say that it is not irreversible or that no issues still arise. For example, in April 2013, the central government protested the Aceh legislature's adoption of the GAM flag as its provincial flag.[75] To date, the two sides are going through legal channels to resolve the conflict. But why has the peace process been so successful? I will focus on seven points:

First, both sides clearly recognized that they had reached a complete stalemate. They could gain nothing more from fighting. Indeed, a continuation of hostilities would have been counterproductive to both sides' interests. That drove both sides to the negotiation table.

Second, the spoilers were neutralized. GAM had surprisingly good command and control over its combatants, or what was left of them. When the cease-fire was established following the tsunami, it broadly held, and large-scale hostilities never resumed, in part because GAM had been militarily weakened, and in part because the insurgents had been traumatized by the devastation and loss of life (their families) in the tsunami. In some ways the hard-line spoilers on the rebels' side were the guys without guns, the exiled leadership. The field commanders were largely committed to the peace process. It was easy to neutralize the old guard because they were living in exile in Europe.

Neutralizing spoilers was far more difficult on the government's side, as the hard-liners there had very deep and vested interests in maintaining the conflict. But President Yudhoyno was able to use his broad base of support in the military to neutralize the commanders who were adamantly against negotiation. The military benefited from the crisis, not only because of budgets, but because of the fact that it received only one-third of its budget from the central government, and Aceh was rich in extrabudgetary opportunities (drug smuggling, illegal logging, and extortion and protection of natural resource extraction, to name but a few).[76] Plenty of the progovernment paramilitaries also resisted the peace process and feared repercussions in any accountability mechanism, as the TNI had used them to do a lot of its dirty work and false-flag operations.

Many potential spoilers who were against the peace process were in parliament. This is where Vice President Kalla proved invaluable. He was the head of Golkar, the largest single party in parliament (and former president Suharto's political vehicle). Golkar held 128 of 545 seats (24.5 percent). The president's party held fifty-seven seats (10.5 percent), so together they commanded over one-third of parliament, and they were able to easily cobble together enough votes from the other parties. And while they did not have to support the agreement, President Yudhoyono did have another strength: he was the first president elected through a popular election, that is, he had an electoral mandate. That was enough to win over a significant number of parliamentarians. As a GAM leader acknowledged: "SBY without Jusuf Kalla: It would not have been possible. Kalla without SBY: not possible. SBY controlled the military. He blocked the Ministry of Foreign Affairs—there was no intervention from them at all." [77]

Third, the peace process itself was attended to at the highest levels of government. In many such negotiations, the task is delegated to junior officials so that should the talks fail, the political leadership is not tarnished or implicated. In this case, President Yudhoyono was deeply involved in all stages and in decision making. He played a critical role in lobbying the senior military leadership. In the end, he tied his political legacy to the peace process. In short, he showed real political courage. But as much credit should go to Vice President Kalla, who was the lead negotiator and parliamentary point man. Kalla was in charge of day-to-day negotiations. He engaged in significant shuttle diplomacy and ran many informal negotiation sessions where the toughest issues were resolved. As one analyst notes, "His enormous energy, entrepreneurial spirit and pragmatic flexibility finally found a way through the entrenched positions toward a mutually acceptable solution. Kalla's position as leader of the Golkar Party, meanwhile, greatly strengthened the administration's ability to win the support of other national political parties." [78] The steadfast commitment of the most senior echelon of the executive branch helped win over enough support within the military—a key political power center even after the fall of Suharto in 1998—and parliament. Many previous governments had negotiated or promised autonomy. This was the first government that could deliver and actually legally implement autonomy.

Fourth, the peace process would never have been successful without being part of a larger political reform package. I do not believe that peace could have been achieved without the democratic transformation of Indonesia. For one thing, a civilian check on military power was now in place; the TNI was less autonomous than it ever had been. Moreover, the TNI was seeking to extricate itself from politics and become more professional while the civilian government was committed to the rule of law, with checks and balances. All regions of Indonesia benefited from significant political and economic decentralization. Aceh could count on other allies across the archipelago pushing for similar goals, whereas before, they might not have been sympathetic to Aceh's bid for independence. What the Acehnese wanted did not threaten democrats the way it threatened the interests of a dictator whose system was based on overcentralization. The central government's Ministry of Home Affairs asserts that it has the authority to annul regional bylaws that contravene Indonesia's constitution. It has largely given the Acehnese legislature and government a bit more autonomy in this regard.

Fifth, the peace process had significant international support, and not solely because of the tsunami. The eight billion dollars in aid was important, but the support went beyond this. The international community had a true sense that out of great tragedy could come a historic opportunity, and it did not let the momentum die. Eight months after the worst natural disaster in modern history, a peace accord was ready. The negotiators did not waste a moment, holding five rounds of talks in very quick succession to keep from losing momentum or allowing opposition by spoilers to materialize. The mediation efforts by former Finnish president Martti Ahtisaari were exemplary. But the commitment in running, staffing, and funding the AMM by the EU (which added global and first-world imprimatur) and ASEAN (which demonstrated the region's commitment to the process) was critical. If the international community is going to involve itself in a peace process, it has to commit itself to doing so for the long haul, though in some cases, such as Aceh's, the conditions are good enough that international support did not need to last that long.

One last point about international support: it took a long time for Indonesia to accept any international mediation or facilitation. In part it was because the country had been so routinely criticized for its human rights abuses. In part, it is the nature of recently independent states to be overly guarded of their sovereignty. For years, Aceh was a matter of purely internal affairs, not subject to any external scrutiny or oversight. Indonesia finally realized that third-party mediation or even the good offices and facilitation of neutral third parties such as Finland or the Henri Dunant Center were useful and that they did not threaten Indonesia's sovereignty. I do not know what changed. Perhaps it was simply a greater sense of security, or perhaps Indonesia recalled its positive role as a mediator in the southern Philippines in 1996. But it made a highly significant difference.

Sixth, GAM was able to quickly and effectively transition into a political party. Retail politics requires a very different skill set from guerrilla warfare. Many rebel movements have trouble reentering civilian life. Yet in six years, GAM has fielded competent administrators. In a poor region of the country, GAM could not rest on its laurels—the legitimacy that it had garnered through its leadership during thirty years of struggle. It actually had to deliver effective governance.

Seventh, the government's establishment of a trust fund to help former GAM combatants reenter civilian life was important. After protracted conflicts, a government always has a twofold concern: (a) that armed men will simply become criminal entities and extort the local population, or (b) that they will demand that the new government employ them all as civil servants or members of a local security force. The latter happened in East Timor, and when the new government did not hire the former FRETILIN rebels, they tried to stage an assassination of the prime minister and mount a coup in 2008. Neither of these happened in Aceh. The government had set aside funds to assist former rebels in buying land and starting businesses, while the AMM's disarmament program was widely successful. The province was not plagued by banditry, and the new government did not become a patronage/jobs program.

NOTES

1. Some Acehnese never accepted the legal inclusion of Aceh into Indonesia. As the Dutch ruled the province indirectly through the sultan, Indonesia had no formal legal right to Aceh upon independence. The Acehnese people were never consulted or given a plebiscite in which they could elect to join the Republic of Indonesia.

2. Another ethnic difference is that very few ethnic Chinese live in Aceh, while other parts of Sumatra and most of Java have significant populations. The presence of the Chinese in Indonesia has always been very sensitive. They were brought to Indonesia by the Dutch to serve as middlemen, wholesalers, and bankers for the indigenous population (collectively known as the Pribumi). M. Adriana Sri Adhiati and Armin Bobsien, "Indonesia's Transmigration Program: An Update," July 2001, at Down to Earth, http://www.downtoearth-indonesia. org/sites/downtoearth-indonesia.org/files/Transmigration%20update%202001.pdf.

3. Kirsten E. Schulze, *The Free Aceh Movement (GAM): Anatomy of a Separatist Organization* (Washington, DC: East-West Center, 2004).

4. The estimates vary widely, from two thousand to ten thousand. As with all insurgencies, a vast discrepancy is evident when determining who is an insurgent. Clearly, all figures include not only armed militants but also members of GAM's support base.

5. Human Rights Watch, "Asia Watch: Countering Human Rights Violations in Aceh," June 19, 1991.

6. While some reports claim that Iran also provided training and assistance, I have never been able to verify this point. It may have provided some arms, and if it did provide training, it was for only a very limited number of personnel. Libya's support to GAM and the MNLF was institutionalized and very much part of Gaddafi's plan to leverage broad international support for his revolutionary model.

7. GAM took advantage of a sizable and fairly wealthy diaspora community living in northern Malaysia, which had ties across the border in Thailand. The border between Malaysia and Thailand was set in an Anglo-Thai agreement of 1909, and the majority of the population of the three southernmost provinces of Thailand are ethnic Malays. They have had a long-running separatist struggle of their own against the Thai government, and many of these rebels lived or took refuge in northern Malaysia. But by the 1990s, their insurgency had been largely quelled (it would erupt again in 2004), and several militants moved into the gun-running business. They brought arms through Thailand and across the Strait of Malacca from the backwater province of Satun, long a haven of smuggling.

8. Amnesty International, "Shock Therapy: Restoring Order in Aceh, 1989–1993" (research report, July 28, 1993).

9. Schulze, *The Free Aceh Movement.*

10. "Blast Rocks Jakarta's Airport," *Jakarta Post*, April 28, 2003.

11. Konrad Huber, "Aceh's Arduous Journey to Peace," *Accord* 20 (2008): 16–21, http:// www.c-r.org/sites/default/files/Accord%2020_ 4Aceh%27s%20arduous%20journey%20to%20peace_2008_ENG.pdf.

12. Fabiola Desy Unidjaja, "Government Steps Up Pressure on GAM," *Jakarta Post* , August 20, 2002.

13. The text is available at the United Nations Peacemaker database of peace agreements, http://peacemaker.un.org/sites/peacemaker.un.org/files/ID_021209_ Cessation%20of%20Hostilities%20Framework%20Gov%20of%20Indonesia%20and%20Free %20Aceh%20Movement.pdf; also see Huber, "Aceh's Arduous Journey."

14. Cited in Hamish McDonald, *Demokrasi: Indonesia in the 21st Century* (Victoria, Australia: 2015), 100.

15. "Aceh Rebels Unmoved by Arrests," *BBC News*, June 16, 2004, http://news.bbc.co.uk/ 2/hi/asia-pacific/3810941.stm.

16. Hamid Awaluddin, "Why Is Peace in Aceh Successful?," *Accord* 20 (2008): 25–27.

17. One of Indonesia's top negotiators, Hamid Awaluddin, wrote a detailed account of the peace process from the Indonesian perspective, *Peace in Aceh: Notes on the Peace Process between the Republic of Indonesia and the Aceh Freedom Movement (GAM) in Helsinki* (Jakarta: Center for Strategic and International Studies, 2009).

18. Cited in Edward Aspinall, "The Helsinki Agreement: A More Promising Basis for Peace in Aceh? Policy Studies No. 20" (working paper, East-West Center, Washington, DC, 2005), http://www.eastwestcenter.org/fileadmin/stored/pdfs/PS020.pdf.

19. Cited in McDonald, *Demokrasi*, 102.

20. Huber, "Aceh's Arduous Journey."

21. Cited in Damien Kingsbury, *Peace in Aceh: A Personal Account of the Helsinki Peace Process* (Sheffield, UK: Equinox, 2006). Kingsbury, an Australian academic, was an adviser to GAM.

22. Kingsbury, *Peace in Aceh*.

23. Aspinall, "The Helsinki Agreement."

24. This is evident in this interview with a GAM field commander in 2005: "Interview: Aceh Rebel Leader," *BBC News*, September 15, 2005, http://news.bbc.co.uk/2/hi/asia-pacific/4247746.stm.

25. "Indonesia: Victims of the Aceh Conflict Still Waiting for Truth, Justice and Reparation," Amnesty International Australia, April 18, 2013, http://www.amnesty.org.au/news/comments/31568/.

26. *Provincial Human Development Report Aceh 2010: Human Development and People Empowerment* (Jakarta: United Nations Development Programme, 2010), http://hdr.undp.org/sites/default/files/nhdr_aceh_2010_english.pdf.

27. Patrick Barron, "Managing the Resources for Peace: Reconstruction and Peacebuilding in Aceh," *Accord* 20 (2008): 58–61, http://www.c-r.org/accord-article/managing-resources-peace-reconstruction-and-peacebuilding-aceh.

28. World Bank, *The Impact of the Conflict, the Tsunami and Reconstruction on Poverty in Aceh: Aceh Poverty Assessment 2008* (Washington, DC: World Bank, 2008).

29. *Provincial Human Development Report*.

30. World Bank, *Impact of the Conflict*.

31. World Bank, *Impact of the Conflict*.

32. The text of the agreement can be found at the website of UNHCR, the UN Refugee Agency, http://www.unhcr.org/50aa090d9.pdf.

33. Edward Aspinall, "Elections: Consolidating Peace," *Accord* 20 (2008): 46–50, http://www.c-r.org/sites/default/files/Accord%2020_13Elections_2008_ENG.pdf.

34. "Aceh Rebels Disband Armed Units," *BBC News*, December 27, 2005, http://news.bbc.co.uk/2/hi/asia-pacific/4561922.stm.

35. The head of the AMM wrote a very good report on the reasons for the success of both the peace process and the AMM in particular. See Pieter Feith, "The Aceh Peace Process: Nothing Less than Success" (special report no. 184, US Institute of Peace, Washington, DC, March 2007), http://www.usip.org/sites/default/files/sr184.pdf.

36. EU Council Secretariat, "EU Monitoring Mission in Aceh (Indonesia)," http://www.aceh-mm.org/english/amm_menu/about.htm.

37. Kirsten E. Schulze, "A Sensitive Mission: Monitoring Aceh's Agreement," *Accord* 20 (2008): 36–39.

38. Bernhard May, "The Law on the Governing of Aceh: The Way Forward or a Source of Conflicts?," *Accord* 20 (2008): 42–45.

39. May, "Governing of Aceh."

40. May, "Governing of Aceh."

41. Amnesty International Australia, "Truth, Justice and Reparation."

42. Schulze, "A Sensitive Mission."

43. Schulze, "A Sensitive Mission."

44. May, "Governing of Aceh."

45. *Provincial Human Development Report*.

46. *Provincial Human Development Report*.

47. "Jika Aceh Perang, Gubernur dan Kapolda Tanggung Jawab," *Serambi Indonesia*, May 27, 2015, http://aceh.tribunnews.com/2015/05/27/jika-aceh-perang-gubernur-dan-kapolda-tanggung-jawab.

48. Sidney Jones, "Keeping the Peace: Security in Aceh," *Accord* 20 (2008): 72–75, http://www.c-r.org/sites/default/files/Accord%2020_22Keeping%20the%20peace_2008_ENG.pdf.

49. Lina Frodin, "The Challenges of Reintegration in Aceh," *Accord* 20 (2008): 54–57, http://www.c-r.org/sites/default/files/Accord%2020_16The%20challenges%20of%20reintegration%20in%20Aceh_2008_ENG.pdf.

50. Frodin, "Challenges of Reintegration."

51. May, "Governing of Aceh."

52. World Bank, *Impact of the Conflict.*

53. World Bank, *Impact of the Conflict.*

54. Aspinall, "Elections: Consolidating Peace."

55. Aspinall, "Elections: Consolidating Peace."

56. Aguswandi, "The Political Process in Aceh: A New Beginning?," Accord 20 (2008): 52–53.

57. See Law on the Governance of Aceh, Articles 67 and 256.

58. Edward Aspinall, "Aceh's No Win Election," *Inside Indonesia* 106 (2011), http://www.insideindonesia.org/aceh-s-no-win-election.

59. Aspinall, "Aceh's No Win Election."

60. Aspinall, "Aceh's No Win Election."

61. "UPDATED—Elections in Aceh: Another Step Forward," International Foundation for Electoral Systems, April 19, 2012, http://www.ifes.org/news/updated-elections-aceh-another-step-forward.

62. "Indonesia: Aceh Parliament Passes Truth Commission Bylaw," Amnesty International Australia, January 8, 2014, http://www.amnesty.org.au/news/comments/33684/.

63. Amnesty International Australia, "Truth, Justice and Reparation."

64. Fadlullah Wilmot, "Shari'ah in Aceh: Panacea or Blight?," *Accord* 20 (2008): 76–79, http://www.c-r.org/sites/default/files/Accord%2020_23Shari%27ah%20in%20Aceh_2008_ENG_0.pdf.

65. "Indonesia: Repeal 'Cruel' New Stoning and Caning Law," Amnesty International Australia, September 17, 2009, http://www.amnesty.org.au/news/comments/21708/.

66. Wilmot, "Shari'ah in Aceh."

67. Amnesty International Australia, "Stoning and Caning Law."

68. "Indonesian Government Must Repeal Caning Bylaws in Aceh," Amnesty International Australia, May 22, 2011, http://www.amnesty.org.au/news/comments/25705/.

69. Hotli Simanjuntak and Ina Parlina, "Aceh Fully Enforces Sharia," *Jakarta Post*, February 7, 2014, http://www.thejakartapost.com/news/2014/02/07/aceh-fully-enforces-sharia.html.

70. "Indonesia: New Law Imposing 100 Lashes for Gay and Extramarital Sex 'Enormous Step Backwards,'" Amnesty International Australia, September 26, 2014, http://www.amnesty.org.au/news/comments/35667/.

71. "Indonesia's North Aceh Separates Sexes in Schools, Similar Ban for Motorbikes to Follow," *Strait Times*, May 4, 2015, http://www.straitstimes.com/news/asia/south-east-asia/story/indonesias-north-aceh-separates-sexes-schools-similar-ban-motorbikes; Muhammad Hamzah, "North Aceh to Segregate Men and Women, Force Kids to Study Koran," *Jakarta Globe*, May 14, 2015, http://thejakartaglobe.beritasatu.com/news/north-aceh-segregate-men-women-force-kids-study-koran/.

72. *Provincial Human Development Report.*

73. "Indonesia's Aceh Province Introduces Curfew Banning Women from Work, Entertainment Venues after 11pm," ABC Australia, June 10, 2015, http://www.abc.net.au/news/2015-06-09/indonesias-aceh-province-introduces-curfew-for-women/6533862.

74. Sebastian Strangio, "Sticks and Stones," *Southeast Asia Globe*, February 19, 2015, http://sea-globe.com/aceh-sharia-indonesia-sebastian-strangio-southeast-asia-globe/.

75. Joe Cochrane, "Rebel Flag Flies over a Province, and Indonesia Wants It Torn Down," *New York Times*, April 14, 2013, http://www.nytimes.com/2013/04/15/world/asia/jakarta-gives-ultimatum-to-aceh-on-rebel-banner.html?ref=world&_r=0.

76. "Aceh: How Not to Win Hearts and Minds" (Asia Briefing No. 27, International Crisis Group, July 23, 2003), 7.

77. Cited in McDonald, *Demokrasi*, 106.

78. Michael Morfit, "A Happy, Peaceful Anniversary in Aceh," *Asia Times*, August 15, 2006.

Chapter Three

Case Study 2—The Moro National Liberation Front (MNLF) and the Moro Islamic Liberation Front (MILF)

Mindanao, the Philippines

1. BACKGROUND TO THE CONFLICT

The Moro insurgency in the southern Philippines has gone on since the early 1970s, but its roots go back to the Spanish colonization of the Philippines in the sixteenth century. Islam first came to the Philippines in the early thirteenth century, almost three hundred years before Magellan's arrival and the introduction of Christianity in 1521. The thriving maritime power, the Sultanate of Sulu, was established sometime around 1450. In 1619, three sultanates were united into the Sultanate of Maguindanao. Ties (mainly through marriage) with sultanates in Brunei and southwestern Sulawesi, Indonesia, reinforced the power of the Muslim aristocracy. Spanish missionaries imposed Catholicism in the northern archipelago, but the Island of Mindanao and the Sulu archipelago, which extends down to what is now the Malaysian state of Sabah, was controlled by the Sultanate of Sulu. The Spanish never exerted firm control over the south.

Muslim separatists use the term "Bangsamoro"—or the "Moro nation." Yet this is a historical misnomer.[1] Thomas McKenna contends that there is no "Moro" nation. The term "Moro," which derives from the Spanish word "Moor," was meant to connote all of the various Muslim tribes that the Spanish were unable to effectively dominate. There is no Moro nation but rather three major linguistic and ten minor linguistic groups along with distinct ethnic differences. Moro as a concept of a nation, or Bangsamoro, is an

65

artificial construct, which partially explains why the different insurgent groups are so ridden with factionalism.

Muslims in the Philippines account for five to six million (6–7 percent) of the total population of eighty-seven million. In the southern part of the country, in Mindanao and the Sulu archipelago, they constitute 20 percent of the region's seventeen million people. The Muslim-dominated territory includes Western Mindanao, Tawi-Tawi, Basilan, and the Sulu archipelago. Today thirteen of the country's sixty-seven provinces have significant, if not majority, Muslim populations. Five provinces and two cities now have Muslim majorities: Maguindanao, Lanao del Sur, Basilan, Sulu, Tawi-Tawi, and the cities of Marawi and Cotabato. "The homeland of the Bangsamoro people consisted of the territories under the jurisdiction of their governments before the emergence of the Philippine state." The Maranaos dominate the Lanao del Sur and Lanao del Norte region. The Tausigs are concentrated in the Zamboanga Peninsula through the Sulu archipelago (Basilan, Jolo, and Tawi-Tawi). The Maguindanaons are concentrated in North Cotabato, Maguindanao, Sultan Kudarat, Davao, and Sarangani.

The common bond among the ethnic groups is religion and a shared history of persecution. As Abhoud Syed Lingga, a Moro academic and counselor to the MILF, put it, "The Muslims claim they belong to a separate nation by virtue of their distinct identity and long history of political independence."[2] It was not until the 1970s, however, that an attempt to unify the groups and articulate the common concerns and aspirations of the Bangsamoro began.

MILF officials and Bangsamoro advocates deny that they are or have ever been Filipino. They have always defined themselves as a distinct racial and religious entity, regardless of the fact that they come from the same Malay stock as the rest of Filipinos, who are like the Bangsamoro, actually a composite of ethnolinguistic groups. The Bangsamoro turn to history to reinforce their ethnonational identity. As MILF founder, Salamat Hashim, wrote:

> Islam was the earliest religion established in the islands, now called the Philippines, and the first political institution, civilization and culture in the area. We must take pride in the historical fact that the Bangsamoro Muslims were an independent people having their system of government and indigenous set of laws long before the rest of the inhabitants in the Philippines had a taste of systematized form of government and social life. This independence, however, was lost due to subsequent plots and machinations of foreign invaders and colonial powers such as the Spaniards and the Americans supported by Filipino collaborators.[3]

Likewise, the MILF ideologue, Nu'ain bin Abdulhaqq, examined Philippine history and argued that as the Spanish never fully colonized the Moros, they are hence a different people and thus a separate nation: "It is a fact established by the course of history that the Bangsamoros were not Filipinos from time immemorial until now."[4]

> The realities were: 1) the *Indios* were subjects of Spanish colonialism unlike the Bangsamoro people who were an independent nation and were *objects* of Spanish colonialism and hegemony; 2) Aguinaldo and his people in *Sangkapuluang Pilipinas*, i.e. *Indios*/Filipinos/Maniolos/Tagalogs were waging a short-lived revolution against the Spanish regime in Manila; while the Moros remained independent but were fighting the combined Spanish-Indio invasion forces in Sulu and Magindanaw; 3) as an independent nation with independent states and governments, the Moros had never seen that Aguinaldo flag until it was flown side by side with the American flag in Marawi in the 1930s. Hence, there is not enough material evidence for the Filipinos to say that the flag includes the Moros than the *acta de la proclamacion de independiencia* itself. The white triangle signified the emblem of Bonifacio's Masonic *Katipunan* of which the Moros were not part of [*sic*].[5]

In a later article, Abdulhaqq argues that the Spanish royal decree of February 26, 1893, never included any Moro lands.[6]

Beginning in the 1860s, "The Sulu and Maguindanao Sultanates were weakened by dynastic dissensions," which allowed for further Spanish consolidation. The wars were also exacerbated by European rivalry: the British, who were in the process of establishing colonies and trading posts on Sabah in Borneo, favored the establishment of a strong and independent Sulu Sultanate and did not formally acknowledge Spanish claims to the southern Philippines until a protocol was signed in 1877.

Following its acquisition of the Philippines in 1898, the United States, too, had trouble imposing law and order in the south.[7] The United States and the sultan of Sulu signed the Kiram-Bates Treaty on August 2, 1899, which allowed for a degree of local autonomy and accepted local customary law, or *adat*, and it was followed by a similar agreement with the sultan of Maguindanao. US forces allied themselves with powerful *datus*, and in return for economic privileges and the conferring of political power, the *datus* accepted US overlordship. Yet President Theodore Roosevelt unilaterally declared the treaty null and void in 1904 and imposed direct rule and control over the Moro islands. Direct rule was never that strong, though, owing to the US preponderance for decentralized rule, and the United States continued to rely on the *datus* as the source of local power. As Benny Bacani notes, the United States was more successful than the Spaniards not only because of superior military technology but also because they implemented "a new model of colonial administration: the Americans allotted considerable administrative powers to governments at the municipal and district levels, which clinched their allegiance to colonial authority."[8]

As the United States prepared the Philippines for independence, the local *datus* who had supported the government became the democratic leaders. McKenna contends that no Moro identity existed during the period of Spanish colonization, that it was forged only during the colonial period. Colonial administrators found that the local population was surprisingly nonreligious and promoted the use of religion and Moro identity as a force for development. On February 1, 1924, in expectation of the United States' eventual decolonization of the Philippines, a group of Muslim leaders met in Zamboanga and issued their "Declaration of Rights and Purposes," a petition to the US president. Fearful of living in a Christian-majority Philippine Republic, the leaders proposed that "the islands of Mindanao, Sulu, and the Island of Palawan be made an unorganized territory of the United States of America."[9] Alternatively, they proposed a referendum for independence to be held fifty years after Philippine independence. Yet US relations with Muslims soured for two reasons in the mid-1930s. First, in 1936, the Philippine government failed to recognize the successor of the sultan of Sulu, Jamal-ul-Kiram, who had died, thus the Sulu court lost its recognition, or rights as an independent entity. Second, US rulers encouraged the mass migration of landless peasants from Luzon, in the Christian north, to Mindanao.

Moros quickly became a minority in lands they claimed as their own. Though they never organized a large-scale revolt, Moros led sporadic and small-scale outbursts against Christian rule. The United States was able to contain the insurgency but never eliminate it. The 1936 elections for constitutional convention delegates included representatives from the Moros, who had hoped to use the democratic process to protect their indigenous rights. Although the majority of the population had shifted due to Christian migration, the Moros largely accepted the new constitution in a referendum.

Following World War II, when the Americans were preparing the Philippines for independence, a coalition of Muslim leaders petitioned the US government to concurrently give them independence. The United States, however, was committed to the territorial integrity of the Philippines and never seriously considered partition, arguing that the legal constitutional framework that they bequeathed the Philippines would protect minority rights.

For the early period, this seemed to work, and the Moros accepted their inclusion in the Philippines. Yet soon after independence, a quasi-communist rebellion broke out in the main island of Luzon and began to spread to other parts of the country. Already in the thick of the Cold War, the United States was fearful of communist gains and Chinese support for the Hukubah rebellion and worked with the new government to quell the insurgency. One of the strategies to defuse the rebellion, which was driven by inequality and landlessness, was to move people to other parts of the country that were more sparsely populated.

While this succeeded in pacifying the Huk rebellion, it sewed the seeds of the Moro rebellion. Large-scale immigration to Mindanao fundamentally altered the demographic mix. In 1968, leaders established the Moro Independence Movement, a nonviolent organization to advocate for secession, but garnered little popular support. By 1972, armed rebellion began. And their grievances were legitimate: by 1976, Moros were only 40 percent of the population, and by the late 1980s, they were a minority in Mindanao; the regions of Mindanao and Sulu where they remained the majority were getting smaller and smaller.

The traditional Muslim zone of control included all of Mindanao as well as the Sulu Archipelago and Palawan, approximately 118,000 square kilometers, or one-third of the total Philippines land area. Today Muslims comprise five to six million people of the country's one hundred million. They have been pushed out of their traditional lands. Only thirteen of the country's sixty-seven provinces have significant Muslim populations, and only five have majority Muslim populations. Though Mindanao is one of the last untapped regions of Southeast Asia, rich in natural resources, it is the poorest part of a relatively poor country. Muslim-majority provinces lag in nearly every measure of human development, according to the UNDP.[10]

2. THE RISE OF ARMED INSURRECTION

The first armed movement was founded by Nur Misuari, a university professor at the University of the Philippines in Manila and a close friend and colleague of Jose Sison, who went on to found the Philippine Communist Party and its armed wing, the New People's Army. The Moro National Liberation Front (MNLF) was largely manned by Muslims, but the group was formally secular, modeled on ethnonational movements of the Middle East, and included Christians and indigenous peoples.

The MNLF benefited from two key elements of external support that bolstered its ranks and capabilities. The first was from Libyan president Muammar Gadaffi's willingness to train anticolonial groups—especially Muslim movements. In 1971, President Gadaffi openly supported the Moro cause and offered one million dollars for training in Malaysia. In 1972, Libya began to provide significant training and arms to the MNLF, whose headquarters was now in Tripoli. Egypt supported both mosque and *madrassa* construction as well as offering scholarships for Moros to study at Egyptian institutions, including Al Azhar, eventually creating a critical mass that would become leaders of the Moro rebellion.

The second source of support came from the governor of the Malaysian state of Sabah, Tun Mustapha, himself an ethnic Tausug who was angered at continued Philippine claims to, as well as covert operations in, Sabah.[11]

Mustafa began to arm and provide sanctuary to small groups of Moro rebels and served as an important conduit for Libyan arms and trainers.

The MNLF's ranks swelled. In 1973, the MNLF had an estimated fifteen thousand men under arms. By 1976, it had an estimated thirty thousand guerrillas and had fought the Armed Forces of the Philippines (AFP) to a standstill, tying down 70–80 percent of government forces.[12] As a result of the insurgency, the military expenditure had to be increased fivefold.

The tide, however, turned on the MNLF.[13] In 1974 the Malaysian government announced a policy of supporting only Moro autonomy, not independence. By 1976, the enlarged and better-armed AFP began to score some military victories. That year, Tun Mustapha lost the governorship of Sabah, and the new government shut down the MNLF's training camps. The MNLF also lost popular support due to a very high civilian casualty rate and a war-wary population. The MNLF had other problems, including weak command and control, as much of the leadership was in Tripoli or Sabah.[14] The field commanders felt alienated and unsupported by the exiled leadership. By 1973 Misuari was in exile in Sabah, and calls for his ouster were growing, though his main opponent stood down for the sake of unity. MNLF combatants I interviewed over the years spoke of an intense war wariness and growing disillusionment with the leadership.

The Philippine government was also under international pressure to reach a negotiated solution. Libya had organized an oil embargo on the Philippines that hurt the economy. In 1976, President Ferdinand Marcos sent his wife, Imelda, to Libya to negotiate with Gadaffi. The result of her seduction[15] — quite literally—was the December 1976 Tripoli Accords that was to give the Muslim south formal autonomy.[16] Mindanao was to receive its own assembly and Islamic courts and a future referendum on autonomy for all thirteen provinces and nine cities in the Moro region, including Basilan, Sulu, Tawi-Tawi, Lanao del Sur, Lanao del Norte, Zamboanga del Sur, Zamboanga del Norte, South Cotabato, Davao del Sur, North Cotabato, Maguindanao, Sultan Kudarat, and Palawan. As part of the Tripoli Accords, the Government of the Republic of the Philippines, or GRP, passed a law in 1977 that established the Code of Muslim Personal Laws, which established *sharia* courts for family law, marriage, and inheritance. The government also established the Philippine Amanah Bank, which operated in accordance with Islamic banking principles.[17]

Yet the peace lasted for a mere nine months until the MNLF realized that Marcos had no real intention of granting the Regional Autonomous Government the political and fiscal autonomy that he had promised in the accord. A massive influx of Christian migrants, starting in 1977, diluted the Muslim population and undermined the plebiscites as Moros had become a minority in most of the territory subject to the Tripoli Accord. Despite Christian support, Marcos rigged the plebiscite that established "autonomy." Fighting resumed in 1977, though the MNLF never regained its momentum and suffered a string of military defeats. [18]

The autonomy agreement also caused a division within the MNLF's ranks. A group of Islamists, led by the MNLF's second in command, Salamat Hashim, an al-Azhar-educated *sharia* scholar, was already angered by the MNLF's alliance with the Philippine Communist Party, which deepened following the Soviet invasion of Afghanistan. [19]

After a failed leadership challenge, Salamat moved to Lahore, Pakistan, where he established a new organization, the Moro Islamic Liberation Front (MILF). [20] The MILF was headquartered in the compound of the Pakistani Islamist organization Jama'at i-Islami and became very influenced by the growth of anti-Soviet *mujahideen*. The MILF, too, began to send members to Pakistan and Afghanistan for education and training and, to a much lesser extent, combat experience. Even if they did not send that many people, it became an important part of the MILF narrative. They saw themselves as part of a global Islamist movement. Through the mid-1990s, the MILF was a small fringe group.

Morale within the MNLF plummeted, as did its military effectiveness. Members made large-scale defections, both to the government and the rival MILF, and resentment grew among the rank and file toward the exiled leadership.

The ouster of dictator Ferdinand Marcos in 1986 and the restoration of democracy under the Corazon Aquino regime rekindled hopes for a negotiated settlement. Aquino met secretly with Misuari on September 5, 1986, resulting in the Jeddah Accord and a cease-fire. Then, in January 1987 under pressure from Malaysia and the Organization of the Islamic Conference (OIC), the MNLF formally relinquished its goal of independence in favor of an autonomy agreement with the government. The 1987 constitution provided for limited autonomy "within the framework of this constitution and the national sovereignty as well as territorial integrity of the Republic of the Philippines."

But peace talks faltered, as Corazon Aquino's government proved weak and ineffective, constantly fending off a string of military coups. She was clearly unwilling to stand up to the AFP and make serious concessions on Mindanao.

And very quietly, the MILF began to assert itself, differentiating itself from the MNLF by demanding independence and escalating attacks. Indeed, after the September 1986 meeting that led to the Jeddah Accord, the MILF launched a major five-day offensive as a show of force and a rejection of autonomy to both the GRP and MNLF. [21] In January 1987, President Aquino met with Ebrahim el-Haj Murad, the MILF chief of staff, to arrange a cease-fire and to invite MILF into the peace process along with the MNLF. The MILF rejected the overture. [22] In March 1987, the government sent emissaries to meet with Salamat Hashim in Pakistan, requesting that the MILF enter peace talks. But the MILF leadership was buoyed by their growth and their support among the population for a string of military successes and so refused.

Following the 1991 bombing of a Pan Am jetliner by Libyan agents, Libya was under intense international pressure to cease support for militant movements, and arms to the MNLF dried up. A battlefield stalemate led to a real desire on the part of the MNLF and the government to come to terms. A surge in the communist New People's Army operations compelled the government to resolve the Moro insurrection. In February 1992, while still on the presidential campaign trail, then secretary of defense Fidel Ramos made a secret trip to Libya, where he met Gadaffi and tried to convince him to put pressure on his Moro clients to return to the negotiating table. Talks resumed in October 1992. The MNLF by this point was a spent force and needed a negotiated settlement. In an attempt to shore up his international image, Gadaffi brokered the 1996 Tripoli Agreement between the Philippine government and the MNLF.

The Tripoli Agreement was, at best, a marginal success. On the one hand, the MNLF did renounce independence, and over five thousand armed combatants stopped fighting. Some 2,200 MNLF combatants were integrated into the AFP and national police force.[23] Nur Misuari became the regional governor of the Autonomous Region of Muslim Mindanao (ARMM).[24] (But this laid the groundwork for future problems as the MNLF believed the governorship and administrative controls were an entitlement to be held in perpetuity).

But once again, it was the issue of a plebiscite for inclusion into the ARMM that proved problematic. With continued Christian migration, the plebiscite included only five provinces, Sulu, Tawi-Tawi, Maguindanao, Basilan, and Lanao del Sur, plus Marawi City, in the ARMM, far short of what the MNLF had expected. Cotabato City, the seat of the ARMM, did not even vote for inclusion. The ARMM accounted for 13,465 square kilometers, roughly 4 percent of Philippine territory, far less than the aspirations of the MNLF and what was originally agreed to in the 1976 Tripoli Agreement.

But the 1996 peace accord was challenged from the start. Nur Misuari was an absolutely incompetent administrator who loved the trappings and the perks for his extended entourage but failed in administration. His inability to govern allowed his inner circle to be extremely corrupt. And Misuari made a critical error in that his own ethnic Tausigs totally dominated his inner circle; the MNLF was no longer a multiethnic organization. It was dominated by chauvinist Tausigs from the Sulu archipelago.[25] Local grievances soared, and few really benefited from the end of hostilities as there was no "peace dividend"; the fruits of the autonomy agreement went to a handful of MNLF leaders. By every measure of human development, the ARMM region remained the poorest region of a poor country.[26]

Moreover, autonomy was a facade. Despite "autonomy," the ARMM still remitted over 60 percent of its revenue to the central government and in turn received only 10 percent back.[27] Despite autonomy, all elections were administered by Manila. The ARMM government was simply an added layer to the Philippines' notoriously corrupt bureaucracy. Manila pledged one hundred million dollars to govern the ARMM, including some sixteen million dollars for education and health programs; yet most was used for administration, leaving less than eighteen million dollars for development projects.[28] As one political analyst put it: "He [Misuari] was obsessed with showcase projects like bullet trains and an international airport for Jolo. But he did little to encourage micro-enterprises, improve educational access and raise the quality of health services for a community with the highest degree of illiteracy, malnutrition, unemployment and infant mortality."[29]

More importantly, the Tripoli Agreement did not end the conflict. The MNLF did not have to disarm or turn over weapons as part of the accord. The "swords to ploughshares" program supported by the United States and donor community, a mere four-and-a-half-million-dollar project, fell far short.[30] While some two thousand were integrated into Philippine security forces, most were not. In Sulu, many MNLF combatants engaged in criminality, some joining the Abu Sayyaf Group (ASG), which vacillated between abject criminality, in particular kidnapping for ransom, and pseudo-Islamist terrorism. MNLF members were drawn by the lure of quick cash in a region with few employment opportunities and pervasive poverty as well as very deep clan ties.

In Central Mindanao, the conflict actually escalated as the MILF rejected the agreement and continued to fight. The MILF more than doubled in size with the signing of the 1996 Tripoli Agreement as large numbers of MNLF combatants rejected the peace process, considering it to be a sellout on the part of Misuari or simply mistrusting the Philippine government's will and capabilities to implement the agreement.

The MILF went from being a fringe organization to the largest armed force in the region. This caught the government completely off guard. For years they focused their efforts on the MNLF and continued to treat the MILF as a fringe organization that would ultimately give up its struggle. The MILF spread through its control of Mindanao's mosques, especially in the Maranao and Maguindanao heartland of Mindanao. According to AFP estimates, the MILF grew from around 5,330 men in 1986 to 8,270 men in 1995 and then almost doubled following the 1996 Tripoli Agreement. Between 1996 and 1999, the MILF's strength grew at an alarming annual growth rate of 21 percent in manpower and 18 percent in firepower. By the end of 1999, it claimed to have 15,690 men with 11,280 firearms, though the number is probably closer to 11,000, and most were part-time guerrillas who were engaged in subsistence farming.

Despite the "peace accord" with the MNLF, a very heavy military and police presence continued in the region, still beset by conflict. In 1997, President Fidel Ramos ordered the AFP to stop attacking MILF positions, and on July 18, 1997, both parties signed a cease-fire.[31] This led to a series of development projects in MILF-held territory, including road construction and hydroelectric projects. In February 1998 they signed a confidence-building agreement. In March they concluded an agreement that established what would later become a formal cease-fire committee.[32] Nonetheless, the MILF was growing in strength and confidence and felt no urgency to make significant concessions. Its view was that the development projects were a form of reparations; it did not view them as ceding sovereignty to the government. And as Ramos's term ended and he became a lame duck, the MILF felt in no rush to restart talks. In August 1998 the two sides signed the General Framework of Agreement of Intent, which was nothing more than a vague commitment to a peace dialogue, without any details or commitments.[33]

By 1999–2000 the MILF controlled enormous swaths of territory in central Mindanao and began to establish a protostate governed by the *sharia*, centered on Camp Abu Bakr in the mountainous region between Maguindanao and Lanao del Sur provinces. In mid-1998, the MILF smuggled its founder, Salamat Hashim, back into the country. The organization saw the pious and dour theologian as a legitimate and morally upright leader in a region that had never had one. The MILF offered limited social services (some *madrassas* and public health clinics) and a three-tiered Islamic court system.[34] While rudimentary, it was not far from the government's dismal offerings in Mindanao. The reality is that much of Mindanao, with its appallingly rudimentary road network and the AFP's lack of capabilities, was an absolutely no-go zone, beyond government control.

The MILF oozed confidence at this time. Salamat Hashim began appearing in public, while the MILF established a body to run mass rallies, the Bangsamoro People's Consultative Assembly. In 1999, the AFP captured the MILF's vice chairman, Ebrahim el Haj Murad, but released him upon being besieged by MILF forces and mobilized locals, who surrounded the police station in Marawi where he was being held.

The MILF began to engage in overt mass politics, establishing the Bangsamoro People's Consultative Assembly, an overt political movement whose leaders and goals are closely affiliated with the MILF, including the commitment to the establishment of an independent Islamic state. The MILF broadened its base of support to include urbanites and people in the middle class through the inculcation of Islamic values and the establishment of a number of front movements and civil society organizations. More importantly, the MILF began to chip away at the MNLF's base of support.

In 1999, the newly elected government of Joseph Estrada began to demarcate a series of MILF camps in order to enact a cease-fire and prevent misencounters.[35] These camps included Abu Bakr al-Seddiqi, Badr, and Omar Bin al-Khattab in Maguindanao; Rajamuda in North Cotabato and Maguindanao; Bilal in Lanao del Norte and Lanao del Sur; and Busrah Somiorang in Lanao del Sur. But immediately the government began to have second thoughts, as the MILF saw the demarcation as government recognition of their sovereignty and the contours of their homeland.

In 2000, photos were published of an execution of drug smugglers, convicted and sentenced in an MILF *sharia* court. President Estrada was infuriated by this sovereign act; the Philippines at the time had abolished the death penalty. Estrada unilaterally broke the cease-fire as an autonomy agreement was being finalized[36] and launched a major invasion of the MILF heartland, capturing its base camp, the heart of the protostate, Camp Abu Bakr. Salamat Hashim fled to the remote Liguasan Marsh area, and the MILF ceased providing what few social services it had offered. To add insult to injury, President Estrada celebrated the capture of Camp Abu Bakr with his troops feasting on *lechon* (roast pig) and beer.

This was a major blow to the MILF, and it never really recovered.[37] The group had staked so much of its reputation on establishing the nucleus of an Islamic state, from which it would gradually expand outward. It had to maintain an effective Islamic government as the counterpoint to the failed and corruption-riddled ARMM government dominated by the MNLF.

Yet a weakness of insurgent groups that desire physical territory and the trappings of government is that they have a fixed position that they have to defend at all costs. Once the MILF had a "state"—with institutions that gave legitimacy to its demand for independence—to defend, it suffered loss after loss. While the MILF proved to be competent guerrillas engaged in small-scale ambushes, its soldiers proved inept at fighting set-piece positional warfare. Territorial defense forced them into static positions that even a poorly armed and trained Philippine military was able to outgun.

Following the loss of much of its liberated zone in 2000, the MILF reorganized into nine separate base commands.[38] While this should have played into the group's military strengths, the separate commands ultimately proved to be its undoing.

First, huge disparities existed among the size and capabilities of the various base commands. Some were large and very well equipped, with soldiers in uniform and kit, while smaller base commands were barely able to engage in guerrilla ambushes from jungle lairs. Second, with the dispersion of forces came the breakdown of centralized command, control, and discipline. Third, the government was able to concentrate its attacks on smaller base commands as it saw fit. Fourth, the base commands received few resources from the MILF headquarters and had to be self-sufficient. This led many base commands to engage in varying degrees of criminality, including extortion, kidnap for ransom, protection rackets, and paid assassinations, which undermined their legitimacy and popular support.

More importantly, it led many base commanders to expand their territories to collect "revolutionary taxes" from the population. While the population did not mind paying taxes within the pre-2000 liberated area when they could witness security and social services, the base commands offered almost nothing in return. The base commanders became increasingly predatory on the local population. Moreover, they competed among one another to control villages. To make matters worse, the base commanders exercised only limited sovereignty, and the population was also taxed by the government. I've conducted field work in villages were people told me that they had paid "taxes" to three separate entities, and these were people who were truly living on the margins of outright poverty. The conflicts between MILF base commanders were then exacerbated by clan feuds, or *rido*.

Even after they tried to revert to smaller guerrilla units, the reality is that after 2000, the MILF never really won another battle. In fact, every major armed confrontation led to significant losses of territory. At the same time, it lost significant popular legitimacy as its provision of social services atrophied.

But what was most frustrating about Estrada's "all-out war" in 1999 was that the MILF had quietly made large concessions. Its twenty-four-page "Position Papers of the Technical Working Groups on Six Clustered Agenda Items" recommended "a political solution reflective of the system of life and governance suitable and acceptable to the Bangsamoro people." While it called for "recognition of the Bangsamoro as a distinct people and nation," the "restitution of the ancestral domain to the Bangsamoro," and "exclusive control over their national governance, security and natural resources," among others, it never raised the demand of the Islamic state, nor did it demand specific territory. [39]

In early 2001, President Estrada was ousted in a popular uprising, and his successor, Gloria Macapagal Arroyo, implemented a unilateral cease-fire. Although formal peace talks did not resume for two more years and low-level skirmishes continued, back-channel talks resumed. Publicly the MILF was far more intransigent. In 2001 Salamat Hashim issued his "Principles for Negotiation," in which he reiterated that the MILF refused to base any negotiation on the Philippine constitution, refused to renounce the goal of independence, and refused to accept any form of autonomy. [40] Yet Murad was secretly meeting with Arroyo's team in Kuala Lumpur. The two sides reached the Agreement on the General Framework for the Resumption of Peace Talks on March 24, 2001, in which both sides committed themselves to a cessation of hostilities, a restart of the peace talks, and the withdrawal of Philippine troops from all the areas they had captured since 1999. [41] In February 2001, President Arroyo ordered the Department of Justice to lift all charges against Salamat Hashim and five other MILF leaders for the December 30, 2000, terrorist bombings in Manila.[42]

Allegations of terrorism were always a factor in the peace process. And without a doubt, they changed the context in which the negotiations took place. The MILF has always denied all acts of terrorism, which it asserts is "un-Islamic." It also used the allegations to distance itself from the more notorious Abu Sayyaf, which engaged in systematic acts of kidnapping and urban terrorism. The MILF never engaged in terrorism against unarmed civilian populations, especially outside of Mindanao, until 2000. The MILF always denied association with the tactic, but the evidence mounted, and it was clearly the beneficiary. And to a degree, the tactic worked. Large-scale terrorist attacks in Davao or Manila put enough political pressure on President Arroyo to halt the offensives. The decision by the MILF to engage in terrorism was driven by both push and pull factors. Pushing it was military necessity. After 2000, the MILF was on the defensive and never regained any battlefield initiative. Every violation of the cease-fire was costly for it. And while the government was ostensibly committed to a peace process, hardliners in the military often continued military operations.

The international environment had clearly shifted against the MILF by 2002. The 9/11 attacks on the United States led to the deployment of the first US Special Forces to the southern Philippines. Although they were deployed ostensibly to combat the Abu Sayyaf—a very small group that had nominal ties to al-Qaeda—the reality is that the MILF had deeper ties to international terrorist networks.

Beginning in the mid-1990s, the MILF hosted a handful of al-Qaeda trainers who conducted small arms and bomb-making classes in MILF base camps. The largest of this type was known as Camp Hudaibiyah. Following Jemaah Islamiyah's (JI's) Bali, Indonesia, bombings that left 202 dead, several top JI suspects fled to Mindanao, where the MILF gave them sanctuary.[43] The presence of two of JI's top bombers, Dulmatin and Umar Patek, in MILF camps in late 2002 to early 2005 gave it further technical expertise. At the time the MILF was looking for some leverage at the negotiating table, and the presence of JI and the willingness to engage in terrorism was a negotiating tool.

The MILF viewed the American presence as directed against it, not the Abu Sayyaf. Pressure on the MILF soared after the October 2002 bombings in Bali. Although Salamat Hashim wrote a letter to President George W. Bush denouncing terrorism, the MILF was on notice, now an intelligence collection priority, and it was increasingly being implicated in terrorist attacks in the Philippines.

But the US presence and post 9/11 environment also impacted the MILF in two very meaningful ways. With the deployment of US Special Forces to the southern Philippines and the arming of their AFP counterparts, the government made attempts to deal with corruption within the AFP. It instituted more accounting procedures, and American advisers told me that they were more confident that the quartermaster's office had (somewhat) better control and accounting of their weapons and equipment. And while the MILF had diverse sources of arms and ammunition, including some limited indigenous production capacity, by the 1990s almost all its weapons systems had changed from Soviet-style AK-47s to M-16s. The Philippine military was riddled with corruption, and the MILF was simply able to employ domestic black markets for its arms and ammunition. The reduction in armed encounters also meant that the MILF captured less weaponry on the battlefield. The international environment also made illicit arms imports more difficult, as global cooperation against small arms black markets stepped up, including greater sanctions on rogue states such as North Korea.[44]

The US presence also impacted the MILF's financing. State sponsorship from Libya dried up after 1996. Some degree of funding came from al-Qaeda through Osama bin Laden's brother-in-law, Mohammed Jamal Khalifa, who opened up a number of branches for Saudi charities, including the International Islamic Relief Organization and the Muslim World League. At the time, Khalifa was in the process of opening a branch of Muwafaq a Jersey Island (UK) investment vehicle used by al-Qaeda. Khalifa married into two MILF families from the Maguindanao and Maranao tribes. Pre-9/11, the MILF was not hiding its ties to al-Qaeda and saw its ties to the global Islamist community as an important asset for propaganda, recruitment, and fund-raising. Khalifa hired MILF members or their siblings to run the local offices of these charities, which funded orphanages, medical clinics, and educational programs. The assumption is that some money was diverted to the armed struggle.

But most of the MILF's funding came from indigenous sources, both licit and illicit. MILF commanders own a number of businesses, from sand, gravel, and cement to trucking and fruit plantations. Again, the assumption is that some of those proceeds go to the struggle, not just the personal coffers of the leadership. The MILF used to control (or at least profit from) the ubiquitous labor agencies in the southern Philippines that sent workers overseas. It engaged in revolutionary taxation of the local population, and it taxed (extorted money from) loggers and miners in territory it controlled. The MILF was involved in a swath of other criminal activities, including extortion of local businesses, kidnapping for ransom, and protection rackets. The MILF also actively raised funds overseas, especially in the Middle East, among the large number of Filipino workers. The Moro issue had long been a cause in the Islamist agenda, and Persian Gulf charities were very supportive of the MILF and Bangsamoro struggle until 9/11, when such aid came under far more international oversight and scrutiny.

Yet despite the setbacks experienced by the MILF, its rival, the MNLF, provided no meaningful counter. In November 2001, frustration over Misuari's mismanagement came to a head, and the MNLF's executive committee ousted him.[45] Misuari denounced the intraparty move as a violation of the Tripoli Agreement and called on followers to pick up arms. After his failed putsch, in which some 400 followers attacked a military base, leaving 113 people dead in three weeks of fighting, he fled to Malaysia, which immediately put him under house arrest and later rendered him to the Philippines. Though he never was tried in a court of law, he was under house arrest until late 2008. The MNLF descended into factional infighting with no leader to date able to unify the movement. Misuari remains a very divisive figure, unaware that he controls only the loyalty of a small following.

3. THE PEACE PROCESS

The complication of the peace process in the Philippines is that it is really two peace processes run side by side but encompassing the same territory. While the MILF rejected the MNLF's 1996 Tripoli Agreement, its process has run in parallel to that agreement. And while it has achieved more than the 1996 agreement, the MNLF is so prideful that it has been unable to join it and create an agreement that supersedes its own failed accord.

Following President Joseph Estrada's ouster in early 2001, President Gloria Macapagal Arroyo declared a unilateral cease-fire in an attempt to restart peace talks, and back-channel talks began. The key issue at this juncture for the MILF was to get government recognition of its liberated base areas. The two sides sent teams around central and southern Mindanao, as well as Basilan and parts of the Sulu archipelago, demarcating MILF territories. At this point, the MILF had not yet renounced its goal of independence and had every reason to hope that these territories would be the nucleus of an independent Bangsamoro state. The government went through the motions to placate the MILF, never intending to cede sovereignty of the territory.

The Tripoli Agreement of June 22, 2001, was a significant breakthrough in negotiations. It reflected the MILF's acknowledgment that it could not win a homeland through military means and that it was far more confident of its popular support. For the first time, a joint document spoke of popular will and the desire to "open new formulas that permanently respond to the aspirations of the Bangsamoro people for freedom," in other words, a referendum. On the other hand, the agreement also recognized that "a Bangsamoro homeland is not necessarily incompatible with Philippine sovereignty and territorial integrity," meaning that a form of autonomy could be acceptable.[46]

In August 2001, the two sides signed the "Implementing Guidelines on the Security Aspect of the GRP-MILF Tripoli Agreement of 2001," which clearly outlined prohibited hostile and aggressive acts, including massive redeployments, harboring or providing assistance to "criminal elements," and terrorism. The agreement established local monitoring teams (LMTs) that included political officers as well as representatives of local NGOs and clergy from the respective sides. The agreement lifted the bounty and dropped all arrest warrants for MILF officials and called on the OIC to deploy cease-fire monitors.[47]

In May 2002, the two sides signed an accord to deal with "lawless elements" and "lost commands" of the MILF.[48] But government forces used the alleged presence of kidnap gangs and terrorist suspects, including members of Jemaah Islamiyah, responsible for the October 2002 bombing in Bali that killed two hundred and two, as the *casus belli* to launch an offensive into MILF territory in February 2003. The attack occurred on the eve of talks in Kuala Lumpur and was viewed by the MILF as a sign of the government's lack of good faith. But more importantly, many saw the attack on the MILF's new headquarters as an attempt to kill or capture Salamat Hashim, something that the government has always denied.[49] The offensive ended in spring 2003, but the MILF demanded a withdrawal of government forces and a return to *status quo ante*.

It is quite possible that the government had no knowledge of the attack or that the AFP was simply trying to weaken the MILF's position at the talks or sabotage them altogether.

But the damage was done as the government captured a major MILF base command that straddled the strategically important cross-island highway, linking Davao and Cotabato for the first time in nearly two decades.[50] Once the highway opened, so did trade and commerce; people could leave MILF-controlled zones, and secular life crept in. Most importantly cell phone and communications towers were installed, bringing people into the Philippine mainstream. The MILF no longer had a monopoly on the flow of information. Its base camps were driven further into the interior, away from the population centers.

The MILF had every reason not to return to the talks, but the reality was that it had few other options as a military victory was out of the question. Since 9/11 the United States had deployed Special Operations forces in the southern Philippines who were there to arm, advise, train, and provide intelligence to the AFP, whose capabilities gradually improved.

By 2003 a formal cease-fire had been signed. The most important aspect of this cease-fire was a joint mechanism to monitor the peace and investigate violations, the Coordinating Committee for the Cessation of Hostilities (CCCH). Both sides put together full-time teams in regional offices that were quick to monitor the peace, to investigate when armed clashes occurred, to try to defuse situations, and also to educate the public about the peace process. The CCCH worked with a host of NGOs that did their own cease-fire monitoring and reporting, most importantly Bantay Ceasefire, which did a fantastic job in investigating and reporting on cease-fire breakdowns. All CCCH activities included equal representation from the government and the MILF. From the AFP's point of view, it was a very important intelligence-gathering mechanism.

In May 2003, Salamat Hashim issued a public statement rejecting terrorism and denying the MILF's ties to any terrorist organizations. He also had an exchange of letters with the White House to convey this point. "The MILF as a liberation organization has repeatedly renounced terrorism publicly as a means of attaining its political ends," he wrote to President George W. Bush.[51]

In what was seen as a major concession to the MILF in 2003 the government agreed that all international assistance to MILF-controlled areas would go through a newly established quasi-autonomous NGO, the Bangsamoro Development Agency (BDA).

Once again, the MILF tried to have its base camps officially demarcated,[52] a process that was begun in 2003 but never completed as government officials saw it as a de facto acceptance of MILF sovereignty.

By the end of 2003, the international context continued to propel the MILF to the negotiating table. Following the October 2002 Bali bombing and the August 2003 bombing of the JW Marriott Hotel in Jakarta by MILF-trained JI bombers, the MILF was under intense international scrutiny, and pressure was growing to have the organization designated as a terrorist organization under the UN's 1267 Committee. Its sources of funding were under greater scrutiny, and the presence of US Special Forces who had spread from Sulu to central Mindanao made MILF fighters edgy.

Another thing pushing the MILF toward negotiating was that its founder, Salamat Hashim, passed away in mid-2003 and was replaced by a more pragmatic and less ideological leader, Ebrahim el Haj Murad. As the vice chairman for military affairs, Murad knew that the balance on the battlefield had turned against the MILF. He was personally committed to forging a negotiated settlement. Under his leadership, the MILF's central committee renounced the bid for independence and accepted autonomy.[53] Some members within Murad's circle advocated a referendum for independence, as had happened in East Timor, Indonesia, in 2000, but even this proved too unrealistic of a negotiating position.[54]

Third, the international community was focused on Mindanao. The US government saw it through the lens of counterterrorism (if there was not a durable political solution, the MILF would never stop working with JI and al-Qaeda), while other bi- and multilateral donors were simply eager to bring peace to the third-largest island in the Philippines and one of the last regions in Southeast Asia endowed with an untapped host of natural resources.

The MILF negotiating strategy was very much derived from lessons it took from the MNLF's 1996 accord. First, MILF was determined to avoid the mistakes of the MNLF. One must understand, this was not only a conflict against the government, this was an internal struggle among the Moros; both the MNLF and MILF were competing for the legitimacy to represent all of the Muslims in the southern Philippines. The MILF studied the MNLF's mistakes, which included getting too close to its government counterparts and being too interested in personal gain, both of which made the MNLF vulnerable to corruption. The MILF's team comprised organic members—all Islamists who really did not want to spend a lot of time with their Christian government counterparts—but it also included nonorganic legal professionals to represent its interests so that it had a firewall between itself and the government.

Second, the MNLF signed a very general agreement and then expected the government to implement the details as they came along in the spirit of the autonomy agreement. That never happened. So the MILF's strategy was lilliputian; it sought to tie the government's hands with a series of small and very narrow agreements. The MILF kept a bound book of joint agreements, MoUs, and other documents at the ready. The government wanted peace first and the details worked out later. But the MILF wanted to hold the government to any previously negotiated point, no matter how trivial.

From 2004 to 2007, round after round of talks took place. They broke the talks into three separate themes: peace and security, development, and "ancestral domain." The government worked hard at getting the MILF fighters out of their jungle camps and allowed them to set up a compound outside of Cotabato City. Many MILF leaders moved back into the towns, and the government even encouraged them to go into business, often providing them with subsidized loans.

Peace and security was the easiest issue to tackle as neither side could afford a return to war. The MILF was a spent force that lost more territory with every cease-fire violation. In addition to the highly effective CCCH, two additional mechanisms were put in place. The first was the Malaysian-led International Monitoring Team (IMT). The IMT was really small, with a headquarters in Cotabato and only three to four field offices. In addition to Malaysians, it included soldiers from Brunei and Libya as well as civilians from Japan and, later, Norway. While it was not large, it was enough of an international presence to assuage the MILF's concerns and made it hard for the government to renew any offensive operations. Armed clashes between the MILF and AFP fell from 698 in 2002 to 559 in 2003, to 15 in 2004, and to 10 in 2005.

The second additional measure for ensuring peace and security was a joint body to deal with criminality, the Ad Hoc Joint Action Group (AH-JAG). The government knew that many MILF commanders were involved in

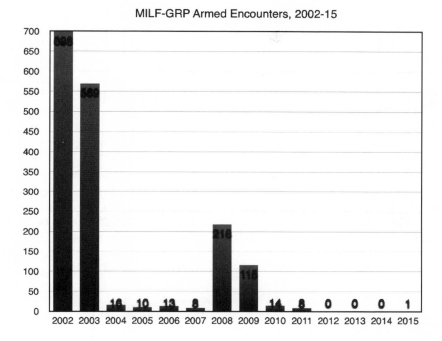

MILF-GRP Armed Encounters, 2002-15

Figure 3.1.   Cease Fire Violations in Mindanao, 2002 to 2007. *Source*: Coordinating Committee of Cessation of Hostilities.

kidnapping and extortion. At the very least, they provided sanctuary to kidnappers in ransom gangs in exchange for a cut of the ransom money. Government forces could not always arrest them for the sake of the peace process, nor could they directly or publicly link them to the MILF. So the two sides created a *kabuki*-esque organization. When intelligence would come in about a new criminal entity, the two sides would work to neutralize the threat. This put the MILF in a hard spot as most of the criminals were linked to it in some way. But the AHJAG made MILF members into responsible stakeholders. The government's position was, "If you want to be autonomous, then you have to start policing your borders." The AHJAG gave the MILF plausible deniability while cracking down on criminality within its own ranks.

The second theme of the talks really came to nought. As mentioned earlier, back in 2003, the government allowed the MILF to control all development projects in its areas, through the Bangsamoro Development Agency. This was an important concession for the MILF that sought to legitimize itself by controlling all development projects in the region. Yet the government systematically worked around the BDA and continued to control both domestically and foreign-funded development projects. The government did a lot of training and human capital development programs for the BDA but really did not allow the agency to control any major capital development funds or projects.

The third issue of the talks was the very thorny one of "ancestral domain." Under the 1996 Tripoli Agreement, the Autonomous Region of Muslim Mindanao was established, and many provinces and regions were eligible to join. The reality is, only five joined after popular plebiscites. The irony is the capital of the ARMM region was Cotabato City, which itself rejected joining the ARMM. Why did only five of the seventeen eligible provinces and cities vote to join the ARMM? The reality is that Christian migration in the southern Philippines made the Muslims a minority in their own land. The core issue of the "ancestral domains talks" was basically how much more territory would be added to the new autonomous region, now called the Bangsamoro Juridical Entity. The MILF argued that in addition to the five provinces that were part of the ARMM, there were 3,978 Muslim-majority villages across the entire region that should be included. The government argued that only 613 of the villages were Muslim majority and called for a census, which the MILF wisely declined.

But more to the point, in negotiating ancestral domain, the MILF had formally renounced its bid for an independent state. It accepted autonomy, though the wording was highly sensitive. "Autonomy" was a poisonous term for the MILF because it sounded like the group was getting no more than the MNLF, and the ARMM had such a terrible reputation. And so the parties agreed on a term: the Bangsamoro Juridical Entity (BJE).

The talks went back and forth for over three years and often threatened to break down.[55] As the talks dragged on in 2006–2007, the number of ceasefire violations and small-scale bombings sharply increased. While statistics from the Office of the Presidential Advisor on the Peace Process state that only one major clash occurred in 2006, it jumped to seven in 2007. Over thirty bombings took place in Mindanao in 2007. The AFP reported thirty-five, sixty, and one hundred clashes with the MILF between 2005 and 2007.[56]

Not all of the MILF membership has endorsed the peace process. Hardliners in the MILF who opposed the peace process (either because they wanted independence, not autonomy, or because they mistrusted the government's willingness to implement any agreement that it signed) argued that the protracted peace process since 2003 would eviscerate the MILF battlefield capabilities.

They were correct in their assessment. The MILF became a hollowed-out organization. Although it still claimed to field twelve thousand to fifteen thousand men, it was clearly much weaker. The cease-fire decimated the MILF's black-market arms networks, and in the tropics ammunition has a very short shelf life. The MILF always took great pride in the fact that it ran two military training camps, with courses for enlisted men and officers. The government put pressure on the MILF to shut down these camps or at least reduce the training as a sign of goodwill during peace talks. MILF combatants have recently been training for internal policing, but that has weakened their ability to return to war.

In 2005 there appears to have been an assassination attempt on Murad by hard-liners who were against the peace process.[57] Though the MILF denied it, afterward the armed wing of the movement underwent a significant reorganization in an attempt to neutralize the hard-liners who saw the MILF's capabilities, arms supplies, training, and command and control all break down with the protracted peace process.

By September 2006, talks had again reached an impasse. Murad released an angry statement complaining that the government still lacked the "political will to push hard for a negotiated political settlement" and that it "continued to cling to such an outmoded template that everything must be tailored fit to the Philippine Constitution."

> The government must take responsibility for this "breakdown" of the talks. It is not serious enough in its formulation or stand on [the] territory of ancestral domain aspect of the Tripoli Agreement of 2001 by offering MILF inclusion of some areas for the proposed Bangsamoro Juridical Entity subject to "constitutional processes." This is a conditional offer that no real revolutionary group worthy of its name can accept. It will only repeat the failure of the GRP-MNLF "Final Peace Agreement of 1996" that until now the government has never complied with fully.[58]

In early 2007, the MILF made a major concession on the number of *barangays* in its "ancestral domain" in return for three concessions from the government: (1) greater geographic contiguity of the *barangays* and fewer isolated communities;[59] (2) financial compensations for lost land that would be put into a public trust fund; and (3) greater assurances that the country's Congress or Supreme Court could not *post facto* water down the agreement, as it did with Republic Act 9054 that weakened the 1996 MNLF agreement. This in itself was important because it was the first time the MILF agreed to negotiate under the ambit of the constitution. But most importantly, the government had made a major concession on the issue of governance, allowing the MILF full autonomy and authority to establish any system of governance of its choosing. This meant that the BJE did not have to follow a system of governance parallel to the Republic of the Philippines, with checks and balances, but could instead establish an Islamic form of governance.

In August 2007, the two sides signed the Memorandum of Agreement on Ancestral Domain (MOA-AD), a draft agreement that would have added roughly 1,100 villages to the current ARMM region.[60] The BJE would have had significant control over finances and enjoy a majority of the proceeds from all subterranean natural resources, which under the Philippine constitution belong to the state.

The MNLF, however, was incensed. Rather than joining the talks, the MNLF demanded that the government participate in "tripartite talks" in Jeddah, Saudi Arabia, under OIC auspices, to revisit the 1996 Tripoli Agreement and compel the government to fully implement it. The GRP all but refused to attend and told the MNLF that such talks would be pointless until a peace pact with the MILF was signed.

Yet President Arroyo's cabinet and the AFP leadership rejected the agreement, which the Supreme Court subsequently ruled as unconstitutional.[61] Three of the most hard-line MILF commanders began a rampage through central Mindanao, targeting Christian enclaves and remote villages.

At this point, the MILF had every reason to quit the peace process and return to hostilities. Yet the hard-liners who warned about the dehabilitating effects of the peace process proved correct. The MILF could barely sustain several months of low-level attacks, in which government forces were highly restrained. The violence petered out by mid 2008.

The MILF also had no popular mandate to resort to an all-out war because of the war wariness of the population. As economic conditions had improved steadily since 2003, no one had an interest in returning to war. Muslim civil society was increasingly independent from the MILF, which for years really tried to control or at least liaise with it.

And while war did not resume, the peace process absolutely stalled. Donors were frustrated, and even the Malaysians threatened to pull out of the IMT, which they had established and led.

Although the IMT did not end its mandate and violence ebbed by 2010, the MILF would not even countenance a return to formal talks until a new president was elected in May 2010. They had high hopes for President Benigno Aquino, son of democracy icon and former president Corazon Aquino, who deposed the dictator Ferdinand Marcos in the 1986 People Power Revolution. Aquino had a host of challenges when he assumed office, and Mindanao was low on his list of priorities, so almost no movement occurred to restart formal talks in Aquino's first year in office.

Then, in a surprise move in August 2011, he met with MILF chairman Murad in Tokyo.[62] While these were not formal peace talks and the details were not publicized, it was a significant meeting, and it led to a resumption of formal talks and a willingness by both sides to make significant concessions. Although the MILF had a significant mistrust, its battlefield realities compelled its leaders to negotiate. And they ended up accepting even less than what had been negotiated in 2007 in the Memorandum of Agreement on Ancestral Domain.

But not all MILF commanders were on board. In 2010–2011, a hard-line group of MILF combatants under the leadership of Ustadz Ameril Umbra Kato broke away and founded the Bangsamoro Islamic Freedom Front (BIFF), rejecting Murad's leadership and the peace process.[63] Others, such as Wahid Tundok, threatened to follow suit but never did. The MILF leadership was able to prevent further defections and rein in the field commanders. But other hard-liners, including the younger brother of the MILF's founder, continued to challenge Murad for leadership. But despite the internal schisms, Murad remained committed to the peace process.

Finally, on October 15, 2012, the parties concluded the Framework Agreement on the Bangsamoro (FAB), paving the way for a formal end to the MILF's insurgency and the establishment of the legal mechanisms to create a new self-governing entity.

4. THE PEACE AGREEMENT

The FAB was a broad agreement of general principles that left many core issues to be worked out. The core of the agreement is summarized below.

1. Governance

- The existing ARMM government would not stand for reelection, as dissolving an elected body posed too many constitutional challenges. The "Bangsamoro," the name of the " new political entity," would replace the ARMM in a multiyear transitional process that was supposed to have concluded with a democratically elected government in 2016.
- The governing law would be the Bangsamoro Basic Law, drafted and approved by the local inhabitants. The Basic Law would protect the democratic rights of the population and outlined the rights and liberties of all inhabitants. The Philippine Congress would have one year to approve the Bangsamoro Basic Law.
- Until the Basic Law was passed, the region would be governed by a "transitory committee," established by executive decree of the president and supported by the Philippine Congress. The two sides acknowledged that a transition period was necessary. The composition of the fifteen-member transitory committee would entirely comprise Moros, seven selected by the government, eight and the chairman selected by the MILF. The transitory committee would be responsible for drafting the Basic Law, working with the government to ensure that the Basic Law was in accordance with the constitution, and coordinating development assistance.

- Once the Basic Law was passed in the Philippine Congress and ratified in the Bangsamoro, the ARMM would be abolished.
- Once the Basic Law was passed and approved, the Bangsamoro Transition Commission would rule until elections could be held. This was supposed to take place in early 2016.
- This new political entity would have a parliamentary system of governance. Roughly fifty regionally elected parliamentarians would elect a chief minister. The reason for this was to make the Bangsamoro inclusive and something that would garner buy-in from the MNLF. It would ensure that the Bangsamoro did not become an MILF-dominated body, as the group had little base of support in Sulu, Tawi-Tawi, and Zamboanga, the MNLF heartland.
- The Bangsamoro would pass a new local governance code, and until it did so, all local governments (villages, towns, cities, provinces) would be governed by existing national laws. The ARMM government would continue to function until dissolution.
- The Bangsamoro territory would include the existing ARMM, six municipalities in Lanao del Norte; all villages of the six municipalities in Maguindanao that voted for inclusion in the ARMM during the 2001 plebiscite; the cities of Cotabato and Isabela; and "all other contiguous areas where there is a resolution of the local government unit or a petition of at least 10 percent of the qualified voters in the area asking for their inclusion." Noncontiguous areas with a Muslim majority could also vote for inclusion.
- The government would be responsible for defense, foreign affairs, the issuance of currency and monetary policy, citizenship, and the post. The central government would be responsible for common market (the ASEAN Free Trade Agreement) and global trade, though the Bangsamoro would be allowed to enter into its own trade agreements.
- The Bangsamoro would be responsible for developing, expanding the reach, and overseeing *sharia* courts that would apply only to the Muslim population. The Bangsamoro would also be responsible for running existing civil courts.

2. Economic Matters

- The Bangsamoro would be in charge of its own fiscal affairs and would be able to set tax rates and levy taxes and fees.
- The Bangsamoro would have the right to receive and manage development assistance from bi- and multilateral donors. It would also be able to borrow money from domestic and foreign markets unless those loans required a sovereign guarantee. To that end, a trust fund would be established.

- The Bangsamoro would share in the proceeds from all natural resource exploitation, though the agreement did not provide a detailed breakdown or an exact formula. A separate annex dealt with wealth sharing.

3. Security and Reconciliation

- The negotiators made a considerable commitment to reconciliation, human rights, human security, and equality of Muslims and non-Muslims alike.
- The government recognized "Bangsamoro identity" and noted that they were "first people," original inhabitants.
- Existing property rights would be respected. The BJE would work to restore land to those who were marginalized or forced off their land. The central government and Bangsamoro would try to jointly address compensation.
- The MILF would gradually demobilize its forces and disarm, putting its weapons "beyond use." This would be phased in as other milestones in the agreement were implemented.
- An independent police force, accountable to both the Bangsamoro and national government, would be established. The PNP would eventually be phased out and an organic police force established. The MILF would not be immediately integrated into the PNP or AFP.
- The CCCH and AHJAG, along with the Malaysian-led IMT, would continue to monitor the peace process and report on cease-fire violations.
- Both parties would work to deal with crime, lawlessness, and private armies. (This is a real problem in the Philippines. An estimated 115,000 guns in Mindanao are outside of government control.)
- The two parties agreed to establish some sort of mechanism to deal with transitional justice and long-standing grievances and human rights violations.
- Third-party monitoring would ensure implementation of the agreement through the 2016 elections.

Following the conclusion of the FAB on October 15, 2012, the two sides began working on four detailed annexes that were concluded by the end of January 2014.

- Transitional Arrangements and Modalities (February 27, 2013) established the Bangsamoro Transition Commission and established rules of operation and membership. This agreement laid out the roadmap for how the Bangsamoro region would be established.
- Revenue Generation and Wealth Sharing (July 14, 2013) generously gave the MILF 75 percent of tax revenues and mineral wealth. In addition, the

two sides concluded an agreement on the "Addendum on Bangsamoro Waters" that demarcates the authority and wealth sharing on the waters that surround future Bangsamoro territories.

- Power Sharing (December 8, 2013) established a parliamentary system of government for the Bangsamoro and outlined the power, functions, and responsibilities of the central government and the Bangsamoro, respectively.
- Normalization (January 25, 2014) outlined the process of decommissioning MILF arms and demobilizing its forces.

An executive order, endorsed by Congress, then established the Bangsamoro Transition Commission, a fifteen-person board comprising seven members from the GRP and eight members from the MILF, headed by their lead negotiator, Mohagher Iqbal, charged with drafting the Bangsamoro Basic Law (BBL) in April 2013.

These annexes led to the March 27, 2014, signing of the formal peace accord, the Comprehensive Agreement on the Bangsamoro (CAB). But a peace agreement is only an agreement between the executive branch and a rebel group; in most political systems it has to go through a ratification or legislative process to turn it into binding law and reconcile it with existing legislation. In the case of the Philippines, it was the eighteen-article BBL that would achieve this.

The BBL was the key to everything as it created the legal mechanism to supersede the Organic Law that established the ARMM government (Republic Act 9054), nullify and supersede the MNLF's 1996 peace agreement, and dissolve the existing ARMM government (technically, not renew it). The BBL would establish the transitional governance mechanism and hold a regional plebiscite that will establish a truly independent governing entity, the Bangsamoro. The BBL had to be approved by the Philippine Congress and upheld by the Supreme Court.

The Bangsamoro Transition Commission submitted its draft of the BBL to President Aquino on April 14, 2014. The draft was signed on April 20, although one of the government's seven members did not sign the agreement.[64] The MILF and the other Transitional Commission members were expecting quick approval by the president. But their hopes were soon dashed, as his legal team scrubbed the document.

The negotiations on the details quickly stalled. By June 2013, the Bangsamoro Transition Committee had held three sessions and was completely deadlocked on issues of governance and wealth sharing.[65] Indeed, according to the MILF, the government had changed some 30 percent of the draft of the wealth-sharing annex that the two sides had agreed on in February 2013. In particular, the MILF was angered at changes in block transfer payments being offered to the Bangsamoro. The MILF's top negotiator was blunt: "The

[MILF] leadership is angry, not only frustrated but angry."[66] The talks were expected to resume in July 2013.[67]

On July 5, the Aquino administration returned the draft BBL to the Bangsamoro Transition Commission that rejected key provisions and "left almost nothing unchanged."[68] Some 70 percent of the ninety-seven-page document was either deleted or significantly revised. Of significant concern was the fact that the Aquino draft had a completely different interpretation of the issues of governance, territory, and resources than had been already agreed upon in the four annexes. The MILF was irate and rejected the government's amendments. MILF chief negotiator Mohagher Iqbal said that he was personally hurt and offended by the government's watered-down draft of the BBL.[69] On July 11, the two sides met in Kuala Lumpur to hammer out an agreement, but none was reached. A week later, a four-day meeting in Manila also failed to bridge the gap.[70]

On July 21, President Aquino spoke of a "middle ground" to break the impasse on the BBL.[71] A summit meeting between him and MILF Chairman Murad was broached, in addition to a "cooling off period" as "significant points of differences" remained.[72]

To be fair, the government's numerous amendments and redrafts were made to assure passage in Congress and to withstand Supreme Court scrutiny.[73] The government's top negotiator, Miriam Coronel-Ferrer, raised a concern that some of the draft BBL were unconstitutional.[74] The government clearly wanted to avoid the debacle of 2008, when the Supreme Court invalidated the MOA-AD, and it ran drafts by former Supreme Court justices and other constitutional scholars. But the amendments were extensive, and the MILF believes that the government's "watered-down" draft was based on a too-strict interpretation of the constitution. Moreover, the MILF contended that the government was revisiting what had been agreed upon in the FAB and the four annexes. The MILF was adamant that nothing already agreed upon could be renegotiated.[75] As the MILF wrote in an op-ed on its website:

> The OP's [Office of the President] comments on the BBL, which is essentially the position pursued by the GPH peace panel, dilute the text and have in many instances departed from the letter and spirit of the Framework Agreement on the Bangsamoro (FAB) and its Annexes, which is the basis of the crafting of the BBL. Moreover, the OP adopted a very conservative interpretation of the Constitution, which is a radical departure from what the government has been saying—and promised—that the flexibility of the Constitution would enable them to implement the FAB and its Annexes. Fourth, many of the delays are caused by issues that were already settled in the FAB and its Annexes but are kept coming back and forth at the instance of the GPH, e.g., ancestral domain to ancestral domains, central to national, Bangsamoro people to Bangsamoro peoples, etc.

The two sides announced a ten-day session, August 1–August 10, to reach an agreement on the BBL and brought in four external lawyers to help mediate the conflict. Yet five days into the talks, the sides had made no progress. The MILF's chief negotiator, Mohagher Iqbal, was blunt: "We cannot accept this proposed law as it is. We will lose face if we agree to this. Their version clearly departed from the letter and spirit of the peace agreement, which was the basis in crafting the proposed law."[76] By the end of the sixth day, the two sides announced that they had reached agreement on 70 percent of the eighteen articles in the BBL but that major differences still remained on governance and resource allocation.

Finally, in September 2014, the parties reached agreement, and the Bangsamoro Basic Law bill was submitted by President Aquino to Congress.

The timetable was key. Although no sunset clause appeared in either the October 2012 Framework Agreement or the March 2014 CAB, the original goal was to have the BBL submitted to Congress for the start of its second session in mid-2014. That would give Congress ample time to deliberate the bill, make necessary amendments, and then organize a plebiscite across seven provinces and multiple cities. And all of this really needed to be done by the first half of 2016. In part, it was the end of President Aquino's term, and the next president was not guaranteed to be committed to implementing the agreement.

But there were technical reasons for the 2016 date. The incumbent ARMM government expired on June 30. The whole idea was that it would simply not run a new election. With the establishment of the Bangsamoro pushed beyond June 2016, it would be difficult to legally dissolve an existing democratically elected body. That could not withstand a constitutional challenge. Moreover, under the Annex on Transitional Arrangements and Modalities, the Bangsamoro Transition Commission was supposed to be replaced by elected officials by July 2016.

The MNLF

But the real challenge to the peace process remained intra-Moro competition. The agreement would lead to the dissolution of the 1996 accord with the MNLF that was established in Republic Act 6734. In a perfect world, the MNLF would endorse this agreement as it gets the Moro people far more, promises far more autonomy, and protects their cultural rights better, but it is not a perfect world, and the MNLF leaders were irate.

This agreement wounded their pride. The current chair of one MNLF faction (the MNLF has three distinct factions, each of which believes it is the rightful leader), Habib Mujahab Hashim, called the agreement a "betrayal" and threatened not only to not cooperate but to return to war: "We have no other recourse but to go back to the original objective of armed struggle."[77]

Another MNLF leader who had a better relationship with the MILF has expressed more of a willingness to cooperate, but under terms. This faction still pushed for "tripartite talks" among themselves, the government, and the Organization of the Islamic Conference.[78] The government and one faction of the MNLF (which claims to represent the whole organization) have negotiated "42 Consensus Points" about the 1996 agreement.[79] The MNLF continued to try to save its pact with the government. Indeed, tripartite talks were still being held in January 2016.

The MNLF also saw the October 2012 agreement as a political threat, though power is not simply handed over to the MILF but eventually to a democratically elected parliament. The MILF has tried to reach out to the MNLF, but it is to little avail. The two sides engaged in armed attacks in May 2013, and every attempt at unity talks failed.[80]

The MNLF repeatedly tried to sabotage the agreement. In December 2012, the MNLF filed a suit at the Supreme Court to invalidate the agreement with the MILF and refused to join the Bangsamoro Transition Commission. Although one senior MNLF member did attend the March 27, 2014, signing of the peace agreement, there was not much of a public endorsement.[81] The MNLF continued to rail about the tripartite talks, refusing to acknowledge that the train had left the station. The BBL would give the MNLF more than it ever got in 1996; it would certainly benefit the Moro, the people the MNLF claims to represent, more than the things Misuari achieved in 1996. But the MNLF would rather spoil the peace process for the sake of its wounded pride.

In July 2013, Misuari declared the founding of the "Bangsamoro Republik,"[82] which existed only in his head. In September 2013, Misuari was so irate about being ignored by the government that he launched an attack on communities in Zamboanga that left scores dead, 180 people taken hostage, and 15,000 displaced people living in absolute squalor.[83]

Beyond the OIC's efforts, others have made multiple attempts to get the two organizations to reach an agreement, but they have always failed. Presidential adviser on the peace process Teresita Quintos "Ging" Deles tried to convince MNLF members that the peace process is "inclusive" and not only for the MILF.[84] But most of the MNLF viewed the MILF accord with a mixture of condescension and suspicion. On January 8, 2014, the MILF issued an editorial on its website imploring the MNLF to join it and stating that the BBL would include the best and most workable aspects of the MNLF's previous accords.

> The only real and desirable thing now is that we produce the best BBL for the future Bangsamoro Government. This law is not for the MILF; it is for our people as a whole. We appeal to our brothers from the Moro National Liberation Front (MNLF) to come to grips with reality that during the current Aquino

administration, the only viable and pursued peace track is the one with the MILF.

The MILF have tried to appeal to reason, arguing that in addition to the existing ARMM region (Basilan, Maguindanao, Lanao del Sur, Sulu, and Tawi-Tawi), the expanded Bangsamoro will also include Isabela City in Basilan, Cotabato City, six towns in Lanao del Norte, and 39 of 208 *barangays* in North Cotabato. The MNLF contends that had the plebiscite not been rigged back in 1996, these regions would already be part of the ARMM and under its control.

Even the Annex on Wealth Sharing, which gives the Moros 75 percent of tax revenues and proceeds from mineral exploration—far more than in the 1996 accord—was not enough to change the minds of the MNLF.[85] The MNLF continued to organize against the MILF. On February 14, when the Bangsamoro Transition Commission held a town-hall meeting in Zamboanga, commission members were booed off the stage by organized demonstrators and were later snubbed by the city's mayor.

In late June 2014, MNLF factions came together and tried to agree on getting behind a single leader. Sadly, they opted for Misuari, who has been hiding in Sulu after leading the "Bangsamoro Republik" rampage in Zamboanga in September 2013.[86] He has since also been implicated in the ASG's spate of kidnappings from eastern Sabah in Malaysia.

The MNLF leaders, nonetheless, began to act more constructively. They agreed to attend another coordinating mechanism established in 2010, the Bangsamoro Coordination Forum, which had been largely defunct. They also asked that the BBL and future documents reference the original 1976 Tripoli Agreement and the 1996 Jakarta Accord.[87]

The OIC was responsible for much of the change in attitude. The OIC tried to harmonize the MNLF and MILF agreements with the GRP.[88] But the MNLF has been stung that the OIC has not come out completely in its corner on this one. The MNLF sent pledges of support for the MILF and BBL from Jeddah, but similar pledges in the past have never been implemented back home.[89]

The United Bangsamoro Justice Party

The MNLF had an added reason for concern. The MILF immediately began work on transitioning itself into a political party in order to contest elections in 2016.[90] That would give the MILF a significant organizational advantage over the MNLF, which never really made the transition and remains in a postrevolutionary organizational malaise. In April 2014, the MILF announced the founding of the United Bangsamoro Justice Party (UBJP).[91] Though the MILF insisted that the party will be inclusive and open to anyone, it is for now very much under the control of the MILF's central committee and should be expected to represent the institutional interests of the MILF.

The MILF combatants were better organized on the battlefield, and MILF was now poised to be more organized politically. The MNLF was never able to transform itself into an effective political party; it merely got absorbed into the weak and fluid party system of the Philippines. Sadly, the Bangsamoro's parliamentary system of government was chosen specifically to entice the MNLF. (In the Annex on Power Sharing, roughly fifty parliamentarians would elect a chief minister.)[92] The geographical representation strongly favors the MNLF in Zamboanga, Basilan, Sulu, and Tawi-Tawi. Were the MNLF to get its act together, it would have significant representation in the Bangsamoro government and an effective check on the MILF.

The UBJP is technically an open party, but it is clearly the political vehicle of the MILF and will forward policies and personnel consistent with MILF interests. What that means, specifically, is not yet clear. By early 2016, the MILF had still not determined the UBJP's platform beyond protecting the rights and interests of the Bangsamoro people. The MILF's vice chairman for political affairs, Ghadzali Jaafar, stated, "This party is based on justice," without going into any more details. "Our goal is to ensure the victory of the candidates that we are going to field . . . the objective is to push the programs of MILF for the Bangsamoro, the new political entity that will replace the ARMM."[93] On another occasion, the MILF announced that the UBJP would "continue the struggle for self-determination, without the use of guns, starting from the 2016 synchronized national and regional elections."[94] This is despite the fact that the MILF renounced its quest for independence and accepted autonomy and despite its knowing that the CAB contains no provision for a referendum on independence. But beyond that, there is no identified platform. Social justice, the application of the *sharia*, and transitional justice are expected to figure prominently in the party agenda. Traditionally, the MILF was a revolutionary party opposed to the traditional aristocratic system in the region. But recently, it has downplayed that issue as it seeks to broaden its base.

The MILF currently has no plans to dissolve, though it is not a legal entity, nor is it clear that it will become one. Many within the leadership want the MILF to become a mass-based organization with the UBJP as its political arm. The UBJP became a formal, legal party, registered at both the Securities and Exchange Commission and the Commission on Elections (COMELEC). But until the relationship between the two entities is defined, there can be no platform.

The senior leadership of the MILF will make up the UBJP's leadership. MILF chairman Ebrahim el-Haj Murad will be the party president, and Ghadzali Jaafar will serve as the vice president. Another senior MILF member, Sammy al-Mansour, who is currently the MILF's top military commander, will serve as the interim committee chairman. All UBJP officials, including the forty local party units, will be appointed by the MILF's central committee.

In March 2014, the Institute of Autonomy and Governance, Institute of Bangsamoro Studies, and Konrad Adenauer Foundation ran a training on party building for thirty-nine senior MILF members. These individuals are expected to be the first to transition to UBJP party work and become the core of the party's leadership. Those thirty-nine individuals, whose names have not been released, hail from both the military and political wings of the MILF. A second party-building conference was concluded in November 2014 in Marawi, again bringing in some forty members of the MILF's central committee, armed forces, and political wings.

Although MILF chairman Murad has long said that he has no interest in becoming the Bangsamoro's chief minister, he was under pressure to run for elected office as only he has the clout to really control competing factions and interests within the MILF, which is much less cohesive than it was a decade ago. That said, his selection would be decisive among MNLF supporters, especially in Sulu, and among traditional warlords in Mindanao. Few, if any, other leaders in the southern Philippines have broad-based appeal that transcends their movement or patronage networks.

In December 2014, the MILF formally registered its new political party, the United Bangsamoro Justice Party, with the Commission on Elections.[95] And the peace process looked like it was moving forward.

Congress

Despite enormous concessions by both sides, intense work by negotiators, and political courage by both President Aquino and MILF chairman Murad, the BBL became the victim of congressional politics.

The BBL actually entered Congress with enormous support and goodwill. Senate president Francisco Drilon promised to make the BBL a legislative priority, and thirteen of twenty-four senators cosponsored the legislation.[96] A large seventy-plus-person *ad hoc* committee in the House was established to push through the agreement.

One concern in particular was whether the BBL created a "state within a state." And some were opposed to the opt-in provisions for the contiguous areas. But for the most part, these views were shared by only a minority of the legislators. Some thirty hearings had been held by December 2015, and expectations were high for the bill's passage. President Aquino's party and allies controlled a majority of the House, and he was confident that the bill would be passed by March 2015, which would give enough time for a plebiscite to be conducted and the agreement implemented before both his and the ARMM government's terms expired in May 2016.

Congressional oversight until this point was largely positive, and there appeared to be no major hurdles for the BBL's passage. But then Mamasapano happened, and everything that seemed certain came undone amid horrific mistrust and political grandstanding.

The Mamasapano Incident and Its Aftermath

On January 25, 2015, an elite unit of the Philippine National Police conducted a raid in MILF-controlled territory. Its targets were two wanted terrorist suspects, including a Malaysian member of Jemaah Islamiyah. The Special Action Forces (SAF) neither told the AFP about the raid nor coordinated it with the Ad Hoc Joint Action Group, a violation of the peace process. The SAF leadership made clear that they intentionally didn't coordinate with the AHJAG: "We don't trust them," explained the force commander, who insinuated that the MILF was either protecting the two or at the very least would tip them off.

The MILF alongside some of the breakaway Bangsamoro Islamic Freedom Fighters (BIFF) (many of whom are tied by kinship and remain neighbors) fought back, and the SAF company immediately found itself pinned down. Forty-four members were killed, the most lethal conflict in years. It was an ill planned, ill conceived, and terribly executed operation. The call for reinforcements came late. The AFP, angered that it was not kept in the loop, refused to provide artillery support.

The national outrage following the clash put the entire peace process in doubt. It was a media spectacle that completely reversed public opinion on the peace process, which through December had been highly supportive of both the process and the government's handling of it.[97] But the image of forty-four flag-draped coffins being unloaded from three C-130 cargo planes changed everything. Congress immediately put the hearings on the BBL on hold indefinitely while it began a series of hearings on the clash.

The MILF's disavowal of terrorism and commitment to the peace process assuaged no one.

Different government organizations produced a series of fact-finding reports and public hearings. The AFP was the first to issue its report, which, not surprisingly, absolved itself of any responsibility.

The Senate's report was the most watched. While people broadly expected the House of Representatives report to be more damning, some hoped that the Senate report would be more thoughtful and considerate of the peace process and the long-term implications. But with five senators eyeing the presidency in the May 2016 election, it became a partisan tool. Indeed, neophyte senator Grace Poe so effectively used her chairing of the hearings that she quickly went from not even being considered as a potential candidate in September 2014 to the leading candidate by the spring of 2015.

The Senate report clearly laid the blame for the incident at the feet of the MILF. It rejected the MILF's assertion that it was a "tragic misencounter" and that the MILF was simply policing its territory against an armed intrusion, acting in self-defense.

The leak of video of indeterminate BIFF or MILF combatants executing wounded SAF that went viral further inflamed the Senate, which labeled Mamasapano as a "massacre."[98]

It bears emphasizing that the first sin in the Mamasapano incident was the fact that the MILF leadership and community allowed themselves to coddle criminals and terrorists. During the hearings, MILF issued blanket denials of knowing about the presence of Marwan, Usman, and a host of other elements in their midst, yet these terrorists have been their residents for almost a decade. Marwan, in fact, had been training recruits in the area and breeding people who would maim and kill.

The sincerity of the MILF's proclaimed quest for peace was, thus, put in serious doubt. A group that claimed to seek peace with the government should have exercised restraint. It should not have massacred police on a legitimate law enforcement operation simply because the police did not give it prior notice about the operations. This also has implications for the safety of government troops who must conduct law enforcement operations within MILF-controlled territory.

If the MILF leadership had already sent word to the ground troops to cease fire but did not have the capability to stop the action of its ground troops, then that showed that the leadership did not exercise a strong command or control of the BIAF.

The MILF issued its own report, which laid the blame on the SAF for its failure to use existing cease-fire and AHJAG mechanisms. The MILF fought only in self-defense, according to its report. The MILF rejected the "massacre" label, arguing that eighteen of its own combatants and civilians were killed in the clash. It stated that the MILF remained committed to the peace process.

But what angered Congress was that the MILF's report did not address its relationship with the BIFF. The MILF said that its only failing was one of intelligence, that is, it had not known the two terrorists were in its territory.[99] But it could not explain why it was fighting beside the BIFF, which had publicly quit the peace process and broken away from the MILF in 2008.

Nothing the MILF said convinced any members of Congress. The MILF's chief negotiator, Mohagher Iqbal, testified repeatedly before both the House and the Senate hearings, and although he originally said that he would do so only in executive session, in all cases he was public and on the record.

Members of both chambers demanded that the MILF turn over those involved in the clash, whom the government considered murderers. One hard-line Christian representative from Mindanao said that failure to do so would be considered an "obstruction of justice" and would be justification for an offensive against the MILF.[100] Others called it a "confidence-building gesture" on the part of the MILF, who refused, again citing the fact that it was acting in self-defense. Indeed, in July 2015, the government issued formal charges against.

Senator Alan Peter Cayetano called for the MILF's immediate disarmament as a precondition for the peace process, not phased out, as had been agreed upon in the Annex on Normalization: "Disarmament cannot be a product of peace. Disarmament must be a precondition for peace."[101] Other senators jumped on board, calling for a total surrender of weaponry, a non-starter for the MILF.

The MILF did turn over sixteen weapons that it seized in the clash as a sign of goodwill, arguing that it had no responsibility to do so under the laws of war. But that it turned over only sixteen of the sixty-three firearms that were lost in the encounter infuriated Congress and other critics of the peace agreement.[102] The MILF argued that it could not compel the BIFF to surrender arms; but critics pointed to the fact that that day they were fighting alongside each other.

In another show of goodwill, the MILF allowed AFP forces to engage in attacks and hot pursuit of BIFF rebels through its territory, as was part of the cease-fire mechanism. Yet in a way, this backfired on it. Congress was infuriated and questioned why permission was now needed to access sovereign Philippine territory. The MILF tried to build confidence by joining the AFP in attacking the BIFF. But the capture of a BIFF bomb factory in MILF-claimed territory led many in Congress to continue to view the MILF as an untrustworthy negotiating partner.[103]

Congressional attacks on the BBL were fueled by public disenchantment. By March 2015, 44 percent of respondents were against the peace process, according to one poll.[104] The president's approval rating fell to an all-time low by 21 percentage points, from 59 percent in November 2014 to 38 percent in March 2015, while his trust rating plunged from 56 percent to 36 percent in the same period.

It was the AFP commander at the time who called the resumption of war against the MILF as "illogical," one of the rare voices of reason who helped prod Congress to remain committed to the peace process in principle.[105] But Congress was dismissive of the third-party IMT's report that found fault on both sides as well as the balanced report of the National Human Rights Commission that apportioned blame equally.

While condemning what happened in Mamasapano, the Commission must caution against broad statements which serve no purpose other than to polarize public opinion. While the Commission commiserates with the families of the victims and acknowledges that the killing of the Fallen 44 was unjustified, categorizing the incident as a "massacre" is excessive. [106]

But most of all, the chair of the Human Rights Commission, Loretta Ann Rosales, was critical of the failure of Congress to look at the peace process in a long-term perspective. Congress "could have weighed on the political maturity of the MILF for its willingness to forego its armed struggle and agree to decommission its forces in exchange for a political settlement in Mindanao, which the organization has been fighting for in more than four decades."

On April 22, the Department of Justice issued its own report on Mamasapano, which added more fuel to the fire. The probe found that SAF did not violate existing cease-fire mechanisms because the AHJAG agreement has an exemption for high-value targets: "The SAF was not in breach of the Ceasefire Agreement. It was in Mamasapano to implement a warrant of arrest against high-value targets, and that kind of police action can be done even without coordination with the Moro Islamic Liberation Front." [107] This formally absolved the SAF of all blame, ergo, the entire onus for the clash was on the MILF. The report found that the MILF/BIFF engaged in "wanton murder" and that as a result, charges for over one hundred were to be filed. [108]

This further bolstered the case of congressional opponents who were hostile to the agreement and added more calls for the MILF to surrender the men. As Senate president Drilon put it:

We hope that the MILF will cooperate with the Department of Justice in seeking justice for what happened in Mamasapano. This is an important step for them as they enter the democratic process. Rather than express doubts on the investigation, the MILF has to move with the rest of the public on this matter. They should abide by the process in accordance with the Constitution and our laws. As our partners in the peace process, now is a good time for them to show that they are genuine in their commitment to securing peace by doing all they can to assist and participate in the legal process that will now take into action. [109]

Former allies of the peace process were now making politically unacceptable demands on the MILF leadership to move forward and resume deliberations on the BBL.

President Aquino had to walk an incredibly fine line. He spoke at the funeral of the SAF members and met with all of their family members. He called the MILF's own report "insufficient." But he made it clear that the peace process had to move forward, so that these forty-four were not the last to die. He had to assuage Congress and let its members vent, grandstand, and politic for the 2016 election because he ultimately needed their support for the passage of the BBL.

It was not until April 2015, four months after the clash, that the Senate resumed its hearings on the BBL. Congress followed suit the following month. But it was clear that the mood had changed, especially in the Senate.

President Aquino was hoping to be able to use his party's majority in the House to push through the BBL largely intact. Despite the vociferous criticism of several Christian politicians from Mindanao, much of the bill passed easily. That was not the case in the Senate, where the twenty-four senators had freer reign from party politics and were in full campaign mode.

Members were calling for the full disarmament of the MILF immediately, not in accordance with the peace process, as was agreed in the Annex on Normalization. Others continued to call for the MILF to turn over its men, which it refused to do. Some accusations were simply red herrings, such as Mohagher Iqbal's use of a *nom de guerre* rather than his real name as evidence that he could not be trusted.[110]

Two of the thirteen senators who originally sponsored the bill had withdrawn their support, and many others had attacked key provisions of it. Nancy Binay, the daughter of the vice president and leading candidate to become president in 2016 despite a host of corruption scandals, attacked the block grants and the government organization established to fund the decommissioning and demobilization of MILF combatants, Sajahatra Bangsamoro.[111] Others challenged the *sharia* court provisions and whether the internal security force of the Bangsamoro would be within the chain of command of the PNP.

But most of all, concern was growing that the BBL itself was unconstitutional. Senator Miriam Defensor-Santiago, herself a presidential candidate, loudly denounced the BBL's illegality. By the end of May, twelve senators had found the BBL to be "unconstitutional."[112] Five of the original thirteen cosponsors had defected.[113]

Ferdinand Marcos Jr., the chair of the Senate Committee on Local Government, which was holding the BBL hearings, said that it was unconstitutional and said he would draft an alternative bill to be presented to the fall 2015 session of the Senate, scrapping the BBL and amending the 1996 ARMM agreement. Despite his grandstanding, his poll numbers for the 2016 presidency remained flat at 3 percent. And the MILF warned that this was completely unacceptable. But when Marcos joined forces and became Vice President Binay's running mate, he continued to push for his drastically watered-down version of the BBL, which offered less than the 1996 ARMM agreement.

No one saw any political cost to being hard-line on the MILF or the peace process. Indeed, most saw intransigent and critical positions as being beneficial. Unlike the House of Representatives, whose members each represent a geographical district, senators are elected on a national slate.

The government's negotiators, Miriam Coronel-Ferrer and Office of the Presidential Adviser on the Peace Process (OPAPP) chief Ging Deles, made herculean efforts to save the peace process. They held one public meeting after another, they appeared before Congress, they provided testimony, and they even had their loyalty to the nation publicly questioned. They suffered vicious attacks on their character, as they were accused of coddling the MILF, murderers, and terrorists, and of not being deferential enough to the slain—no, it's the Philippines—martyred forty-four SAF. In one hearing, Senator Francis Escudero blasted Coronel-Ferrer for speaking again on behalf of the MILF.[114] Another Christian politician from Mindanao and a sharp critic of the BBL, Rep. Celso Lobregat, said the OPAPP report on Mamasapano was "acting in defense of the MILF" and demeaning of the forty-four SAF "martyrs." Senators Francis Escudero and Alan Peter Cayetano urged President Aquino to replace the negotiating team, accusing them of siding with the rebels and acting like "spokespersons, lawyers, and campaign managers" for the MILF.[115]

Yet they pressed on. By the end of July 2015, they had held or participated in 553 public consultative activities to educate various stakeholders, inform the public, and build up support for the peace process. They were unflappable.

But most of all, they had to defend the BBL's basic constitutionality: they had to deny that it created a state within a state, which could allow for a future declaration of independence, and that it would be an Islamic state that governed by the *sharia*, violating the principles of the secular constitution. They argued instead that the BBL would be responsible to and in accordance with Philippine national laws, under the jurisdiction of Congress and the Supreme Court, that the BBL would protect minority rights of Christians and indigenous peoples (*lumads*), and that nothing about having a parliamentary form of government was explicitly unconstitutional.

While the bill stalled in Congress, the MILF continued to prove its commitment to the peace process. It killed a wanted terrorist in early May 2015.[116] But members of Congress viewed it as insufficient. The MILF continued to meet with its counterparts regarding disarmament and demobilization.

And in a very high-profile ceremony in the MILF headquarters, Camp Darapanan, on June 15, 2015, the MILF put 75 weapons beyond use, under the lock and key of independent and international monitors, while demobilizing the first 145 combatants.[117]

But most of all, the MILF leadership repeated that no matter what happened with the BBL in Congress, it was not preparing to return to war. In

March 2015, it had its combatants register to vote, while in May 2015, the UBJP finalized its registration process as a legal political party.

And still, none of these was sufficient, especially in the midst of a presidential election.

In August 2015, murder charges against 102 MILF combatants involved in Mamasapano were filed, while Senator Marcos rolled out his substitute version of the BBL, 80 percent of which he said had to be changed. The bill, which had ten coauthors, gutted the original BBL.

Although the parliamentary form of autonomous government remained intact, it had a significant reallocation of seats. The Bangsamoro government lost significant autonomy, and the concept of intergovernmental relations was diluted. The powers of the chief minister, especially over the autonomous police force, were weakened. Although the Bangsamoro block grant remained intact, other fiscal powers, including taxation and the ability to get grants and enter into economic agreements, were removed. Marcos's substitute BBL reasserted sole central government control over strategic minerals, including hydrocarbons. And the bill demanded a front-loaded rather than phased-in decommissioning process.

The Bangsamoro Transition Commission urged Congress to pass the BBL "in its original form," saying that it is the version consistent with the peace agreements and is constitutional. In a letter to both chambers, the BTC wrote that it "stands firm that the proposed BBL in its original form is the most appropriate version based on the Framework Agreement on the Bangsamoro (FAB) and Comprehensive Agreement on the Bangsamoro (CAB)."[118] The BTC warned that the proposed amendments "constitute a clear transgression of the signed agreements."

More ominously, the MILF issue a scathing criticism of the BBL redrafting and warned that "the MILF will not accept a diluted BBL." "If a law is based on the report of the [House] Ad Hoc Committee on the BBL, which is 50 percent bad, the MILF will outright reject it."[119] The MILF were irate over the Ad Hoc Committee's redrafting of revenue sharing, saying that the current bill "not only maintains the status quo, but [is] an outright deprivation of what remains of the wealth in our lands, which have been raped by outsiders." Likewise, the imposition of national laws, such as the Indigenous Peoples Rights Act (IPRA) and the labor code, "destroys the essence of autonomy."

President Aquino called on Congress to pass the BBL in his last State of the Nation Address, in July 2015, but the peace process, which had been so central to his administration, seemed to be written off. It got only the briefest and most *pro forma* endorsement. And congressional intransigence in light of Aquino's lack of political capital and lame duck status only grew, all the more so once election season was in full swing. Ever since Mamasapano, Aquino never invested the necessary political clout or used his bully pulpit to cajole legislators into approving the agreement. And the nature of the Philippine political system, with its weak party structure and constant defections, gives party leaders few tools to enforce discipline on key votes.

International donors have tried to remain positive. The Asian Development Bank announced that part of its three billion dollars in loans to the Philippines between 2016 and 2019 would go to support the peace process. The World Bank has continued to support agricultural development. Other bilateral donors have maintained their commitment. The third-party monitoring team has continued its rounds of dialogue and engagement, but the mood has become very somber.

The costs of congressional intransigence remained very low. The Asia Foundation and Social Weather Stations (SWS) survey found that following Mamasapano, public support for negotiation as the best way for dealing with the MILF dropped sharply, and, unsurprisingly, those who said military means were the best way increased. Public disapproval of the BBL remained high, with only 23 percent and 24 percent in favor in March and June 2015 polls, respectively. Disapproval of the BBL remained fixed at 48 and 47 percent, respectively. Yet within the territory that would be the core of the BBL, support for the agreement is overwhelming. Only in Sulu and Isabela City was support under 38 percent; every other region overwhelmingly supported passage of the BBL. And politicians could capitalize on public mistrust, in large part fueled by anti-Muslim biases, toward the MILF. Trust in the MILF plunged after Mamasapano. In the March survey, only 16 percent had trust in them, 61 percent had little trust, and the remainder were undecided. "Net trust in the MILF fell by 15 points to –45 in March 2015, from –30 in September 2014."[120]

Meanwhile, frustration on the part of the MILF has grown. In its eyes, it has done nothing wrong. It acted in self-defense and on the basis of the cease-fire mechanisms. It has done everything it can to demonstrate goodwill and commitment to the peace process. But it was never enough, and the goalposts constantly changed, as Congress saw no costs, except for some votes in Mindanao, to opposing the BBL. And as this happened, the Islamic State in Iraq and the Levant (ISIL) arose across Southeast Asia, including many organizations that publicly pledged loyalty to ISIL: Mujahidin Indonesia Timur (MIT), Jamaah Ansharut Tauhid (JAT) in Indonesia, the Abu Sayyaf, the Bangsamoro Islamic Freedom Front, and the Ansuar al-Khalifa in the Philippines. Philippine leaders who decry the rise of ISIL have only themselves to blame for thwarting the peaceful aspirations of the Bangsamoro. Murad has repeatedly called on his combatants to maintain the cease-fire, but frustration and mistrust of government intentions have soared, while incentives to remain in the chain of command are ebbing. Murad's command and control are dissipating quickly.

An opportunity to achieve a far-reaching and progressive peace process, which could have been a model for the resolution of conflicts around the world, was squandered for short-term political gains and endemic prejudice among the majority-Christian lawmakers. As Pangalian Balindong, a Muslim congressman from Lanao del Sur and a staunch supporter of the peace process, said, barely holding back his tears:

> Today, with a heavy heart and a disturbing sense of foreboding, I close the book of hope for the passage of the Bangsamoro Basic law. Fifty-one public hearings, 200 hours of committee level debates and 8 months of consultations are all put to waste—thrown into the abyss of uncertainty and darkness. This is the lowest and saddest day of my legislative work. . . . We have foreclosed all possible peaceful, legal and constitutional avenues for peace. No matter how we stand to legal reasoning, no matter how we shout for our constitutionally guaranteed right to genuine political autonomy, the reality is that there are only ten Moro legislators against the more than 280 members of this house. We are only ten lone voices in the wilderness of bias, prejudice and hatred. . . . We have failed the next generation who will obviously inherit this vicious cycle of war and conflict. The BBL should have been our vehicle to peace. [121]

The Philippine negotiator Miriam Coronel-Ferrer laid the blame clearly on "the sheer indifference and chronic absenteeism of a majority of the legislators."[122]

While political opponents have long tried to pin the Mamasapano incident on President Aquino, no real evidence exists that he signed off on the original operation. But his lack of leadership and oversight, sins of both omission and commission, cost him what could have been his presidential legacy: lasting peace in Mindanao.

5. PRESIDENT DUTERTE, FEDERALISM, AND THE FUTURE OF THE BBL

The toxic atmosphere following the Mamasapano incident was amplified during the heated presidential election campaign. In December 2015, the House failed to pass the Bangsamoro Basic Law (BBL), meaning that by law the legislation had to be resubmitted to the next Congress, which would have to start from scratch in terms of hearings and the legislative process. No presidential candidate condemned the inaction by the Congress.

The Aquino administration did try to assure the MILF that the Comprehensive Agreement on the Bangsamoro (CAB) remained in place and was binding despite the failure to pass implementing legislation. But the MILF's concerns were palpable. And as the BBL went unpassed, the MILF had no legal obligation to disarm, which continued to irritate Philippine politicians.

While none of the presidential candidates was against the peace process, their support for it was highly qualified. Only one, President Aquino's hand-chosen successor, Mar Roxas, campaigned promising to push the BBL through Congress at the next session. All other candidates pledged support for the peace process in principle but were short on details. Several of the senators most involved in the scuttling of the BBL were presidential candidates (Grace Poe, Miriam Defensor-Santiago) or vice-presidential candidates (Alan Peter Cayetano, Ferdinand Marcos Jr.). Only two candidates traveled to meet with the MILF during the campaign, Roxas and Davao mayor Rodrigo Duterte. Duterte spoke empathetically of injustices and his centerpiece proposal of political devolution through the establishment of a federal system: "I know you are very frustrated and I know you are hurt. This could have created a problem had it not been for the moderation of the Central Committee."[123] More importantly, he said that the BBL was a "template" for the country. But even here he said that he would push for passage of the BBL only if Congress embraced federalism. As he said: if federalism "will be undertaken by a Constitutional Commission, and thereafter if I am contented and it is gaining ground, BBL will be incorporated into the Constitution as an organic law of the Federal Republic of the Philippines." Then he immediately contradicted himself: "If it [a constitutional amendment] takes time, and if only to defuse tension, in my government I will convince Congress to pass the BBL then make it as a template for federal states."

Overall, the peace process was a nonissue in the campaign, reinforcing the concern among the Moro that there is no place for them within the Philippine national narrative or construct. The MILF, for its part, did not endorse a candidate. And the MILF's legally registered political party, the United Bangsamoro Justice Party (UBJP) ran no candidates.

Upon Duterte's victory in the presidential election, the MILF welcomed him as a "true son of Mindanao." Chairman Ebrahim el Haj Murad said Duterte's "message of justice, freedom, equality and social justice resonates with our aspiration for genuine change."[124] Murad said that the MILF shared Duterte's belief that the "status quo is unacceptable." In a May 11 letter to the president elect, Murad wrote that the MILF was "highly optimistic and confident that your victory would carry with it our hopes and aspirations for peace and justice in Mindanao."

But the MILF's hopes were soon dashed. While Duterte put key allies from Mindanao in his cabinet, they are largely hostile to the MILF and the peace process. Duterte immediately selected Jesus Dureza as his adviser on the peace process. Dureza held the same position in the cabinet of Gloria Macapagal Arroyo from 2001 to 2003. Dureza had a terrible reputation as a back-channel wheeler dealer whose strategy tended to focus on corruption and co-optation. Duterte and Dureza's quick appeal to the Moro National Liberation Front (MNLF), including offering to meet Nur Misuari, still a fugitive from justice, reminded the MILF of Dureza's history of trying to pit Moro groups against one another.

In addition, Duterte selected a Cotabato-based Christian politician as his secretary of agriculture. Manuel Piñol had cut his teeth as an elected official in North Cotabato, where some of the most fierce fighting between the government and the MILF, and later the Bangsamoro Islamic Freedom Fighters, took place. Piñol has been a leading critic of the BBL and a hard-line Christian advocate within Congress to oppose the peace process. Finally, Duterte named Salvador Panelo, the former defense lawyer for the Ampatuan clan, which was responsible for the murder of fifty-eight people, including thirty-two journalists, in 2009 and archrivals of the MILF, as his presidential spokesman.

It is more than the cabinet's lack of commitment to the BBL or empathy with the plight of the Moros that has given the MILF leadership cause for concern but the issue of federalism that has caused the greatest consternation. The MILF is not opposed to Duterte's plan. But it always saw the plan as something that would augment the BBL and the establishment of the Bangsamoro, not supplant it. The MILF was in for a shock when Duterte's candidate to be the speaker of the house, Congressman Pantaleon Alvarez, stated that the Duterte administration had no plan to resubmit the BBL to Congress. He said the CAB had been "rendered moot" as the Duterte administration was simply going to pursue a constitutional amendment and popular referendum by 2019 to establish a federal system.[125] The MILF felt betrayed. In his February meeting with the MILF leadership Duterte said, "I have been proposing federalism. But your territory will not be touched." On May 28, Duterte backtracked and said that he would resubmit a version of the BBL. However, he was not enthusiastic and seemed unwilling to use his electoral mandate to push for its passage. He again defaulted to federalism: "If Congress cannot enact into law the proposed Bangsamoro Basic Law, then we can pursue our collective dream of peace and prosperity via federalism."

Any constitutional amendment is by definition a tall order, requiring three-fourths approval by both houses of Congress or a constitutional convention and then a popular referendum. Despite several attempts to amend the 1987 constitution, none have made it to the referendum phase.

And the MILF were incensed that the future of the peace process was going to be dependent on such a fraught process with little likelihood of success. In an editorial on its website, the MILF called the proposal a "nonstarter" that "does not build confidence that the Duterte administration understands the Bangsamoro problem."[126] While the MILF couched its criticism, saying that Alvarez might not have been speaking for the Duterte administration, it was clearly signaling that anything short of the implementation of the CAB would be unacceptable to it. "There are peculiarities that are unique to the Bangsamoro but are not present in the other possible federal states, which are predominantly Christians, such as the issues of shariah, madrasah systems, [the] need for Bangsamoro police, etc. Even in terms of narrative, the Moros have their distinct history."[127] And they warned that without implementation of the CAB, there would be no disarmament or demobilization. "How would he address the issue of MILF's weapons and combatants and the need to normalize the situation?"

A federal system may be beneficial for the country as a whole, but it does not give the MILF the sense of special cultural identity, distinct from the Philippines, or that the government is trying to address historical wrongs. Moreover, the MNLF's quick embrace of federalism, with Duterte's olive branch to them, has angered many in the MILF leadership.

From May 29 to May 30, the respective peace panels met in Kuala Lumpur, where they issued a statement calling for the continuity of the peace process. It was the last meeting with the stalwart defenders of the peace process and advocates for the passage of the BBL, Ging Deles and Miriam Ferrer Coronel, who were condemned by critics in Congress as "traitors." The parties signed the Declaration of Continuity of the Partnership of the GPH and MILF in the Bangsamoro Peace Process that pledged both sides to continue to fully implement the Comprehensive Agreement on the Bangsamoro. Though he did not attend the meeting, Jes Dureza sent a note to the meeting. While he did not explicitly state that the Duterte administration would push for congressional passage of the BBL, he said: "We intend to continue with the gains and build on those already done and achieved. The roadmap that we will traverse hereon will take policy guidance and direction from the new President when he assumes office on June 30, 2016."[128]

On June 18, Duterte hosted leaders of both the MILF and the MNLF in Davao for a two-hour meeting. The MNLF representative Datu Abul Khayr Alonto, as quick to endorse the president-elect's plan for federalism, said: "The centralized form of government has been a dismal failure. That is precisely (the reason) why you still have war in Mindanao."[129] The MILF continued to be more suspect and reiterated that it would continue to push for passage of the BBL as originally submitted. In July 2016, the MILF signed an agreement with one faction of the MNLF to coordinate their roadmap to peace, but Muslimin Semma's faction is only one of three.[130]

Even if the Duterte administration decides to submit the implementing legislation to Congress, it is very likely not going to be the original piece of legislation submitted in September 2014. The government will most likely submit a watered-down draft, stripping away much of the MILF's autonomy, arguing that the original bill could not garner sufficient congressional support. This, in itself, will be a major irritant to the MILF leadership and their rank and file.

To be fair, Duterte does care about the plight of the Moro. As a fellow Mindanaoan, he has a vitriolic mistrust of Manila and blames the country's ills on decades of overcentralization. He does have a commitment to peace, but his advisers, politics, and competing interests seem to be pulling him in many different directions. It is to be seen whether he is willing to expend his political capital early on and push for the passage of the BBL.

But with the peace process on indefinite hold, Duterte faced a worsening regional security situation. The Abu Sayyaf Group engaged in a spate of kidnappings, including three Westerners from a Davao resort. By early 2016, the Abu Sayyaf had held twenty-four foreigners. Although the MILF had nothing to do with this, it also had no incentive to police its territory or be a stakeholder in regional peace and order. The Abu Sayyaf's brutal beheading of its two Canadian hostages in April and June 2016 and the regular release of videos with hostages in front of ISIL flags or wearing orange jumpsuits made ubiquitous by ISIL in its videos of beheadings raised alarm bells of the return of ungoverned space to Mindanao. The kidnapping of twenty-one Indonesian and four Malaysian mariners by Abu Sayyaf caused consternation in Jakarta and Kuala Lumpur, which once again looked to Mindanao as being the weak link to regional security. The weapons used in the January 2016 terrorist attack in Jakarta came from Mindanao, and increasingly, IS cells in Malaysia and Indonesia were linked to Mindanao. While the Abu Sayyaf pledged *baiyat* to ISIL in mid-2014, this was widely seen as a tactic to raise ransom payments. The real concern is that IS cells are now spreading to central Mindanao, including MILF territory.

On April 4, a video surfaced, showing two Philippine hostages clad in the ubiquitous orange jumpsuits beheaded in front of a camera in a remote region of Lanao del Sur Province. The two men, who were among six sawmill workers who had been abducted, were declared "spies" and executed. Though the black flags of ISIL were absent, the video was eerily modeled on ISIL execution videos.

A new group, Dawlah Islamiyah, more commonly referred to as the Maute Group, which pledged allegiance to ISIL, claimed responsibility. The group's relationship to the MILF is uncertain. Butig, in Lanao del Sur, is the MILF's heartland, and the most prominent base commander there is Abdullah Macapagar, a hard-liner and critic of the peace process, who with Ustadz Ameril Umbra Kato went on a rampage against Christian communities in 2007–2008 when the Arroyo cabinet rejected the draft peace accord. Armed clashes between the government and MILF jumped from eight in 2017 to 218 in 2008, with Kato's and Macapagar's forces responsible for the majority. While Kato broke from the MILF and founded the BIFF, Macapagar was reined in by the MILF leadership. But he has remained a critic of the peace process, and with the nonpassage of the BBL, the MILF leadership is struggling to rein in restive and disillusioned field commanders and youth. In a rare TV interview, Macapagar said that ISIL was very active in the area, though he did not reference Dawlah Islamiyah or its leader, Abdullah Maute.

Though filmed in front of the MILF flag, signaling that he still views himself as loyal to the organization and was still part of its chain of command, Macapagar said that ISIL had "similar goals" and hoped that one day the groups would be "united."[131] Kato, who died in early 2015, had already pledged the BIFF's allegiance to the Islamic State in an August 2014 YouTube video.

In January 2016, *Al-Naba*, an official IS newspaper, reported that four Philippine groups, which it labeled "battalions" of God's fighters—"*mujahideen*"—had been unified.[132] Although the statement did fall short of declaring any part of the southeast a *wilayat*, a province of the IS caliphate, it was the first time that ISIL had recognized any Philippine-based group. In January 2016, video footage of these groups coming together and engaging in joint training in a jungle camp emerged as evidence of the union.

Without a durable political solution, the southern Philippines looks likely to regress into pervasive insecurity, a growth of ungoverned space, with both national and regional security implications. Duterte's statement that the Philippines will push for its claim to Sabah, which had been dormant since the first Aquino administration, is likely to infuriate Kuala Lumpur, already lacking enthusiasm to continue funding the international monitoring team or facilitating the peace process.

Only one clash occurred between GRP and MILF forces between 2012 and 2015, but that clash continues to impact security in the region and has made the peace process seem increasingly uncertain. This raises a highly troubling question of how the MILF leadership can continue to manage expectations and maintain command and control over its combatants, who may defect to more radical groups. Individually, these groups pose no real threat, but if they are united or receive an infusion of personnel from the MILF, then the security situation in the southern Philippines looks likely to devolve and a peace that was once in their grasp slips away.

6. ASSESSMENT

The FAB and CAB were innovative agreements that offered creative solutions for complex issues. Despite the Philippine Congress's abject failure to deliver the BBL, I still consider it to be a model agreement, against which all others should be measured. It was thoughtful, creative, and equitable, and it protected the rights and interests of all. It was born of great statesmanship and political courage. It created important monitoring arms, decommissioning bodies, and third-party observers, as well as institutions to disarm, demobilize, and retrain combatants. The Bangsamoro people are once again reminded that they are the victims of Manila's "treachery." Promises made are promises unkept. The disappointment is palpable. The region was so close to a durable and lasting peace that had the potential to bridge the differences between the competing Moro organizations. But most of all, it had the power to bring peace and prosperity to the poorest part of a poor country. While all-out war is unlikely, more rank and file will continue to join the BIFF and Abu Sayyaf, while ISIL's message resonates more widely as the hopes and dividends of peace fade. The short-term political gains are coming at the expense of an equitable and lasting peace.

So why did the MILF leaders sign the FAB and CAB? I believe it was for six distinct reasons: The first and most pressing is that they had become a shadow of their former selves. They commanded less popular support and military capabilities than at any time in the past sixteen years. The MILF was unable to revert to war over a sustained period. Were all-out war to break out again, the MILF would lose—even more than they lost in 2000 and 2003. Even in 2007–2008, when they had every reason to revert to war, they could not sustain combat operations. The MILF's greatest asset at the negotiating table was the threat of returning to war. That threat rang hollow by 2012.

Nor would the population necessarily support them if war were to break out. After decades of conflict, the population in Muslim Mindanao is exhausted by conflict. Although no formal peace exists, the area has seen a substantial "peace dividend" since 2003. The people had no stomach for a return to war, and the MILF leadership knew it. The MILF, like many revolutionary groups, has an overexaggerated sense of its popular support.

The change in the battlefield was reflected in the negotiations: in each iteration of the talks, the government has had to offer the MILF less. What was on the table in 2004 and 2005, an eventual referendum, was dropped. The size and scope of the MILF's ancestral domain shrinks, as does its demand for control over natural resources. If the leaders did not conclude a deal soon, the government would offer even less in the future. With a growing economy and more resources, time was on the government's side, not the MILF's.

Fourth, MILF chair Ebrahim el-Haj Murad had staked his entire reputation and leadership on delivering peace. He had already been challenged by hard-liners in the movement, and each setback weakened him. More importantly, the MILF bench is not that deep, and it is hard to see a next-generation leader who could hold the group together and negotiate peace.

Fifth, the MILF was desperate to get its hands on the mineral resources that are coming out of the ground and, more importantly, from under the seabed. In particular, the MILF has its eyes set on several offshore service contracts in the Sulu Sea, near the Malaysian state of Sabah, which all have tested and proven reserves and where drilling will soon commence. And unlike the Catholic Church or communist New People's Army, which have been vociferous in their criticism of mining, the MILF seems eager as long as there is equitable wealth sharing.

Finally, the international community's interest in supporting a peace process was waning, support the MILF needs as a guarantor. From 2004 to 2007, the United States, Japan, the European Union, and a host of multilateral donors were actively engaged and ready to pour significant funds into the region. The protracted talks and pessimism following the failure of the MOA-AD have led to donor fatigue. More to the point, simply less money was available in 2012 than in 2007. It is hard to imagine any donor being able and willing to match what it put on the table from 2004 to 2007.

The government, too, had its reasons for signing. The president had accomplished a number of his domestic priorities and realized that should he not get the ball rolling, he would soon be in the lame-duck phase of his six-year term. Aquino, too, needed to secure his legacy and build on his mother's first overtures to the Moros three decades prior.

But there were two more pressing reasons: first, the government is currently confronted by a very aggressive China in the South China Sea. China has grabbed a number of atolls and islands claimed by the Philippines and clearly on its continental shelf. The Philippines has every reason to solve the Moro issue and dedicate the country's limited resources to external threats, no small order, given the fifty-plus-year legacy of the Philippines to not invest in its military. While the Philippines embarked on a courageous strategy of challenging the Chinese claims at the Permanent Court of Arbitration at The Hague, it has paltry ability to defend its claims or defend its fishermen and enforce sovereignty. Aquino embarked on a sixty-billion-peso modernization program that would have been unthinkable with insurgencies dominating the national security budgets.

Second, the government was confronted with a double-edged sword: a weaker MILF meant making fewer concessions, but the flip side was that a weaker MILF would not be able to implement an agreement. The government had already seen a surge in intra-MILF clan wars and *rido* (honor) conflicts. For all its faults and weaknesses, the MILF offered the best chance to implement a lasting peace in Mindanao.

I am always loath to write about the peace process in the Philippines, as it is very complicated, involving at least two groups and factions there that have fought and negotiated separate agreements. Both the MILF and the MNLF see themselves as vanguard organizations representing the interests of all Muslims in the southern Philippines. Both organizations clearly overestimate their popular support. The Philippine government has always had a policy of divide and conquer, believing that if it can reach an accord, it will deal with the hard-line breakaway factions at a later point. And with each round of talks, the size and threat posed by the groups remaining in the fight diminishes. Yet the Philippine government has limited capabilities and resources, and divide and conquer has never achieved a lasting peace. In the past, the Philippines has failed in establishing a holistic strategy for pacifying the south. The Philippines has a weak government that has repeatedly failed to implement the agreements it has signed. This always sows the seeds of the next conflict.

One could write a book about all the missed opportunities and mistakes made in the quest for peace in Mindanao.

NOTES

1. Thomas M. McKenna, *Muslim Rulers and Rebels: Everyday Politics and Armed Separatism in the Southern Philippines* (Berkeley: University of California Press, 1998).
2. Abhoud Syed Lingga, "Muslim Minority in the Philippines" (paper presented to the SEACSN Conference, Penang, Malaysia, January 12–15, 2004), 7.
3. Salamat Hashim, *The Bangsamoro Mujahid: His Objectives and Responsibilities* (Mindanao: Bangsomoro Publications, 1985), 18–19.
4. Nu'ain bin Abdulhaqq, "The Philippine Centennial: A Century of Indio/Filipino Colonial Tyranny against the Bangsamoro People," Bangsamoro.com, May 8, 2005, http://www.bangsamoro.com/old/mvoice/mv_050805.php.
5. Abdulhaqq, "The Philippine Centennial."
6. Nu'ain bin Abdulhaqq, "Bangsamoro Homeland Is Not Part of the Spanish Dominions under the Royal Decree of February 26, 1886 and the Maura Law of 1893," Luwaran.com, July 21, 2005, http://www.luwaran.com/modules.php?name=Content&pa=showpage&pid=50.
7. Cesar Adib Majul, *Muslims in the Philippines* (Quezon City: University of the Philippines Press, 1999); Nasser A. Marohomsalic, *Aristocrats of the Malay Race: A History of the Bangsa Moro in the Philippines* (Quezon City: VJ Graphics Arts, 1995).
8. Benedicto Bacani, "The Mindanao Peace Talks: Another Opportunity to Resolve the Moro Conflict in the Philippines" (special report 131, United States Institute of Peace, Washington, DC, January 2005), 3.
9. The document can be found in full in Salah Jubair, *Bangsamoro: A Nation under Endless Tyranny*, 3rd ed. (Kuala Lumpur: IQ Marin, 1999), 293–97.
10. *Philippine Human Development Report, 2005* (New York: United Nations Development Program, 2005).
11. In the nineteenth century, the British colonized the eastern portion of the Island of Borneo, what is today the Malaysian states of Sabah, Sarawak, and the independent Sultanate of Brunei. Sabah was once part of the Sultanate of Sulu. The British established the North Borneo Corporation (NBC), a Crown-chartered company, to administer Sabah. The Sultanate of Sulu claimed that the NBC leased Sabah from them. The NBC asserted that the territory was ceded to them. The British gave Malaya independence in 1957, but they did not know what to do with a handful of other colonies in the region, including Sabah, Sarawak, and Singapore. In 1963 they convinced Malaya to incorporate these territories into a new federation, Malaysia. In 1963 the Cobold Commission conducted a referendum in Sabah in which the people overwhelmingly decided to join the Federation of Malaysia, which they formally did on September 16, 1963. Angered, the Philippine government broke off diplomatic relations with Malaysia twice. Indonesia also failed to recognize Malaysia and soon after began its policy of Konfrontasi until the 1965 coup d'état that brought Gen Suharto to power. Suharto restored ties with Malaysia. In 1966, the new Philippine president, Ferdinand Marcos, recognized Malaysia, though the Philippines, as the successor state of the Sultanate of Sulu, maintained its claim to the ownership of Sabah. Yet Marcos was also preparing to launch covert operations in the Sabah. In 1968 a group of between fourteen and twenty-eight Muslim commandos in the Philippine Armed Forces (AFP), though under the nominal command of the Civil Affairs Office, were killed in mysterious circumstances on Corregidor Island, an incident known as the Jabidah Massacre. The Philippines formally continued to claim the territory until the Corazon Aquino administration withdrew the claim. The 1987 constitution does not mention Sabah or assert a territorial claim to it. In November 1987, Aquino submitted a bill to the legislature to

formally renounce the Sabah, though the Congress never acted on it. To this day, the Philippines has not renounced its claim to the Sabah, but the claim is dormant. In 2013, followers of the Sultanate of Sulu launched an armed raid into Sabah. Though it was put down by Malaysian security forces, it is indicative of how emotional the issue remains for some Tausigs.

12.   General Fortunato U. Abat, *The Day We Nearly Lost Mindanao: The CEMCON Story*, 3rd ed. (Manila: FCA, 1999), 165–66.

13.   The Philippine version of this period can be found in Abat, *Day We Nearly Lost Mindanao*.

14.   Jubair, *Bangsamoro*, 151.

15.   Imelda Marcos's account of the meeting can be found in James Hamilton-Paterson, *America 's Boy: A Century of United States Colonialism in the Philippines* (New York: Henry Holt, 1999), 343.

16.   Under the December 1976 Tripoli Agreement, Mindanao was to receive their own assembly and Islamic courts, and a future referendum on autonomy for all 13 provinces and nine cities in the Moro region, including Basilan, Sulu, Tawi-Tawi, Lanao del Sur, Lanao del Norte, Zamboanga del Sur, Zamboanga del Norte, South Cotabato, Davao del Sur, North Cotabato, Maguindanao, Sultan Kudarat, and Palawan. Only 5 provinces voted to join the ARMM.

17.   Lingga, " Muslim Minority in the Philippines," 7.

18.   The best history of this era is McKenna, *Muslim Rulers and Rebels*.

19.   Jubair, *Bangsamoro*, 154.

20.   The MILF's official history can be found in Jubair, *Bangsamoro*; Nu'ain bin Abdulhaqq, "The Philippine Centennial." Another MILF history can be found in Lingga, "Muslim Minority in the Philippines." Lingga was an aid to and biographer of Salamat Hashim.

21.   Jubair, *Bangsamoro*, 186.

22.   Jubair, *Bangsamoro*, 186.

23.   The UNDP's *Philippine Human Development Report, 2005*, cites the figure as 7,250. This was a sore point for the MILF. In 2008, I conducted extensive interviews with MNLF commanders, including Nur Misuari (who was under house arrest at the time), and they expected that almost all of their forces would be integrated into the Philippine National Police (PNP) and AFP. I subsequently interviewed government officials who played roles in the integration, and they found that illiteracy, poor health, and other issues precluded most MNLF from integration.

24.   The ARMM was established on November 6, 1990, by Republic Act 6734. It was legally possible because of the promulgation of a new constitution in 1987 that allowed for the establishment of autonomous regions.

25.   In April 2001, the MNLF fifteen-man executive council voted to oust Misuari for mismanagement, electing him "honorary chairman" of the ARMM. On November 19, 2001, Nur Misuari led some five hundred MNLF combatants to take up arms again due to the government's "violation" of the peace treaty. In nearly two weeks of fighting, some 147 people were killed. He fled to Malaysia and was rendered to the Philippines.

26.   *Philippine Human Development Report, 2005*.

27.   ARMM Media Affairs Officer, interview with the author, Cotabato, January 9, 2002.

28.   *Philippine Human Development Report, 2005*.

29.   Luz Baguioro, "Misuari's Downfall," *Straits Times*, November 27, 2001.

30.   Deidre Sheehan, "Swords into Ploughshares," *Far Eastern Economic Review* (FEER), September 20, 2001, 30–31; Dan Murphy, "Filipinos Swap Guns for Rakes," *Christian Science Monitor* (CSM), March 5, 2002.

31.   "Implementing Operational Guidelines of the GRP-MILF Agreement on the General Cessation of Hostilities," Marawi, November 14, 1997.

32.   "Agreement Creating a Quick Response Team," Sultan Kudarat, Maguindanao, March 11, 1998.

33.   "General Framework of Agreement of Intent between the Government of the Republic of the Philippines and the Moro Islamic Liberation Front," Sultan Kudarat, Maguindanao, August 27, 1998.

34. For more on the MILF's organization, see Zachary Abuza, "The MILF at 20: State of the Revolution," *Studies in Conflict and Terrorism* 28, no. 6 (2005): 453–79.

35. The MILF defined a base camp as a "contiguous area which may be composed of two or more adjacent municipalities or portions thereof, covered and secured by a division or expanded brigade of the BIAF [Bangsamoro Islamic Armed Forces], where its/their headquarters are located, including but not limited to military installations, encampments, structures, and facilities, and such other areas or positions occupied and used by MILF civilian workers or followers, such as, among others, agro-industrial establishments, educational institutions, political offices, medical centers, commercial establishments, agricultural lands, forests, marshes, lakes and other ancestral possessions of the Bangsamoro people, all falling within the perimeter defense of the camp." "Joint Acknowledgment," Sultan Kudarat, Maguindanao, February 10, 1999; "MILF Mujahideen to Maintain Identified Camps," Luwaran.com, August 10, 2004, http://www.luwaran.com; Jubair, *Bangsamoro*, 232; "Rules and Procedures in the Determination and Verification of the Coverage of the Cessation of Hostilities," Cotabato, May 18, 1999.

36. "Aide Memoir," Cotabato, April 27, 2000.

37. Salamat Hashim, "First Statement of the Latest Jihad Development in the Invaded Bangsamoro Homeland," in *The Bangsamoro People's Struggle Against Oppression and Colonialism* (Camp Abu Bakr al-Seddiqi: MILF Agency for Youth Affairs, 2001), 17.

38. Salamat, "First Statement," 17.

39. Soliman M. Santos, "Dynamics and Directions of the Peace Negotiations Between the Philippine Government and the Moro Islamic Liberation Front" (historical analysis presented for Catholic Peacebuilding Network, Quezon City, September 24, 2004), 11.

40. "The Seventh Statement Especially on the Negotiations between the MILF and the Philippine Government," June 10, 2001, in Salamat, *The Bangsamoro People's Struggle*, 30.

41. "Agreement on the General Framework for the Resumption of Peace Talks between the Government of the Republic of the Philippines and the Moro Islamic Liberation Front," Kuala Lumpur, Malaysia, March 24, 2001.

42. See Abhoud Syed M. Lingga, "The Mindanao Peace Process: Needing a New Formula" (paper presented at the SEACSN Conference, Penang, Malaysia, January 2004), 6.

43. "Southern Philippine Backgrounder: Terrorism and the Peace Process" (Asia Report No. 80, International Crisis Group, July 13, 2004); "The Jemaah Islamiyah Arrests and the Treat of Terrorism" (white paper, Republic of Singapore, Ministry of Home Affairs, 2003).

44. See Lino Miani, *The Sulu Arms Market: National Responses to a Regional Problem* (Singapore: Institute of Southeast Asian Studies, 2011).

45. "Special Report: Nur Misuari, Muslimin Sema and the Future of the MNLF," *Mindanao Examiner*, April 28, 2008.

46. Bacani, "The Mindanao Peace Talks," 6.

47. Bacani, "The Mindanao Peace Talks," 6.

48. "Joint Communique," Cyberjaya, Malaysia, May 6, 2002.

49. Lt. Gen. Rudolfo Garcia, Vice Chief of Staff AFP, Chairman GRP-CCCH, interviewed by the author, Quezon City, June 29, 2004.

50. For a complete listing of all AFP positions in the Rajah Muda and Buliok Complex region, see Mary Ann Arnado et al., *Bantay Ceasefire 2003* (Davao, March 2004), 48. Arnado independently verified these forward positions. The AFP withdrew in August 2004.

51. Letter from Salamat Hashim, Chairman, MILF, to President George W. Bush, May 20, 2003.

52. Abu Bakr Al Seddiqi, Badr, and Omar Bin Al Khattab in Maguindanao; Rajamuda in North Cotabato and Maguindanao; Bilal in Lanao del Norte and Lanao del Sur; and Busrah Somiorang in Lanao del Sur.

53. Lingga, "The Mindanao Peace Process," 6.

54. "Interview with Salamat Hashim: The Muslim Separatist Rebel Leader Wants the 'East Timor Formula,'" *AsiaWeek*, March 31, 2000; Eid Kabalu, MILF Spokesman, interviewed by the author, Cotabato, January 9, 2002; Abhoud Sayed M. Lingga, interviewed by the author, Cotabato, January 9, 2002.

55. Lingga, "The Mindanao Peace Process," 6.

56. "No Peace Pact This Year: Rebel Group," *Sun-Star*, August 8, 2006; "Gov 't, MILF Not Likely to Sign Peace Deal in September," Luwaran.com, May 31, 2006, http://www.luwaran.com; " Peace Talks Head for Impasse, MILF Fears," Luwaran.com, July 31, 2006, http://www.luwaran.com.

57. "MILF Faces Turmoil, Reports of Coup Surface," *Sun-Star*, March 10, 2006. For the MILF's official denial, see the editorial "No Coup in a Revolutionary Movement," *Maradika*, March 2006. *Maradika* is the official publication of the MILF's central committee.

58. Ebrahim el Haj Murad, "Peace Talks Can Swing Either Way," press release, Luwaran.com, September 18, 2006, http://www.luwaran.com.

59. "MILF Sees Hard Bargaining Ahead in Talks," Luwaran.com, December 6, 2006, http://www.luwaran.com/modules.php?name=News&file=article&sid=109.

60. "Philippines in 'Separatist Deal,'" *BBC News*, November 15, 2007, http://news.bbc.co.uk/2/hi/asia-pacific/7096069.stm.

61. The Supreme Court's ruling can be found at http://sc.judiciary.gov.ph/jurisprudence/2008/october2008/183591.htm; Manny Mogato, "MILF: Peace Talks Now in 'Purgatory,'" Reuters, August 31, 2008.

62. Norman Bordadora, "Aquino, MILF Chief Talk Peace in Tokyo, *Philippine Daily Inquirer*, August 6, 2011, http://newsinfo.inquirer.net/36947/aquino-milf-chief-talk-peace-in-tokyo.

63. "MILF Admits Major Split Ahead of Talks," Agence France Presse, February 5, 2011.

64. "Final Draft of Bangsamoro Law Submitted to Palace," *Philippines Star*, April 21, 2014, http://www.philstar.com/nation/2014/04/21/1314432/final-draft-bangsamoro-law-submitted-palace.

65. Angela Casauay, "MILF on Stalled Talks: 'Frustrated, Angry,'" Rappler, June 16, 2013, http://www.rappler.com/nation/special-coverage/peacetalks/31452-ph-milf-peace-talks-delay.

66. Casauay, "MILF on Stalled Talks."

67. Angela Casauay, "Gov't, MILF to Resume Talks 'Early July,'" Rappler, June 21, 2013.

68. Nikko Dizon, "Palace Overhauls Draft of Bangsmoro Basic Law," *Philippine Daily Inquirer*, July 5, 2014, http://newsinfo.inquirer.net/617204/palace-overhauls-draft-of-bangsamoro-basic-law.

69. Nikko Dizon, "MILF Chief Negotiator Hurt by Revisions of Draft Bangsamoro Charter," *Philippine Daily Inquirer*, July 22, 2014.

70. Carolyn O. Arguillas, "GPH-MILF 'Workshop' in KL ends; Panels to Meet Again in Manila," *Minda News*, July 11, 2014; Carolyn O. Arguillas, "GPH, MILF End Four-Day 'Workshop' in Manila; Major Issues Unresolved," *Minda News*, July 22, 2014, http://www.mindanews.com/peace-process/2014/07/22/gph-milf-end-four-day-workshop-in-manila-major-issues-unresolved/.

71. Christian V. Esguerra and Nikko Dizon, "Middle Ground with MILF Sought," *Philippine Daily Inquirer*, July 22, 2014.

72. Angela Casauay, "Proposed Bangsamoro Law Still in Limbo," Rappler, August 1, 2014, http://www.rappler.com/nation/special-coverage/peacetalks/63994-bangsamoro-law-limbo.

73. "Gov't, MILF Disagree on Draft Bangsamoro Basic Law," *Philippine Star*, July 21, 2014, http://www.philstar.com/headlines/2014/07/21/1348987/govt-milf-disagree-draft-bangsamoro-basic-law.

74. Andreo Calonzo, "Some Provisions in Bangsamoro Bill May Be Unconstitutional—Govt Negotiator," *GMA News Online*, July 22, 2014, http://www.gmanetwork.com/news/story/371491/news/nation/some-provisions-in-bangsamoro-bill-may-be-unconstitutional-govt-negotiator.

75. Nikko Dizon, "Bangsamoro Gov't Expected in Place by 2016—MILF Negotiator," *Philippine Daily Inquirer*, July 22, 2014, http://newsinfo.inquirer.net/622384/bangsamoro-govt-expected-in-place-by-2016-milf-negotiator.

76. Manuel Mogato, "Philippine Peace Deal in Jeopardy as Muslim Rebels Cry Foul," Reuters, August 6, 2014, http://uk.mobile.reuters.com/article/idUKKBN0G60EZ20140806?irpc=932.

77. Aileen Estoquia, "World Welcomes PHL-MILF Peace Deal; Politicians, MNLF Subdued," *GMA News Online*, October 16, 2012, http://www.gmanetwork.com/news/story/278370/news/nation/world-welcomes-phl-milf-peace-deal-politicians-mnlf-subdued.

78. In 2006–2007, the MNLF was calling on the government to attend the tripartite talks in Libya. The talks, attended by the MNLF, the Philippine government, and the Organization of the Islamic Conference (OIC), were supposed to address the myriad issues and parts of the agreement that had gone unimplemented since the 1996 Tripoli Agreement was signed. The MNLF wanted to use this international forum to pressure the government, which was loath to attend. The government kept on telling the MNLF to forget about the tripartite talks and await the conclusion of the peace agreement with the MILF. This was simply unacceptable to the MNLF, which simply could not keep its ego in check and work with the MILF. In part this was ethnic chauvinism, and in part it was delusions of grandeur.

79. John Unson, "Gov't, MNLF List 42 Consensus Points," *Philippine Star*, June 16, 2012, http://www.philstar.com/breaking-news/2012/06/16/817696/govt-mnlf-list-42-consensus-points.

80. Karlos Manlupig, "MILF, MNLF Forces Clash; Hundreds Evacuate," Rappler, May 6, 2013, http://www.rappler.com/nation/28305-evacuations-clashes-erupt-milf-mnlf-cotabato.

81. Angela Casauay, "MILF, MNLF Move to Iron Out Differences," Rappler, June 16, 2014, http://www.rappler.com/nation/60708-milf-mnlf-talks-jeddah-oic.

82. Roel Pareño, "Nur Declares Independence of 'Bangsamoro Republik,'" *Philippine Star*, August 15, 2013, http://www.philstar.com/nation/2013/08/15/1094161/nur-declares-independence-bangsamoro-republik.

83. Carmela Fonbuena, "MNLF Rebels Burn Houses, Step Up Attacks," Rappler, September 12, 2013, http://www.rappler.com/newsbreak/38547-milf-mnlf-peace-agreements); http://www.rappler.com/nation/38765-rebels-more-attacks-zamboanga.

84. "Stakeholders Express Support for MNLF-MILF Deal," *Philippine Star*, June 18, 2014, http://www.philstar.com/nation/2014/06/18/1336238/stakeholders-express-support-mnlf-milf-deal.

85. Angela Casauay, "Bangsamoro Gets 75% of Taxes, Resources," Rappler, July 15, 2013, http://www.rappler.com/nation/special-coverage/peacetalks/33714-bangsamoro-gets-75-of-taxes-natural-resources.

86. Julie S. Alipala, "3 MNLF Factions Agree to Re-unite with Misuari as Leader," *Inquirer Mindanao*, June 26, 2014, http://newsinfo.inquirer.net/614656/3-mnlf-factions-agree-to-re-unite-with-misuari-as-leader.

87. Luwaran.com, http://luwaran.com/index.php/editorial/item/1039-bangsamoro-coordination-forum.

88. Roel Pareño, "MNLF-MILF Deal Reaches Breakthrough," *Philippine Star*, June 16, 2014, http://www.philstar.com/nation/2014/06/16/1335453/mnlf-milf-deal-reaches-breakthrough.

89. Perseus Echeminada, "MNLF Groups Back OIC Stand on CAB," *Philippine Star*, July 3, 2014, http://www.philstar.com/nation/2014/07/03/1341667/mnlf-groups-back-oic-stand-cab; Casauay, "MILF, MNLF Move to Iron Out Differences."

90. Luwaran.com, http://luwaran.com/index.php/welcome/item/365-milf-to-form-political-party-chairman-murad.

91. Karlos Manlupig, "MILF Forms United Bangsamoro Justice Party," Rappler, April 9, 2014, http://www.rappler.com/nation/55028-milf-forms-united-bangsamoro-justice-party.

92. The text of the Annex on Power Sharing is available at Scribd.com, http://www.scribd.com/doc/208285324/Annex-on-Power-Sharing.

93. Amita O. Legaspi, "MILF Sets Up Political Party for Bangsamoro Polls in 2016," *GMA News*, April 9, 2014, http://www. gmanetwork.com/news/story/356125/news/nation/ milf-sets-up-political-party-for-bangsamoro-polls- in-2016.

94. "MILF's United Bangsamoro Justice Party," *Manila Bulletin*, April 12, 2014, http://www.mb.com.ph/ milfs-united-bangsamoro-justice-party/.

95. Edwin Fernandez and Nash Maulana, "MILF Takes Next Step to Polls, Seeks Comelec Nod for Party," *Philippine Daily Inquirer*, December 18, 2014, http://newsinfo.inquirer.net/657841/milf-takes-next-step-to-polls-seeks-comelec-nod-for-party. For more on the UBJB, see

Zachary Abuza, "From Bullets to Ballots in Muslim Mindanao: The New Challenge of Democratic Politics," *Focus Asia*, no. 11 (November 2014), http://www.isdp.eu/images/stories/isdp-main-pdf/2014-abuza-from-bullets-to-ballots-mindanao.pdf.

96.   Maila Ager, "Drilon Urges Swift Passage of Bangsamoro Basic Law," Inquirer.net, July 23, 2014, http://newsinfo.inquirer.net/622749/drilon-urges-swift-passage-of-bangsamoro-basic-law.

97.   SWS (Social Weather Stations) poll.

98.   Angela Casauay, "Battalion Chief Confirms SAF Member in Mamasapano Video," Rappler, February 11, 2015, http://www.rappler.com/nation/83626-batallion-commander-confirms-saf-member-mamasapano-clash-video.

99.   "Full Text: MILF Report on Mamasapano," Rappler, March 24, 2015, http://www.rappler.com/nation/87812-full-report-milf-mamasapano.

100.   Xianne Arcangel, "MILF 'to Be Hit' if It Blocks Arrest of Members Involved in Mamasapano, Lawmaker Warns," *GMA News Online*, March 29, 2015, http://www.gmanetwork.com/news/story/461130/news/nation/milf-to-be-hit-if-it-blocks-arrest-of-members-involved-in-mamasapano-lawmaker-warns.

101.   Ayee Macaraig, "Cayetano: Disarm MILF before Passing Bangsamoro Bill," Rappler, March 11, 2015, http://www.rappler.com/nation/86528-cayetano-disarmament-milf.

102.   "Gov't, MILF Must Do More to Regain Trust—IMT," Rappler, February 19, 2015, http://www.rappler.com/nation/84387-government-milf-regain-trust-peace-process?utm_source=twitter&utm_medium=referral&utm_medium=share_bar.

103.   Carmela Fonbuena, "Bomb Factory Captured in Mamasapano—Military," Rappler, March 2, 2015, http://www.rappler.com/nation/85516-bomb-factory-captured-mamasapano.

104.   Angela Casauay, "62% of Mindanao Residents Oppose BBL—Pulse Asia," Rappler, March 19, 2015, http://www.rappler.com/nation/87310-pulse-asia-survey-bangsamoro-basic-law.

105.   Carmela Fonbuena, "AFP Chief: 'Illogical' to Go Back to War with MILF," Rappler, March 6, 2015, http://www.rappler.com/nation/85939-afp-catapang-supports-peace-process-milf.

106.   "Mamasapano Report Based on 'Emotions, Not Facts,'" Rappler, March 22, 2015, http://www.rappler.com/nation/87594-chr-reaction-senate-report-mamasapano.

107.   Bea Cupin, "SAF Didn't Breach Ceasefire Deal in 'Oplan Exodus'—DOJ Report," Rappler, April 22, 2015, http://www.rappler.com/nation/90813-saf-ceasefire-mamasapano-doj-report.

108.   "Death of SAF Troops 'Murder All the Way and Around,'" Rappler, April 22, 2015, http://www.rappler.com/nation/90756-doj-nbi-nps-mamasapano-charges?.

109.   Dennis Carcamo, "Drilon to MILF: Cooperate in Seeking Justice for SAF 44," April 23, 2015, http://www.philstar.com/headlines/2015/04/23/1447055/drilon-milf-cooperate-seeking-justice-saf-44.

110.   Xianne Arcangel, "What's Wrong with Aliases? Iqbal Says Even Heroes Have One," *GMA News Online*, April 8, 2015, http://www.gmanetwork.com/news/story/466258/news/nation/what-s-wrong-with-aliases-iqbal-says-even-heroes-have-one.

111.   Leila B. Salaverria, "Nancy Binay Seeks Probe of Aquino Dole-Out to MILF," *Philippine Daily Inquirer*, March 31, 2015, http://newsinfo.inquirer.net/682619/nancy-binay-seeks-probe-of-welfare-program-limited-to-milf.

112.   Angela Casauay, "5 Co-authors Signed Senate Report on BBL Unconstitutionality," Rappler, May 28, 2015, http://www.rappler.com/move-ph/issues/mindanao/94611-co-authors-bbl-unconstitutional?utm_source=twitter&utm_medium=referral&utm_medium=share_bar.

113.   Michael Bueza, "Senators on Bangsamoro Basic Law: Where Do They Stand?," Rappler, June 5, 2015, http://www.rappler.com/move-ph/issues/mindanao/94651-senators-bbl-statements-stand?utm_source=twitter&utm_medium=referral&utm_medium=share_bar.

114.   Macon Ramos-Araneta and Maricel V. Cruz, "Escudero: Panel Still Speaking for MILF," *Manila Standard*, April 7, 2015, http://manilastandardtoday.com/2015/04/07/escudero-panel-still-speaking-for-milf/.

115. Elizabeth Marcelo, "Lobregat: OPAPP's Mamasapano Report Branded MILF Fighters as Martyrs," *GMA News Online*, April 9, 2015, http://www.gmanetwork.com/news/story/467174/news/nation/lobregat-opapp-s-mamasapano-report-branded-milf-fighters-as-martyrs.

116. "Philippine Rebels Kill Most Wanted Islamist Militant in South," Reuters, May 3, 2015, http://www.trust.org/item/20150503141616-ytc65/?source=shtw; Andreo Calonzo, "MILF's Role in Killing Usman to Boost Confidence in Peace Process—Palace," *GMA News Online*, May 4, 2015, http://www.gmanetwork.com/news/story/481166/news/nation/milf-s-role-in-killing-usman-to-boost-confidence-in-peace-process-palace; Maila Ager, "Killing Usman 'Positive Step' in Peace Process—Marcos," Inquirer.net, May 4, 2015, http://newsinfo.inquirer.net/689116/probe-milf-role-in-usmans-killing-escudero-says#ixzz3ZB4aSreC; Floyd Whaley, "Filipino Bomb Maker, Sought by U.S., Is Said to Die in Fight with Rebels," *New York Times*, May 4, 2015, http://www.nytimes.com/2015/05/05/world/asia/abdul-basit-usman-philippines-dies.html?_r=0; Edwin O. Fernandez and Karlos Manlupig, "Bomber Basit Usman Killed by MILF," *Inquirer Mindanao*, May 4, 2015, http://newsinfo.inquirer.net/689010/maguindanao-police-chief-confirms-usmans-death.

117. "MILF Starts Decommissioning of Weapons, Combatants Despite Delay in BBL," OPAPP, June 15, 2015, http://www.opapp.gov.ph/milf/news/milf-starts-decommissioning-weapons-combatants-despite-delay-bbl; Angela Casauay, "Aquino Witnesses Historic MILF Arms Turnover," Rappler, June 16, 2015, http://www.rappler.com/move-ph/issues/mindanao/96482-milf-first-decommissioning.

118. Dee Ayroso, "'We Will Not Accept a Diluted BBL'—MILF," Bulatlat, August 7, 2015.

119. Luwaran.com, http://www.luwaran.com/index.php/editorial/item/503-critical-period.

120. Christian Hope Reyes, "Philippines: Polling the Peace Process," Asia Foundation, September 9, 2015, http://asiafoundation.org/in-asia/2015/09/09/philippines-polling-the-peace-process/.

121. Carolyn O. Arguillas, "Balindong: 'This House of Representatives Has Collectively Failed the Bangsamoro People,'" *Minda News*, January 27, 2016, http://www.mindanews.com/peace-process/2016/01/27/balindong-this-house-of-representatives-has-collectively-failed-the-bangsamoro-people/.

122. "Philippines Fears New Fighting with Stalled Muslim Autonomy," Voice of America, February 23, 2016, http://www.voanews.com/content/philippines-fears-new-fighting-with-stalled-muslim-autonomy/3174743.html.

123. "Duterte, MILF Want to Bring Peace in Mindanao," *Philippine Star*, February 29, 2016, http://www.philstar.com:8080/headlines/2016/02/29/1557993/duterte-milf-want-bring-peace-mindanao .

124. Karlos Manlupig, "MILF Congratulates 'True Son of Mindanao' Duterte," *Philippine Daily Inquirer*, May 12, 2016, http://newsinfo.inquirer.net/785329/milf-congratulates-true-son-of-mindanao-duterte .

125. Nikko Dizon, "Duterte Can't Just Scrap BBL, Says MILF," *Philippine Daily Inquirer*, May 20, 2016, http://newsinfo.inquirer.net/786652/duterte-cant-just-scrap-bbl-says-milf .

126. Editorial, "A Non-Starter Statement," Luwaran.com, May 24, 2016, http://www.luwaran.com/home/index.php/editorial/26-january-24-31/740-a-non-starter-statement.

127. Editorial, "A Non-Starter Statement."

128. Joel M. Sy Egco, "Duterte Govt to Push BBL," *Manila Times*, May 31, 2016, http://www.manilatimes.net/duterte-govt-to-push-bbl/265319/.

129. Karlos Manlupig, "MILF to Push for 'Original' BBL under Duterte Gov't," *Philippine Daily Inquirer*, June 20, 2016, http://newsinfo.inquirer.net/791484/milf-vows-to-push-for-original-bbl-under-duterte-govt.

130. Charlie C. Senase, "Pact Raises Hope for Moro Reb Unity," *Inquirer Mindanao*, July 3, 2016, http://newsinfo.inquirer.net/793958/pact-raises-hope-for-moro-reb-unity .

131. "Philippines: Moro Islamic Liberation Front Dreams of 'Caliphate' on Mindanao," YouTube video, 5:08, posted by France 24 English, May 19, 2016, https://www.youtube.com/watch?v=Qva06hh7Ubw&feature=youtu.be&utm_content=buffer65cd9&utm_medium=social&utm_source=twitter.com&utm_campaign=buffer .

132. "Islamic State Spreads Its Wings in South East Asia," NewsGram, March 12, 2016, http://www.newsgram.com/islamic-state-spreads-its-wings-in-south-east-asia/.

Chapter Four

Case Study 3—The Barisan Revolusi Nasional (BRN), Pattani United Liberation Organization (PULO), and other Malay Militant Groups

Southern Thailand

1. BACKGROUND TO THE CONFLICT

Since January 2004 insurgency in southern Thailand has claimed the lives of more than 6,500 people and left almost 12,000 people wounded. It has destroyed the social fabric in the south, and an estimated 20 percent of the region's Buddhist community has fled, with the remainder having largely moved into district and provincial towns or heavily fortified enclaves. A total of 176 teachers have been killed in attacks that have hobbled the education system, while the public health system is in crisis. Although the level of violence is down sharply from its peak in 2007, since 2009 violence has largely plateaued. Violence in the south is a slow burn, low-level endemic violence that, despite over seventy thousand security forces and large budgets, the state is unable to quell. Insurgents have achieved many of their short-term goals: weakening state institutions, driving many Buddhists from the region, creating a greater rift between the Malay community and the Thai state, eliminating moderates within the Muslim community, and raising political and ethnocultural consciousness.

But the insurgents have clear weaknesses. They are geographically hemmed in, have a limited pool of supporters and recruits, have no state support, and operate with limited resources. The insurgents are horizontal in their organizational structure, riddled with factionalism and disputes over leadership. Their media and propaganda arms are eighteenth century in their sophistication. Moreover, they are up against a well-resourced, though politically inclined, military with more than six billion dollars for its annual budget. On a per capita basis, Thai security forces are far better resourced than their Philippine and Indonesian counterparts, with a much smaller area of insurgent operations.

Insurgency is not new in southern Thailand, a region that was colonized by the Siamese Kingdom in the eighteenth and nineteenth centuries.[1]

The Kingdom of Pattani converted to Islam in 1457, giving rise to the Muslim Kingdom of Pattani (Pattani Darussalam), the geography of which included the present-day Thai provinces of Narathiwat, Pattani, and Yala and the northern Malaysian states.[2] Beginning with the Ayutthaya Kingdom (1350–1767) in the fifteenth century, the Kingdom of Siam began to exert strong influence over the Malay Peninsula. The Kingdom of Siam was strengthened following the founding of the Chakri Dynasty in 1782, however, and by 1789 it had conquered the Kingdom of Pattani, imposing a tributary system over what are now the northern Malay states of Kedah, Kelantan, and Terengganu. When the Siamese court was strong and not itself under attack from Burmese and other neighbors, it expanded south into the Malay peninsula.[3] By 1800, Siamese control extended deep into what are today's Malaysian states of Kelantan and Terengganu, and by 1892, it included Perak and Kedah.

Although Siamese officials worked to bring Thai culture and language to the southern region, Thai rule was fairly benign as long as the Malay rulers accepted Siamese suzerainty and traveled to Bangkok every three years to make obeisance (*tawai bangkom*).[4] *Sharia* courts, for example, remained in operation under the Pattani sultan. Starting in 1816, Siam began to enact policies to integrate the Deep South into the national administrative structure, thereby decreasing local autonomy. The government established seven provinces in the region to facilitate tax collection, leading to large-scale revolts in 1832. King Chulalongkorn's government reforms in the 1890s led to the establishment of a strong centralized bureaucracy with even greater central control over the provinces, a legacy that continues to this day. Indirect rule ended as the Ministry of Interior put Malay vassals under its direct control and began to directly appoint and dispatch governors and administrators from Bangkok. Thailand treated the Deep South as a colony, dispatching officials from Bangkok to administer the restive region.

British colonization of Malaysia prevented Siam's drive deeper into the Malayan Peninsula. In 1897, the British and Thais signed a secret agreement that recognized Thai suzerainty over Kelantan and Terengganu as long as the Thais denied commercial access to the region to Britain's European competitors. The Siamese court feared the growing closeness of the British and the

Pattani sultans and in 1902 put down a rebellion. Siamese aggression prompted the Malay court to request "British protection and a British Resident."[5] The current border was codified—largely under duress—in a 1909 agreement.

But after the 1909 agreement, the Siamese court was even more determined to implement Thai political and legal institutions in the three Muslim Malay majority provinces, including shutting down the *sharia* court system.

The Thai colonial project has been a failed experiment in assimilation. Although Malay ethnic, social, and cultural identities initially remained largely unaffected, by the 1909 treaty, as residents on both sides regularly crossed the border, the Thai state gradually began to push the development of a Thai national identity in the southern provinces. In 1921, for example, Thailand imposed a national curriculum in the Thai language and more controls and restrictions on Islamic schools.[6] Thai authorities also crushed a Muslim tax rebellion in 1922–1923, though King Vajiravudh, increasingly fearful of British aggression, did lessen the tax burden to win popular support among the Malay. After the fall of the absolute monarchy in the 1932 revolution, the *sapiban* system that had given the Malay aristocracy a degree of local political and religious control was scrapped and replaced by a more restrictive provincial system.[7]

The highly centralized nature of the Phibul Songkran dictatorship degraded local autonomy further by pressuring Malays to assimilate and by abolishing all Islamic laws. Mandate 3 of the National Culture Act (Thai Ratthaniyom) in 1939, meanwhile, banned the use of the Malay language and the wearing of Malay dress (such as sarongs) and forced all Thai citizens, regardless of ethnicity or religion, to adopt common Siamese customs.

Phibul was strongly influenced by the rise of ethnocentric fascism in Germany and Japan in the 1930s. In an irridentist pique, he changed the name of the country from Siam to Thailand in 1939, in a Hitleresque attempt to create *lebensraum* , living space needed to ensure national survival for all Thais, including pockets of minorities in Cambodia, Laos, the Shan State of Burma, and up to Xishuangbanna in China's Yunnan Province. At the core of Phibul's policies was an intense ethnic chauvinism, if not a sense of ethnic and cultural superiority.[8] During World War II, Phibul aligned Thailand with Japan largely in the hopes that Japan would reward Thai loyalty with ethnic Thai territories lost to or simply held by Britain and France. Indeed, during World War II, Thais working with the Japanese retook the northern Malay British colonial provinces of Kelantan, Terengganu, Kedah, and Perlis.

Thai policy toward the Deep South has always been based on the idea of total assimilation, not accommodation or the protection of minority rights or cultural identity. With Buddhism becoming the state religion and the symbol of the nation, ethnic Thai chauvinism—and the irredentist nature of the new regime—increased. In 1944 Thai civil law was instituted, and the establishment of the national educational curriculum, taught in Thai (and not just Thai, but Central Thai), has been an attempt to end even the colloquial use of Bahasa Melayu. One can see this even in the architecture: all the Thai government buildings in the Deep South are constructed in Central Thai style.

After World War II concluded, both the British and the Americans supported the territorial integrity of Thailand—though not the irridentist claims. Neither country supported Pattani independence or its union with the new Federation of Malaya. Although public opinion in Pattani endorsed joining the federation, the British rejected that bid for the sake of stronger ties with the Thai government.[9]

The government sought to placate Malay demands by reintroducing *sharia* for family law in 1946, but this did little to quell their demands.[10] That year, Haji Sulong Tokmina, the first national-level Malay leader to emerge, led a brief uprising, the Dusun Nyur Rebellion. Quickly quashed, Sulong switched to a peaceful political strategy.[11] In early 1947, Sulong established the Pattani People's Movement (PPM), which called for self-rule, language and cultural rights, and *sharia* law.

Sulong presented a fundamental challenge to Phibul's conception of the Thai state that after World War II refocused its attentions on political centralization, development, and the promotion of Thai national identity.[12] Thai authorities arrested Sulong in January 1946. He was acquitted of treason but still served seven years on lesser charges. By 1948, a quarter-million Thais had petitioned the United Nations to join the new Federation of Malaya, and revolts became commonplace, including one in 1948 that left four hundred people dead and some two thousand to six thousand refugees in Malaysia.

Yet the rapid emergence of the Cold War and threat posed by Mao's communist China, which was exporting revolution throughout Southeast Asia, transformed Thailand into a key ally for both the United States and Great Britain. Thailand was a frontline state in the Cold War and a bastion of anticommunism. The quid pro quo was Western support for Thailand's territorial integrity.

Political power in Thailand in most of the post–World War II era was dominated by anticommunist and development-oriented military officers who were determined to maintain centralized control over the country. As part of the counterinsurgency campaign, in the 1950s, the Nikhom program saw the resettlement of 102,000 Buddhists from the northeastern part of the country into the Malay-dominated south.[13] The military never countenanced autonomy for any ethnic or regional group, much less the Malay, and the military had near-total political control from the 1950s through the 1980s. The harsh policies of Field Marshals Phibul Songkran and Sarit Thanarat in the 1950s and 1960s "crushed the moderate leadership of the Malay Muslims in the southern border region . . . (and) more radical leaders rose to prominence."[14]

Although the government released Sulong in 1952, almost immediately he was "disappeared," sadly, a routine practice of Thai security forces to this day. Eliminating the most vocal and articulate leader of Pattani rights may have been a tactical victory for the Thai government, but it was a strategic loss. In 1957, Sulong 's son, who successfully ran as a member of parliament (MP), was jailed for three years for raising Muslim demands in parliament.[15] He later fled to Malaysia. These acts ended peaceful struggle for autonomy. Armed rebellion began with the founding of the first armed movement, the Barisan Nasional Pembebasan Pattani, in 1959.

All-out insurgency erupted in the 1960s. It was no longer led by the traditional elites but instead by Islamic clerics trained in the Middle East (mainly Egypt and Pakistan), who served as a counter-elite. Originally, three main Muslim separatist groups operated in Thailand: Bertubuhan Pembebasan Pattani Bersatu (Pattani United Liberation Organization, PULO), led by Haji Hadi Mindosali and Haji Sama-ae Thanam; the smaller Barisan Nasional Pembebasan Pattani (Pattani National Liberation Front, BNPP), founded by Malay aristocrats; and the Barisan Revolusi Nasional (National Revolution Front, BRN).[16]

The insurgency in the period of the 1950s to 1990s was quantitatively and qualitatively different. For one thing, it was a very small-scale insurgency. For example, between October 1976 and December 1981, the insurgents committed only 127 violent incidents, including a number of bombings of government buildings and schools that led to the death of 200 people and the wounding of roughly 300 others. The insurgency was very much a rural phenomenon, and the targeting was much more selective.

By the 1990s, the insurgency had largely petered out for eight key reasons: first, the insurgents never enjoyed a secure base area in Malaysia because of the strong cooperation between the Malaysian and Thai governments. Thais assisted Malaysia in routing out the Communist Party of Malaya insurgents who had sought sanctuary in southern Thailand. Indeed, from 1964 to 1976, Malaysian police had the right to hot pursuit across the border. In 1977 the two countries established the Thai-Malaysia General Border Committee and began joint military operations.[17] The quid pro quo was, of course, Malaysian cooperation and the arrest of insurgent leaders, including the head of PULO, Haji Sama-ae Thanam; new PULO chief Haji Abdul Rohman Bazo; new PULO deputy Haji Mae Yala; and Haji Dato Thanan. In short, bilateral cooperation led to the virtual annihilation of both states' security concerns along the border.

Second, the Thai government avoided large-scale repression of Muslims that would have created a broad anti-Thai movement; indeed, most Muslim leaders worked with the Thai state. The Thai military had significant experience and was organized for counterinsurgency. More importantly, it never approached the south with a completely military mindset; it always left some degree of civilian control. In 1981, Gen. Prem Tinsulanonda, himself a southerner, established the Southern Border Provinces Administrative Committee (SBPAC) to govern the south and coordinate all economic development there. (He also established its armed wing, CPM-43, a unified military-police-civilian command in charge of all security operations in the south.) In 1987, Prem as prime minister shifted the Internal Security Operating Command from the military's Supreme Command to the Office of the Prime Minister.

Third, Thailand's rapid and sustained economic development tended to help raise the standard of living for all citizens. Beginning with Prime Minister Sarit Thanarat in the late 1950s, the government had a stated goal of bringing development (*phattana*) to all parts of the country to counter the appeal of insurgent movements.

Fourth, through the mid-1990s, the various insurgent groups were woefully divided in terms of both ideology and goals and included Islamists, more secular ethnonationalists, and groups affiliated with the Malayan Communist Party. Some favored independence, others union with Malaysia, and others simply greater autonomy. More importantly, the groups lacked a cohesive social, political, and economic objective and plan, which kept them from developing a mass following. Islam is not repressed, and there is no limit on mosque construction or *madrassa* enrollment. Thai policy is one of theocratic pluralism. The constitution requires the government "to patronize and protect Buddhism and other religions." The government provides some support for Islamic education (roughly 80 percent of Islamic schools receive some government funding) and the maintenance of central provincial mosques and their clergy. Some *sharia* courts handle family law, and the government permits Islamic banks.

Fifth, Muslims are not politically marginalized and have held influential positions at the national level. They have always had parliamentary representation.

Sixth, though the insurgents received some financial and military sponsorship from Libya and Syria in the 1970s (including military training), state sponsorship was very limited, and most weapons were purchased from illegal brokers within Thailand itself. Saudi Arabia has been less welcoming, and none of the insurgent groups have ever had the active support of the Organization of the Islamic Conference (OIC) or have had permanent representation in the organization.

Seventh, the insurgency has been constrained by the physical geography of the Malay Peninsula. Although many commentators note that the porousness of the Thai-Malaysian border aids the insurgents, the border itself is only 506 kilometers long, and Malaysia is a fairly inhospitable operating environment. While the forest cover is dense and the terrain mountainous, the region is small enough that the Thai military's superior mobility has ensured that the insurgents do not have a secure rear-base area.

Finally, building on the government's successful use of amnesties to quell the communist insurgency in the north and northeast in 1952 and 1982, Prime Minister Prem Tinsulanonda issued Order No. 65/2525 in 1984 to grant amnesty for Malay separatists. A second offer of amnesty in 1993 further depleted PULO's ranks.

The leading insurgent group at the time, PULO was dealt a series of further blows with the arrests of key leaders in the mid-1990s. A newly elected group of leaders tried to reverse the movement's setbacks by authorizing a major offensive, Operation Falling Leaves. By the end of 1997, PULO claimed to have killed 146 Thai soldiers and wounded more than 80 in 33 separate attacks.[18] Despite this brief paroxysm of violence, by 1998 the Thai insurgency under PULO was in its death throes. Arrests of senior leaders by both Malaysian and Thai authorities continued to weaken the movement. More than nine hundred combatants accepted amnesty programs and were given land and other livelihood assistance projects.

Although low-level and sporadic attacks continued in 1998–1999, by 2000, the government of Prime Minister Thaksin Shinawatra had declared the insurgency over. But this declaration had an adverse impact, allowing the prime minister to dismantle SBPAC and put his cronies in the police in charge of southern security. Competition between the army and the police over control of the lucrative smuggling networks broke into the open. Effective institutions that once resolved disputes and served as a system of checks and balances broke down.

But it is essential to understand that though violence dissipated, a peace treaty or legal agreement was not responsible for ending the violence and, more importantly, addressing the grievances of the Malay people. This is, sadly, a very Thai way of doing things. They assume that the absence of violence is peace: it is anything but.

The Thais have been immensely frustrated that unlike every other ethnic minority that assimilated for the sake of citizenship, the Malay have steadfastly refused assimilation. For hill tribes in Chiang Mai and Chiang Rai or the Lao people of Issarn, citizenship and integration was a key component of the Thai national security strategy. But culturally, assimilation was much easier for these people than for the Malay. The commitment and total loyalty to the king (who is in essence a Hindu god-king), the de facto national religion of Buddhism and the overly centralized Thai state are anathema to the goals and values of the Malay in the Deep South. If anything, the emphasis on these three pillars only serves to create a greater sense of disenfranchisement among the Malay, who make up 1.3 million of the total 1.8 million population in the south. Although Islam was part of the identity of the separatist groups, it was not the central factor in their political struggle. As Joseph Liow has written, "It is not Islam *per se* that has politicized the Muslims in the south, but the fact that these Muslims identify themselves as Malay and relate to the Thai state and the Thai nationalist project as Malays that is of utmost importance."[19]

And while the era of ethnonationalist struggle, led by the old Malay aristocrats, had largely come to an end, local grievances remained deep-seated, and a small cadre of Islamists and Afghan veterans went underground, organizing among the youth in *madrassas*, private Islamic schools, and mosques. And as in the Philippines, where the Datu-led MNLF gave way to the distinctly Islamist movement of the Moro Islamic Liberation Front (MILF), a new generation of insurgents in southern Thailand emerged with a more Islamist stance.

After a decade-long incubation, in 2004 the insurgency reignited. Though the insurgency began on a small scale, Thai government missteps and egregious human rights violations, compounded by political posturing, led to an increase in the scope of violence and degree of support for the insurgency.

2. THE RISE OF ARMED INSURRECTION

On January 4, 2004, a group of militants raided an army base in Narathiwat's Rueso district. It was an exceptionally well-planned operation, and the militants made off with 413 assault rifles and other firearms. It revealed the corruption and ineptness of the security forces under Thaksin's reforms. And sadly, the military allowed the police to flounder in the first year before pushing them to the side and reasserting control. But by then, the insurgency had gained momentum, capitalizing on the government's heavy-handed response and missteps.

The insurgency that erupted in 2004 is qualitatively and quantitatively different from its predecessors. The insurgency is far more violent than we've seen anytime in the past, with far higher casualty rates. In the 1960s–1990s, insurgency was confined to the countryside, with insurgents living in very remote mountainous base camps and with government forces the primary targets. But since 2004, targeting is much broader and now includes civilians, women, children, medical personnel, and Buddhist clergy. Attacks are sectarian in nature as well as indiscriminate. The clear goal is to drive Buddhists from the countryside. By 2015, few if any mixed villages existed anymore, as Buddhist fled en masse either out of the Deep South altogether, or to cities or provincial towns where security is higher, or to heavily guarded Buddhist enclaves in the countryside. While attacks in the countryside are targeted, attacks in the city employ indiscriminate IEDs to terrorize the population.

When the insurgency erupted, the immediate response of the security force was to go and arrest the known surviving members of the previous generation of insurgents. This was a failed policy. The former PULO insurgents had been caught as much off guard by the eruption of violence as the government.

The BRN had transformed itself from the 1990s. It gained strength through recruitment in religious schools, in particular the Thamiwttiyah Foundation School in Yala and the Samphan Wittiyah School in Narathiwat. The headmasters of the two schools, Masae Useng and Sapaeng Basoe, are believed to be the BRN's top leaders; both have gone underground since 2004. The BRN's process of indoctrination was rooted in the political awakening of Pattani nationalism. As one insurgent told me, "We were determined to rise up again but this time from within, as opposed to the previous generation, which really ran its guerrilla war from Malaysia. The BRN was determined that this movement would really be homegrown and tied to the local community."

With the insurgency under way, PULO did restart military operations, but it has always been a minor player, seeking to leverage greater political space for itself without bringing much to the fight. But despite its name, PULO is woefully factionalized, with different groups vying for power and influence. There is nothing "united" about PULO. Its top leadership is largely languishing in Thai prisons. Other faction heads are exiled across the Middle East and Scandinavia. The group's "foreign affairs spokesman," Kasturi Mahkota, who had been trying to leverage his own position by holding secret peace talks with the Thai government since 2006, broke away in October 2011. The group's vice president Lukman bin-Lima heads another faction. None of these factions command militants in the field, but a few smaller PULO factions do. One, often referred to as "New PULO," or "PULO 4-Star," has been led by Samsudin Khan since mid-2009. Kamae Yuso leads another faction, "Pulo 5-Star."

The Gerakan Mujahideen Islam Pattani (GMIP) emerged in the early 1990s, not as an ideological movement but as a gang linked primarily to gun running for Acehnese separatists (Gerakan Aceh Merdeka, or GAM) and the occasional contract killing in southern Thailand. The group was taken over by Jehku Mae Kuteh, also known as Doramae Kuteh, and some of the few veterans of the Afghan *mujahideen* from Thailand.

The final group, the Barisan Islam Pembangunan Pattani (BIPP), is very small and is not known to command any militants in the field. But the organization remains highly influential at the ideological level. Its leaders still command religious and ideological respect and, as such, remain relevant.

A former insurgent leader, Wan Kadir Che Man, tried to establish an umbrella grouping, Bersatu, though he controls no militants on the ground. Bersatu largely failed. In 2015, the Malaysian government tried to establish another umbrella grouping, MARA Pattani, which includes PULO factions and the BIPP but is dominated by the BRN.

None of these groups is large, well resourced, or broadly based. Most—though not all—are riddled with factionalism, based as much on ego and power seeking as on ideology. Not all have armed combatants on the ground but instead rely on their influence as elder religious leaders. But the sheer number of organizations and factions thereof makes command and control, coordination, and consensus very hard to achieve.

But what is different from in the past is that the various organizations and their factions are more united in their goal. They might discredit one another behind closed doors, and they certainly compete, but they are not out to undermine or discredit each other in public, and their goals are no longer at cross-purposes.

The insurgency began at very low levels, but the government's response was disastrous and led to a growth in insurgent operations and support for the movement. What began as a slow boil in 2004 gained momentum with the disastrous handling of the Krue Se Mosque incident and Tak Bai massacre. In the former, twenty-two armed militants holed up in a thirteenth-century mosque outside of the city of Pattani. Security forces made no attempt at trying to negotiate their surrender and shot up the mosque, killing all twenty-two. They were buried with the designation "*shaheeds*." In the latter incident, in October 2004, several hundred unarmed men were protesting government policies and mistreatment, were subdued by government forces, and, with their shirts binding their arms, made to serpentine across the ground. They were packed into army trucks so tightly that eighty-seven died of asphyxiation. The Tak Bai incident was caught on video, and what is striking is the fact that despite so many different security forces being at the scene, no one was willing to take charge. The incompetence of the security forces in the early years of the insurgency was staggering.

The government's failures in five key and interconnected areas directly led to the growth of the insurgency. The first was the interagency turf war over command, control, and the budgets. The RTA very clearly let the police, who had taken over responsibility for security in the south starting in 2001, fall on their face, which they did. The RTA quickly imposed martial law in the south, wresting back control, and eventually re-established the Southern Border Provinces Administrative Centre. There were between 60-70,000 security forces in the south, but the competition amongst them precluded cooperation. Indeed, at times there was more than a lack of coordination, and closer to all out war. In 2004, Royal Thai Army (RTA) personnel raided the regional offices of the National Intelligence Agency, which was investigating official crimes, and hauled off all its files and computers. The RTA exerted nearly full control of all resources, including development funds for the south. Despite this new authority and soaring budgets, the leadership had no continuity. Fourth Army commanders were cycled through at a dizzying rate, with the result being no policy continuity.

Second, the government's intelligence was disastrous. When the insurgency broke out, the first response was to round up all the former insurgents known to security forces, mainly members of PULO. But PULO had nothing to do with the insurgency and commanded almost none of the militants on the ground. It has constantly tried to leverage political gains since 2004, but it is responsible for only a fraction of the violence. But the arrest of these community leaders alienated the population and was a waste of intelligence into the new movements. Indeed, it was not until 2007–2008 that Thai security officials even acknowledged that the BRN was most responsible for the violence. As a result of their paucity of intelligence, the security forces engaged in sweeps, arresting tens, sometimes fifty or sixty people at a time, which indicated that they were simply profiling a certain demographic and not known suspects. This fueled the ranks of the insurgency. Young men either were disaffected by government action or were mistrusted by the insurgents upon their release and had to prove their loyalty to the movement.

Third, Thai counterinsurgency tactics were flat-out shoddy and unprofessional. They relied on static positions and rarely patrolled, and their checkpoints were all fixed. They rarely set up rolling checkpoints. Security forces were deployed in pickup trucks, often unarmored, and more frequently only on motorcycles. Armored personnel carriers and armored vehicles were rarely seen in the first ten years. It took a decade before proper protective equipment, kevlar flak jackets and helmets, new weapons, and so on filtered down to forces in the south.

Fourth, the government allowed a culture of impunity to flourish, alienating the general public. In July 2005, prime minister Thaksin Shinawatra pushed the Emergency Decree through parliament, which not only gave the security forces substantial new powers in the south but gave all security forces immunity for official acts. In the following twelve years, immunity has been waived in only an estimated twenty cases, in which, in most cases, charges were dropped. Of the few cases that went to trial, all were acquitted on appeal. This has created a culture of impunity that has done more to alienate the population than anything else.

Finally, the beleaguered Buddhist community practiced significant amounts of vigilantism. Some of this was in response to the government's poor handling of the insurgency—Buddhists simply took matters into their own hands. But some of it was—to a degree—state sanctioned, with both the Ministry of Interior and the Queen's Guards arming Buddhist villagers. The fact that much of the training was done in Buddhist temple compounds severely alienated the majority-Muslim population, who were made to feel like the enemy.

Violence grew throughout 2005 and 2006. Following the September 2006 coup, violence spiked, peaking in mid-2007. Between 2004 and 2008, an average 1,1926 violent incidents per year occurred, significantly higher than the twelve-year average of 1,281.[20] At its peak in 2007, according to SBPAC data, 471 armed clashes took place between militants and security forces, which fell to 167 in 2015.[21]

At the time, an average of over 70 people were killed each month, and it really seemed as though the Thai government had lost control: social services ground to a halt, the sense of insecurity was pervasive, Buddhists flew from the region en masse, and the population had a sense that the insurgents could strike at will. The RTA surged its forces in the south in the second half of 2007. But it's also clear that the insurgents had overplayed their hand: the high level and grisly nature of violence was starting to alienate their base of support, and they were hitting logistical limits to the growth of operations. With no external or state support and an insecure base area in Malaysia, they had hit the limits of how much they could do militarily. Violence fell in the second half of 2007 and into 2008.

Since 2009 the level of violence has been amazingly consistent. It is calibrated to be a level at which it can continue to pressure the Thai state and force Buddhists out or convince them at least not to return, diminish the effectiveness or provision of government services, eliminate rivals within

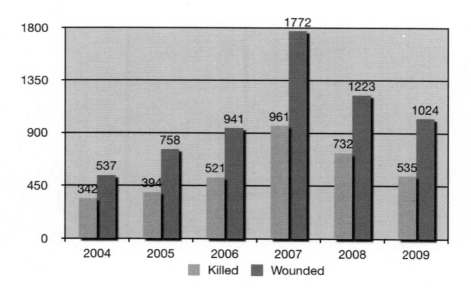

Figure 4.1.   Casualties 2004 to 2009 *Source*: Southern Border Provinces Administrative Centre

their own community, maintain the respect of the community or at least the narrative, and convey that they can still cause incredible harm to the Thai government, the general public, and security forces. The level of violence is at a sustainable level, clearly within the means of the insurgency.

Between January 2009 and December 2015, over 2,200 people have been killed and nearly 5,000 people wounded. An average eighty-six casualties per month occur, of which security forces make up only 40 percent. Insurgents have launched more than 1,100 IED attacks, with an additional 160 defused or failed IEDs. They have made nearly five hundred arson attacks, including thirty-three schools. They have destroyed ninety cell or electric towers and countless CCTV cameras as well as made twelve major attacks on railway lines. Insurgents, who are inherently cautious, have launched eighty-eight attacks on hardened security force outposts, including several attacks that were utter humiliations for the Thai government. In that time, insurgents have beheaded twelve victims, bringing the total to forty-two since 2004. They have desecrated the corpses of fifty-seven more.

All of this has happened as the security situation has greatly improved across the south, which now has more security forces better equipped and with more mobility, a thorough network of checkpoints and monitoring of people, enormous DNA and forensic databases, and greater professionalism. Since 2004, the government has spent 2,649.4 billion baht in the Deep South ($7.3 billion). The budget for all security operations, including development

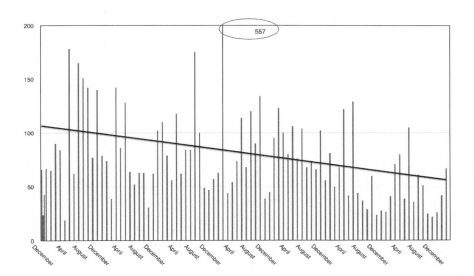

Figure 4.2.   Total Casualties, December 2008 to March 2016, with Trendline.
Source: **Author's open source dataset.**

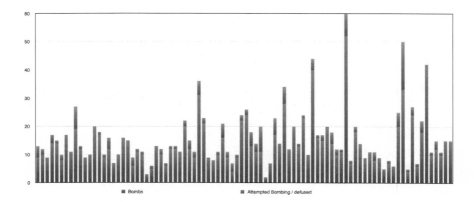

Figure 4.3.   Successful Bombings and Defused/Unexploded IEDs, January 2009 to March 2016. *Source*: **Author's open source dataset.**

projects, for FY2016 is baht 30.1 billion ($832 million), an increase of baht 4.4 billion over FY2015, which was already the highest ever. The military's own budget has increased from baht 78.55 billion in 2004 to baht 193 billion in 2015, a 161 percent increase. Yet the government still cannot stem the violence, which is highly calibrated to government actions and countermeasures.

At the root of the government's failure to stem the violence is truly a lack of political will to do so. The government's goals remain very limited and at odds with its public pronouncements (1) to prevent secessionism but also maintain the unitary nature of the Thai state; (2) to reduce violence to tolerable levels that can be attributed to criminality; (3) to assimilate the Malay-dominated south into the Thai nation-state; and (4) to shore up the dwindling Buddhist community in the south while reseeding the population with new migrants.

The overarching goal of the Thai government is to prevent the insurgents from successfully seceding. It has little chance of succeeding in this endeavor. But as important to the military is to prevent any devolution of political power. It intends to bring an end to the conflict on its own terms and without making any political concessions or ceding any political control and creating a precedent for autonomy elsewhere, in particular Issarn and the north, the epicenter of the "Red Shirt" movement, which is aligned with ousted prime minister Thaksin Shinawatra . As the former RTA chief Gen. Udomdej Sita-butr blunt ly put it: "The Army will not tolerate the separation of the territory. That is impossible because the constitution makes it clear and local people do not want independence."[22] The cornerstone of the government, and in partic-

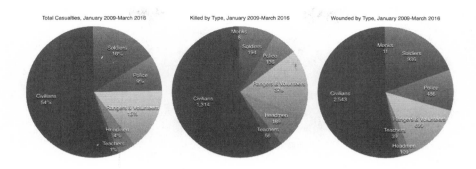

Figure 4.4.   Casualties by Type, January 2009 to March 2016. *Source*: Author's open source dataset.

ular the junta that seized power in 2014, is to maintain the unitary nature of the Thai state.[23]

The security services, especially the army, strongly believe that they can militarily defeat the insurgency without ever having to make concessions. As long as the majority of violence is directed at security forces or against perceived legitimate targets, such as informants, and is largely away from urban population centers, the government can deflect pressure to change its policies, negotiate, and reach a durable political settlement. As one CSO activist tied to the BRN told me: "The army doesn't care about peace; they just want the violence to go down."[24]

The third goal is to assimilate the south into the Thai nation-state. Thailand has long been frustrated that the Malay are the only minority group that has consistently resisted assimilation. The Malay do not see any space for them in the construct of the Thai state: the monarchy (a Hindu god-king), religion (Buddhism), and nation (Thai), whose southern border was codified in the Anglo-Siamese Treaty of 1909 and which Pattani nationalists believe to be occupied territory. Indeed, most Thais and Thai officials will not refer to the local population as Malay. The spokesman of Internal Security Operation Command (ISOC) Region 4 refused to identify them as Malay, insisting that they were "Thai Muslims." Thai Muslims are ethnic Thai who profess the Islamic faith, and such communities exist in central and northern Thailand. The three southernmost provinces and parts of Songkhla are dominated by ethnic Malay. Yet they are listed as " Thai" on their identity card, with no option for Malay. The government has resisted using Malay and its Arabic-based written script of Yawi, and those who do are restricted from being employed in government or in schools. And while the Thai deny the Malay their own identity and try to enforce their integration, the Thai are at the same

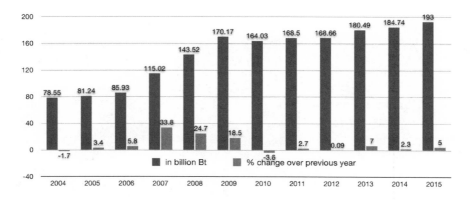

Figure 4.5.   Thai Military Expenditure, 2004 to 2015 in Thai Baht (billions).
Source: **Stockholm International Peace Research Institute, Military expenditures data set at www.sipri.org.**

time highly prejudiced toward the Malay. The Thai see the Malay as lazy and call them *khaek*, a derogatory term.[25]

The final goal is to shore up the Buddhist community in the Deep South. Buddhists, both Thai and ethnic Chinese, who are a very distinct minority, made up 20 percent of the population of 2.2 million in 2004. The exodus has slowed. In the first eighteen months of the crisis, a Ministry of Interior survey estimated that 10 percent of the Buddhist community, or thirty-four thousand people, had fled the south.[26] By 2010, according to a survey by the National Statistical Office, only 288,000 Buddhists lived in the three provinces, 20 percent fewer than in the 2000 census.[27] Today, Buddhists represent less than 15 percent, and in particular the Thai have fled the countryside in droves, in favor of the cities. The number of mixed communities across the three and one-half provinces in the conflict zone have dwindled, and most Buddhists who remain in the countryside reside in heavily garrisoned Buddhist communities or in district towns. Senior RTA officers now estimate that by the end of 2014, Buddhists were down to 10 percent of the population, roughly 190,000.[28] But the demographic trends are clear: the Malay community's birth rate is estimated to be over four children per woman, while among Thai women, the fertility rate is 1.5, far below the replacement rate.[29] The government's policy is both to convince those remaining Thai Buddhists to not leave the region and to transplant residents from the poor and overpopulated Issarn region. The RTA believes the dearth of Buddhists in the Deep South threatens national security and territorial integrity. Thus, rebuilding the Buddhist community is a top priority. It also helps to dissipate some of the antimilitary sentiment that centers in the poor and overpopulated Issarn region.

3. THE PEACE PROCESS

Technically, peace talks have been under way since 2005, but the reality is that it's never been a formal process that has included the requisite actors on the insurgents' side. And on the government side, these peace talks have been completely at the mercy of Thailand's tumultuous domestic politics, with both the civilian government and the military conducting back-channel negotiations to politically undermine the other.

From 2004 to the October 2006 coup that forced him from power, Thaksin Shinawatra engaged in back-channel peace talks. But this strategy had two major problems. First, his team truly did not know with whom to talk. It had no idea who was behind the insurgency, and so it approached any known figures or people who sent feelers to the government. For example, members of PULO were very quick to try to leverage the talks for themselves, even though they had nothing to do with the violence. One PULO faction leader, Lukman bin Lima, announced his willingness to negotiate with the Thai government, as did other PULO leaders. The BRN responded with a wave of assassinations to put PULO in its place. And the talks went nowhere. But the military was incensed that Thaksin, who had a fundamental mistrust of the military, was trying to do an end run around it by neither consulting with it nor getting it to endorse the talks.

Another track of peace talks was held at the impetus of former Malaysian prime minister Mahathir Mohamad and the Thai military at the behest of the Thai monarchy. Thaksin's government was kept out of the loop. The "Langkawi process," as it was known, was not a "formal negotiation" but "an attempt to identify common ground between the two sides and designed to reconcile differences." Although independence was not discussed, a myriad of issues were, including amnesty, the use of Melayu as a working language, social justice, education, and economic development. The two sides came up with the Joint Peace and Development Plan for South Thailand in September 2006, although it was never made public or implemented.

And once again the talks came to nothing as only previous-generation insurgents and others who sought to leverage a place at the table bothered to attend; the BRN was not involved. The defen se minister at the time, Boonrawd Somtas, acknowledged as much: " In the past, we have had negotiations with insurgent groups, but we held talks with the wrong groups such as Bersatu and PULO which did not launch attacks. We need to talk with the BRN Coordinate, who are the real ones behind the bloody attacks. But it has refused negotiations so far as it is gaining the upper hand and winning greater support from local residents."

The talks were ideologically fraught, as both sides entered with nonnegotiable preconditions. The Thai government demanded a one-month cease-fire—reduced to a two-week period—as a show of goodwill and proof of command and control. The "insurgents" could not deliver a day of peace. Violence actually spiked as the BRN sought to discredit and undermine what it considered to be pretenders, the "insurgent" groups that showed up in Langkawi. The government's demand for a surrender of weapons and materiel was a nonstarter. The insurgents, for their part, were as unrealistic in their preconditions: a blanket amnesty, the adoption of Melayu as an official working language, and the scrapping of the government's draconian Emergency Decree.

The BRN had clearly concluded that it had nothing to gain from the talks and that it was clearly gaining the upper hand on the battlefield.

Violent attacks increased steadily from 2004 to 2006 and spiked dramatically in the six to eight months following the 2006 coup d'état. The level of violence soared following the coup, and it appeared that the military and government had lost all control. Insurgents were able to attack at will.

In July 2007, the RTA launched its own surge in the south, dramatically increasing deployments. But the insurgents had clearly overextended themselves. Violence fell sharply in the second half of 2007 and remained fairly low in 2008 before climbing again in 2009.

Following the October 2006 coup, the appointed prime minister and former army chief Surayud Chulanont made a public apology for the government's missteps in the south. This did not win over the public in the south, but it played very well in Kuala Lumpur, which was critical as bilateral relations from 2004 to 2006 had spiraled downward. Malaysian foreign minister Syed Hamid Albar responded to Surayud's apology positively and opened the door to Malaysian cooperation: "His step is a step in the right direction. It is an attitude of humility. . . . I am very glad that he has taken the first very, very constructive step. It is not easy to make a public apology for something that had happened."

Surayud also extended an olive branch to Indonesia, seeking further international support for a peace process. He assured Indonesian president Susilo Bambang Yudhoyono that he would not pursue the heavy-handed strategy of the Thaksin government and that he was "inspired by the peace process in Aceh province."

Yet the Langkawi process collapsed. The different insurgent groups that did attend were there to leverage a position for themselves out of a weak military position on the ground and to garner Malaysian government support. The BRN saw no use in attending. Moreover, while the insurgents were happy to meet with the Malaysians, they showed little support for talks with the Thai government.

Despite the coup, the legal disbanding of Thaksin's Thai Rak Thai political machine, the five-year political ban of more than one hundred of its top members, a new constitution drafted to weaken the power of parties, and blatant military intimidation of the electorate, Thaksin's allies won election with their new political vehicle, the People's Power Party, when elections were finally held in December 2007. The military was apoplectic. As such, governments since then have given the military a free hand in dealing with the south.

The short-lived governments of Samak Sundaravej and his successor, following his military-orchestrated ouster in mid 2007, were weak and fearful of running afoul of the military. The two People's Power Party governments pushed through no policies for the south and displayed almost no oversight over the Deep South; they certainly were unwilling to enter into even back-channel talks with the insurgents. And with violence down and the monarch increasingly incapacitated, the military felt little pressure to enter into talks.

The opposition Democrat Party, whose primary base of support is in the south, came to power in December 2008, but only after the military compelled one of the PPP's coalition partners in the parliament to defect from Thaksin's camp. As such, the Democrats were completely beholden to the military and steered clear of anything to do with the south. Although talk of peace talks continued, along with some back-channel talks throughout 2010, the reality was that the government was consumed with elite-level politics in Bangkok.

In 2011, the newest reincarnation of Thaksin's Thai Rak Thai Party swept to power. Led by his younger sister Yingluck Shinawatra, the Pheu Thai dominated the July 2011 polls. Despite the 2006 coup and all that the military had done to disqualify and dismember Thaksin's political machine, it won every election after the coup, an enormous setback for the military, which remained preoccupied with elite politics, not the insurgency in the Deep South.

Yingluck visited the south once during the 2011 electoral campaign and made a vague promise of decentralization and the establishment of a "special administrative center." But there were no details and clearly no follow-up after her electoral victory. Like her predecessors, Yingluck was fearful of running afoul of the military and went out of her way to repair ties with it. To that end, she steered clear of interfering in military promotions, acceded to its demands for huge budget increases, and had little to say about the military's handling of the south. Indeed, Yingluck concurrently served as the minister of defense and offered little in the way of oversight.

In February 2012, Yingluck traveled to Kuala Lumpur to meet with Prime Minister Najib Razak, who made an unequivocal statement that Malaysia viewed the unrest as a "domestic matter" for Thailand and rejected any secessionist agenda on the part of the insurgents. "They must reject violence and extremism."[30]

Having secured further Malaysian cooperation, the government started to develop some plans for the south. In March, the Pheu Thai Party drafted two bills for the south, including one that would overhaul the SBPAC and the other a controversial bill that would create a special administrative zone in the south, called " Pattani Maha Nakhon."[31] Both the bills sought to strip power in the south from the military and, as such, were immediately rebuked by the RTA leadership and subsequently scrapped.[32]

In April 2012, Yingluck came under attack from the opposition Democrat Party when word got out that back-channel talks were taking place.[33] But the real concern was that they were being organized by her brother Thaksin, who had been exiled since the 2006 coup and was a fugitive from Thai justice. Clearly he had an ulterior political motive in trying to deliver peace. The government denied conducting talks until August 2012, when it acknowledged that it was in "talks," though not "negotiations," with some, but unspecified, insurgent groups. As Deputy Prime Minister General Yuthasak Sasiprapha explained, "Don't call it negotiations . . . but there are talks to achieve peace, which is a crucial government policy."[34]

The secret negotiations were conducted by the SBPAC chairman, Police Colonel Thawee Sodsong, a close ally and confidante of Thaksin and Yingluck. But he was an important figure in his own right as head of the SBPAC. In that capacity, he did an excellent job in reaching out to the Malay community and civil society organizations and in trying to rein in the excesses of the military and security forces. Thawee began to push back against the culture of impunity enjoyed by the security forces, which won him plaudits from the local community. He spoke of the importance of human rights and fostering a political dialogue. He engaged the OIC. He was a transformative figure, whom many people I have interviewed credit with single-handedly changing the tenor of Thai policy and making a political dialogue possible.

And those efforts paid dividends. On February 28, 2013, in a complete surprise, the secretary general of the Thai National Security Council, Lt. Gen. Paradorn Pattanatabut, signed a "general consensus" agreement with Ustadz Hassan Taib, the Malaysian liaison of the Barisan Revolusi Nasional, in Kuala Lumpur, to begin a formal peace process.[35] It was the first time in ten years that the BRN, the group most responsible for the violence in the south, formally endorsed a political solution to end the conflict. And in a major concession, it agreed that the talks would take place "under the [2007] Thai Constitution," which explicitly forbade separatism. And to the government's credit, it acknowledged that the conflict could be resolved only through a political solution.[36]

The first round of talks was held on March 28. And despite the fanfare and high expectations generated by the peace process, the first round of talks made clear the enormous divide between the two sides and just how complicated the talks were going to be. While talks usually begin with maximalist demands, each side was tremendously naive regarding what the other side was able and willing to deliver on.

The insurgents were represented by Hasan Taib, who identified himself as the deputy secretary general of the BRN, and one other BRN member, as well as one member each from PULO and the BIPP, and they put forward nine demands:[37]

1. The Thai government should send only appointed representatives;
2. The Thai side should recognize the identity, race, and language of the Melayu people;
3. Thailand should withdraw its troops from the restive region and revoke its special security laws;
4. Thailand should let local security forces take over peacekeeping duties;
5. Thailand should designate the south as a special administrative region;
6. Thailand and Malaysia should assign their prime minister's offices to carry on the dialogue to avoid disruption from any change of government;
7. Thailand should ensure that the dialogue proceeds without intervention from the Office of Islamic Countries and the European Union;
8. Thailand should offer amnesty to insurgents; and
9. Thailand should model the southern administration on the autonomous region of Aceh in Indonesia.[38]

The fifteen-member Thai peace panel had only one representative from the military, which suggests both the Yingluck government's fundamental mistrust of the military and also the lack of any military support for the peace process. But the military immediately put its foot down on most of these demands. The government rejected the militants' demands to free all detainees, drop charges against others, issue a blanket amnesty, and withdraw all RTA forces.[39] In particular, the military completely rejected any form of autonomy, something that government negotiators had hinted might be worth discussing, seeing it as a first step to independence. As RTA chief Gen. Prayuth Chan-ocha made clear: "It is impossible to give up [territory] to anyone. Everything must be discussed at the negotiation table, under the law and constitution."[40] Once the RTA made clear its firm opposition to amnesty, the NSC chief retracted his statement. And days before the talks began, a court acquitted a police officer for his alleged role in the 2004 disappearance of Muslim human rights lawyer Somchai Neelapaijit, whose Muslim Attorney Centre does pro bono work for suspected insurgents, aggravating local sentiment that a culture of impunity pervades the security forces.[41]

Despite the vast gulf between the two sides, they agreed to meet again in April. But the Thai army had already signaled its opposition to the talks moving forward, pointing to the continued violence. Indeed, despite a pledge by Hasan Taib on March 5 that he would "signal" the commanders in the field to reduce the violence, violence spiked that month. Insurgents killed thirty-eight people, well above the 2012 average of twenty-eight, and wounded eighty-five people.

The Thai NSC chief and lead negotiator, Paradorn Pattanatabut, was realistic. Though he publicly called on the militants to reduce their attacks, he conceded after the conclusion of the March 28 talks: "It is impossible to hope that major violence will not occur in the restive region. Talks will continue though the unrest hasn't improved yet."[42]

The second round of peace talks resumed in Kuala Lumpur on April 29, even though the violence continued unabated. Indeed, hard-liners in the movement assassinated the highest ranking official since the insurgency began in 2004, the deputy governor of Pattani.[43] Although the prime minister incredulously asserted that the assassination was not connected to the peace process, Paradorn conceded that "radical militants are flexing their muscles to oppose the peace plan." But the government team was under immense pressure from the military. Paradorn warned, "There will be problems concerning the peace talks if the violence continues. It is BRN's duty to ease violence."[44] But the government remained committed to the talks and appeared to have the backing of the public. A survey conducted by the Prince of Songkhla University in late March, but released on April 10, found that 67 percent of the respondents across the Deep South supported the peace talks.[45]

Yet the second round of talks began on a very unauspicious note. On the eve of the peace talks, the BRN released a short video on YouTube that laid out five new demands:[46]

1. The "Siamese government" must accept the role of the Malaysian government as a "mediator" and not just as a "facilitator" of the peace talks.
2. Participants of the peace talks can include only Melayus led by BRN and Thai government authorities.
3. Representatives from ASEAN and the OIC and other NGOs should be allowed to observe the talks.
4. The Thai government must release all detained suspects without conditions and must suspend and stop issuing additional arrest warrants for other suspects.
5. The BRN's status must be recognized as a Pattani liberation movement, not an insurgent group.

The video clearly caught the government team off guard and should have scuttled the talks as they violated most of agreed principles in the February 28 agreement. Paradorn quickly responded, "I will ask Hasan Taib if he really meant what he said," warning that "their demands are hard to accept. And if they want to have it all, I think it will disrupt the talks. . . . It was agreed that talks would be in line with the Thai constitution."[47] He tried to put a positive spin on the video: " At least we know what they think and want. It's a gesture of their willingness to talk, otherwise they would not issue the demands."[48]

Yet all five demands, which were then presented in written form at the talks, were completely rejected by the military after it convened an urgent meeting on the talks.[49] The military had been steadfast all along of not allowing the conflict to be internationalized. While it allowed Malaysia to play a role in facilitating the talks, that was a practical matter as it had leverage over and direct contact with the insurgents; no one ever countenanced a role for it as a mediator. The military had, likewise, rejected any observers or peace monitoring by outsiders, whether NGOs, international organizations, or states.

The second demand was rejected because the Thai delegation included ethnic Thais from the Deep South, whose rights the insurgents do not recognize. The insurgents deem them colonial occupiers, hence their fifth demand, that the BRN be acknowledged as a "liberation movement." This de facto implies that the Deep South was colonized by Thailand, that it had been illegally annexed, and that its continued rule was illegitimate.

But the real showstopper was the demand that all detained suspects would have to be released and that the government should stop issuing arrest warrants for suspects, even though the insurgents refused to curtail the violence.

Taib concluded his video with a statement that almost ended the talks: "The struggle of the BRN can lead to peace and justice, to the establishment of a state, God willing."[50] The Thai side was both incredulous and infuriated as the February 28 agreement promised that the talks would stay strictly within the Thai constitution.[51]

The parties agreed to a third round of talks, though it was clear that military opposition was growing and would likely thwart anything that the civilian negotiators agreed to.

On May 27, ahead of the third round of talks, the BRN released yet another video. This one had a more aggressive and, frankly, a more arrogant tone, going further than the original five demands. Abdulkarim Khalid, a core member of the BRN and a member of the peace talks team, accused the government of perpetrating a number of violent incidents, including the massacre at the Al Furqon mosque in Narathiwat's Cho Airong district and the May 1 killing of six people in front of a grocery store in Pattani. He warned the government to stop all forms of violence against "the people of Pattani" or face the consequences. Hasan Taib said the BRN was formed to fight for the liberation of "Pattani" from the "Siamese colonialists."[52]

The video and the ongoing attacks targeting security forces at unprecedented levels put the government in a tight spot. But the talks proceeded nonetheless.[53]

The composition of the insurgent negotiating panel was also different in the third round of talks. In addition to Taib, it included Ahmad en-Awan, believed to represent the BRN's youth arm called Permuda, and a member of the BRN's secretariat. But it also included five members of PULO. No explanation was given for the different personnel, but it clearly reflected ongoing jockeying for power behind the scenes.

While the government asserted that the talks "did not fail," it was hard to put them in a positive light. The government gave the BRN an ultimatum to stop the violence as proof of the BRN's command and control abilities and sincerity toward a peaceful resolution. The government also rejected all five of the demands. The BRN reiterated its position that it would call on its men to stop attacking civilians.

The third—and final—round of peace talks was held in Kuala Lumpur on June 13. The government was desperate to keep the talks alive as the violence continued to soar. The bleeding had to stop. Yet, the government knew that if it could not reduce the violence quickly, the military would continue to oppose the talks. The government appealed to local imams to use their authority to call on the BRN to support a Ramadan cease-fire.[54]

As it turned out, the BRN did agree to suspend its violent attacks during the holy month of Ramadan, from early July to early August. In return, the government would "soften security measures and scrutiny, except for risk areas and government buildings."[55] The Thai government continued to refuse a blanket amnesty and, even worse, made a nonsensical concession that it would "revoke charges against those found to be innocent."[56] The Thai side, for its part, did agree to bring the insurgents' five-point proposal under consideration, but clearly, how far that could go with the RTA's total opposition was limited.

On June 19, Hasan Taib gave a rare thirty-eight-minute television interview—speaking to a Muslim politician from the New Aspiration Party.[57] Although he publicly committed the BRN to the peace process, he did acknowledge that some hard-liners did not support the peace process. But where the decision to escalate violent attacks was coming from, whether hard-line field commanders or the BRN's top leadership body, the Dewan Penilian Party (DPP), was unclear.

The interview revealed continued contradictions. While reiterating that it would continue to push for its five demands, Hasan Taib said that the BRN would consider autonomy. "But the final goal and main path of the BRN remains independence in freedom of education, economics and the social and religious way of life."[58]

On June 22, the BRN submitted, via the Malaysian facilitators, its detailed plan to curb violence during Ramadan. But at the same time, it also listed an additional seven demands to be met by Thai authorities before it would order the militants to stand down:

1. The government had to withdrawal all soldiers, rangers, and police assigned from regions 1, 2 and 3; only Fourth Army personnel and local police could remain in the south.
2. The RTA had to withdrawal all troops in the countryside.
3. The police and border patrol police had to withdraw from all villages.
4. All Muslim defense volunteers must be exempted from work during Ramadan.
5. The government could not conduct any operations, restrict movement (run checkpoints), or make any arrests during Ramadan.
6. The government could not conduct any social welfare during Ramadan.
7. The prime minister had to publicly accept these demands and sign them by July 3.

Hasan Taib reiterated these demands publicly in a five-minute video posted on YouTube on June 25 and warned that peace talks between the BRN and the Thai government would not take place unless the demands and conditions were met.[59]

The demands were clearly unacceptable to the Thai side and rejected outright across the government and military. The minister of defense at the time, Air Chief Marshal Sukumpol, was blunt: "I announce on behalf of security authorities that I do not accept the conditions of the insurgents because they are not right and are insincere. . . . We are not interested. I stand firm: the conditions are unacceptable to us. They must know who they are talking to and what their status is."[60] Then RTA chief Gen. Prayuth Chanocha dismissed the BRN demands out of hand: "The BRN has no advantage over us. They only have a mouth that outdoes us because they speak without holding any principles. Let's see if they are able to stop violence during Ramadan. Then, [their status] may be worth reviewing and gain some more credibility."[61] Gen. Akanit Muansawat, a member of the House Committee on State Security, said the BRN's demands showed that Taib could not control the militants: "It's obvious that this is the way out for Mr. Taib, because he knows he could not order the active militants to stop their operations. That's why he proposed demands that were impossible to achieve by the Thai government again and again."[62]

The Thai side was enormously frustrated. It had little room to maneuver due to pressure from the military. But it had no clear understanding of where these continued and outrageous demands were coming from. Was it the fact that the insurgents simply could not agree on a course of action and that they were constantly making concessions to others to get their buy-in? Was it done intentionally to scuttle the peace talks but make it look as though it was the government that walked away? Or was it the fact that these insurgents were simply rank amateurs, who had absolutely no experience in negotiation and were out of their depth?

Despite government's rejection of the BRN's new demands, the BRN and the Thai government, under Malaysian auspices, signed the Ramadan Peace Initiative on July 12 to establish a forty-day cease-fire until August 18.[63] In the agreement, the BRN pledged to " put an effort and consideration not to create any violence including armed attack, bombing and ambush towards the security forces and the public. Party B also will put an effort not to sabotage or damage government's properties and public amenities. Party B guarantees the rights, freedom and safety of non-Muslims will always be respected, valued and protected."[64]

Despite the cease-fire agreement, violence continued at roughly normal levels throughout the forty-day period. On July 20, the BRN issued a letter of protest to the Malaysian facilitators, blaming the government for cease-fire violations, though without giving any specifics, thereby justifying insurgent retaliation. The government asserted that it would continue to defend itself but pledged not to engage in offensive operations.[65]

By July 26, the government was coming under pressure due to the continued violence, and the RTA began to redeploy troops who had been brought back to base as part of the cease-fire by order of the prime minister/defense minister. The government went out of its way to attribute all but five of the attacks between July 12 and 26 to other factions in order to justify the resumption of talks in August.[66] In all, the south experienced sixty-nine incidents of violence causing the death of twenty-three, mainly government and security forces.[67] Due to the violence, Malaysian prime minister Najib Razak canceled an August 1 Ramadan visit to southern Thailand. On August 7, BRN negotiator Hasan Taib submitted a letter of protest to the Malaysians, contending that the government had failed to protect Muslims from violence.

Despite the violence and overall lack of progress, the Thai government indicated its intention to hold a new round of talks in August after Ramadan. An adviser to the NSC had publicly commented that two of the five demands, an amnesty and the declaration of the BRN as a "liberation movement," were being considered.[68]

By this point, however, the RTA was convinced that the talks needed to end. RTA chief Gen. Prayuth Chan-ocha unequivocally stated: "The scope of the talks must be ironed out in order that we have a clear answer that it will involve neither a special administrative zone nor independence [for the southern border states]."[69] A few days later, he sent a clear warning to both the government negotiators and the BRN that the BRN's five demands were totally unacceptable.[70]

The fourth round of talks, which was supposed to take place immediately after the conclusion of Ramadan but was never set, was then pushed back to September. The Malaysian government was fearful that the talks had hit an impasse. On August 23, the deputy prime minister traveled to Bangkok to pledge Malaysia's continued support for the peace process. But its refusal to make any concessions on the issue of dual citizenship was an irritant to the Thai military, and the parties made little progress on resuming the talks. [71]

The Thai government had real debates over how to proceed with the talks, now set back to late October. Much of the debate centered on the BRN's five demands, in particular whether they were in breach of the constitution. [72] NSC chief Paradorn, perhaps trying to keep hope of the talks alive, publicly stated, "Personally, I don't think the demands are in breach of the constitution, but a thorough study of the legal implications is still needed." [73] He indicated that from his vantage point, a negotiated agreement could possibly be found for four of the five points. On October 6, another deputy prime minister stated that the BRN's five demands were "acceptable overall" in total contravention of what the RTA had been saying. [74]

Also debated was whether the insurgent panel should be broadened to include other groups, [75] and if so, how broad the panel should be. On the one hand, if it was totally inclusive, comprising the various PULO factions, the BIPP, and the GMIP as well as the BRN, a common platform or consensus agreement would be all but impossible to reach. Yet they needed these groups in order to get buy-in to the peace process. And the inclusion of all would make the attribution question more clear when violence broke out. The Thai side finally agreed to increase the size of the panels to fifteen members per side to ensure as broad a representation on the part of insurgents as possible.

The October talks were scrapped, and the peace process was put on hold indefinitely. [76] On the insurgents' side, they were unable to put together a peace panel whose composition was acceptable to all factions. The Thai side, for its part, was still very divided on how to proceed with the BRN's five demands.

But it was domestic politics that really tripped up the peace process. The government of Yingluck Shinawatra, which until then had maintained a surprising detente with the military, had antagonized the military leadership when a group of Thaksin loyalist back benchers tried to push through an amnesty bill. Although the amnesty bill was defeated, it proved to be a strategic mistake that changed the course of Thai politics. Yingluck shrugged off the bill's defeat and moved on. But the bill, which was widely seen by the political opposition, military, and ultramonarchists as a means to return her brother to the country with a full amnesty, provoked street protests and a high-level elite political feud.

The military has always attributed the breakdown of the peace talks to the country's political instability. But the real onus was on the military itself. The military's total unwillingness to make any concessions on the BRN's five demands had led to a breakdown in the talks. It was the military's own intransigence, not the political stalemate, which actually did not transpire until the first quarter of 2014. Formal talks had been on hold since June, long before the government pushed through the amnesty bill.

Indeed, on October 11, Gen. Prayuth said (in a news item that garnered almost no scrutiny) that the talks to date had "failed" and that they were postponed indefinitely. More to the point, he had instructed military forces to go on the offensive.[77]

Then an incredible disconnect happened. On October 29, the Thai panel told the Malaysian facilitators that it was ready for a new round of talks in mid-November. In early November, Malaysia quietly sent a high-level delegation, which included the head of the Royal Malaysian Armed Forces and the Malaysian External Intelligence Organization, the official facilitator of the talks, to Bangkok on November 7 to get the peace process back on track. Bangkok agreed to allow PULO and the BIPP to be part of the insurgents ' fifteen-member negotiating team, led by the BRN. But the government still refused to accede to the insurgent's five demands. On November 27, the secretary general of the National Security Council and the government's chief negotiator, Paradorn Pattanatabut, said the fourth round of talks had been postponed indefinitely due to the political unrest in Bangkok.[78]

On December 2, 2013, the BRN's Hasan Taib issued yet another video on YouTube demanding the full implementation of the five demands. Either unaware of the growing political stasis in Bangkok or simply because of it and the indefinite postponement of talks, the BRN's position clearly was hardening. Taib concluded with a highly confrontational position: "The BRN is a liberation movement for the Pattani nation, to liberate it from the shackles of Siamese colonialism, to realize justice and prosperity in the form of the independent Pattani. This is the true meaning of 'genuine peace,' not the peace under the colonial rule of the Siamese."[79]

The government announced that talks would resume following the February 2014 election that would put a new government in power. But elite and military machinations led to the February 2015 polls being scrapped. This led to the ongoing political stasis that was used to justify the military's coup d'état on May 22, 2014, its second in eight years.

The BRN's intransigence was born of frustration. But why was the military so intransigent? Ostensibly it was opposed to the peace process because the violence continued unabated.

By every measure, the violence did surge in the six months following the February 28 agreement. A total of 231 people were killed and 426 people were wounded between March and September, according to the author's open source database. To put it into perspective, only 334 people were killed and 705 wounded in all of 2012. But the military leadership was correct in that they were taking the majority of casualties. Of the 231 people killed in that six-month period, 118 were members of the security forces (51 percent).

Security forces accounted for a staggering 71 percent of the 426 wounded. To put those figures into perspective, between 2009 and 2012, security forces made up only 28 percent of those killed and 38 percent of those wounded. In other words, the casualty rate for members of the RTA and police doubled from the average over the past four years during the peace process. From the military's perspective, there was nothing peaceful about it.

In all other categories, too, violence was up. Between March and September, insurgents made 120 IED attacks and some 8 attempted bombings. In all of 2012, they made only 139 successful IED attacks and 33 attempts. There were eleven attacks on hardened military positions and twenty-nine deprecate firefights with security forces, more than in all of 2012 (eight and sixteen, respectively).

To the military leadership this was ample evidence of both the BRN's lack of command and control and its lack of sincerity in seeking a durable political dispute.

The BRN disputes both counts. For it, the security forces remained a legitimate target as they were an illegal occupation force. And the BRN cites the fact that it was able to concentrate its attacks on security forces while dramatically scaling back attacks on citizens as evidence of command and control. Paradorn *de facto* accepted this reasoning, calling on the militants to simply reduce civilian casualties, which infuriated the military and deepened its mistrust of the government's intentions.

Yet the ongoing violence was a smokescreen for its real opposition: the military saw the peace talks as an existential threat. It was deemed to be part of Yingluck Shinawatra's overall national reconciliation program that would see her fugitive brother returned to Thailand a free man. From the February 2013 announcement, the military saw the talks as about Thaksin, not about bringing peace to the war-torn region.[80] The military did not see the southern peace process in isolation but rather as part of a national process that would roll back everything the military had tried to politically emasculate Thaksin and his movement since 2006. It was bad enough that Thaksin was key to the back-channel negotiations that led to the February 2013 agreement and that he was trying to present himself as a national savior to whom the government would have no choice but to give amnesty. Second, they saw any political solution as a wedge that would lead to a devolution of political power at a time when their goal was to centralize power, and in particular their own authority. Anything that potentially changed the unitary nature of the Thai state was a threat that had to be neutralized.

Following the coup, the peace process was at a standstill. While the junta issued a statement on June 30 that it was interested in restarting talks, it was lip service. The military government's overwhelming priority was to consolidate power and purge the Yingluck government from office.

Prior to the coup, the military had forced Paradorn out of the NSC and subsequently dismissed him as the lead negotiator. The junta purged SBPAC secretary general Col. Thawee Sodsong, who had won over a lot of support from the Malay community, and transferred him to an inactive post in Bangkok immediately following the coup on May 24, 2014. The junta replaced him with with Panu Uthairat, the Interior Ministry inspector general and an ultraroyalist. Panu immediately rolled back the progressive policies that had been implemented in the past few years.

The National Council for Peace and Order, or NCPO, did state its goal to bring peace to the south, but it was a very low priority and one that the increasingly inept and gaffe-prone junta seemed unable and unwilling to meet. Their priority remained the consolidation of power. And they made very clear that any talks had to be bound by the Thai constitution—terribly ironic since the junta had just overthrown a lawful and democratically elected government and scrapped the constitution. A junta spokesman made it very clear that any talks would have to be predicated on the "common understanding that Thailand is a single, inseparable state."[81]

The NCPO issued Order 230 on November 26, 2014, to establish a peace panel and appointed a close confidante of Gen. Prayuth, Gen. Aksara, as its chairman.[82] Later Prayuth appointed another confidante, Gen. Akanit Muansawat, a member of the National Legislative Council and adviser to the National Security Council (NSC) to head the back-channel talks. But his selection created a confusing chain of command. More importantly, it was an insult to the BRN, who rejected his conclusion. Akanit had been involved in previous rounds of talks and was a known hard-liner, unwilling to make any concessions. The BRN viewed him as having an "arrogant attitude," partly because he condescendingly referring to Pattani freedom fighters as *jone khaek*—"Muslim bandits."[83]

The appointment of two people very close to Prayuth made very clear that nothing could even be tabled that was not in the interest or ideological worldview of the junta leadership. Nonetheless, the talks, according to the junta, were set to resume in late December.

Prayuth traveled to Kuala Lumpur in December 2014 to meet with Prime Minister Najib Razak, whom he hosted the following month.[84] Gen. Aksara had made several trips to Kuala Lumpur to arrange for the talks, but little came of them.

Malaysian prime minister Najib pledged to work with the military junta, though only if Malaysia remained the sole external party involved in the talks. Otherwise, Najib's three principles remained very much in line with the junta's: a period of no violence as well as respect for the law was mandatory; all factions must be included at the talks; and all the demands of the insurgent groups must be collated into one set "that would be the basis of starting the actual substantive negotiations with the Thai government."[85] The issue of dual citizenship remained a bilateral irritant, and the two nations made no progress on the issue, including Prayuth's demand that Malaysia track and return some 250 dual citizens suspected of insurgent activities. [86]

In mid-December, Aksara held secret talks with Malaysian peace talks facilitator Ahmad Zamzamin but refused to disclose what had been agreed on. [87] According to the BIPP's Abu Hafez al-Hakim and is known to be very close to the BRN, the insurgents in the south were divided over whether to participate in the government's peace dialogue. "There has been serious debate among the movement circles whether it is to their advantage to talk to the military junta at this juncture or better to wait for a legitimate democratically elected government in 1–2 years time."

In January 2015, the National Security Council endorsed talks, calling them "necessary," and focused on efforts needed to restart them. It outlined three steps:

1. Trust building following Malaysian-facilitated talks, in which all the various insurgent groups show up;
2. A cease-fire agreement for a complete cessation of hostilities; and
3. The implementation of a "road map," which will involve measures to end violence and "cope with various demands through enforcement of law and judicial processes," and the reduction of "social disparities," with full respect for "local identities, culture and traditions." [88]

In the Thai context, these were very progressive and should have offered some inducements to the insurgents to come back to the table. Yet the insurgents still had deep misgivings, completely understandable considering the political context after the coup.

The government announced that the first round of talks would commence in April 2015, yet the talks were pushed back to May, and even then, they remained informal, back-channel talks. [89]

While talks remained stalled, there was progress behind the scenes. In May 2015, the Malaysian government brokered an agreement between six separate rebel groups and factions to form a single umbrella grouping: Majlis Amanah Rakyat Pattani (MARA Pattani). [90] MARA Pattani included the BRN and three separate Pattani United Liberation Orgnisation (PULO) factions—PULO 5-Star, led by Kamae Yuso, PULO 4-Star under Samsudin Khan, and another PULO faction under Kasturi Mahkota—the Barisan Islam Pembangunan Pattani (BIPP), and the Gerakan Mujahideen Islam Pattani (GMIP). [91]

The BRN, being the largest and most militarily capable of the groups, held three of the seven seats, including the chairman and the lead negotiator.

With MARA Pattani established, Lt. Gen. Aksara Kerdphol traveled to Kuala Lumpur on June 8–9, 2015, for another round of back-channel talks.

But the insurgents remained very pessimistic on prospects for peace and showed little interest in resuming formal talks.[92] In late June, a second round of secret talks was held in Kuala Lumpur, but again no agreement on restarting the peace process was reached. MARA Pattani rejected the government's proposal for a Ramadan cease-fire.

The government tried to put a positive spin on the meetings. As a senior Thai negotiator put it:

> Since then, we have continually followed up. At the early stage, there have been meetings, discussions and getting to know each other. . . . We are now at the stage of building trust. But . . . [Malaysia] is the facilitator that glues us together, which is very effective. We trust Malaysia and so do the dissidents living there. When we met the dissidents, Malaysia brought us together perfectly.[93]

And Prayuth clearly wanted to put the blame on the insurgents. "We are talking with the leadership and coordinator level of different groups. Right now, many have joined the discussion. Even people who join it don't agree with each other. There's not much unity on their side. . . . You cannot hope to finish this tomorrow or the day after tomorrow. The more we press them, the more they will pressure us with violence, because it's us who wants it to be over. I am telling you today, the country has to stick together. If you have a problem, fix it through the legal process and the justice system. If you keep fighting, it will damage all of us."[94] The irony of the coup leader saying that political disputes had to be resolved through the "legal process and the justice system" and not through violence was rich indeed.

But it was so clear that the government had absolutely no political will to see the talks through or to make any meaningful concession. Indeed, the junta leader, who had publicly complained in the past that the insurgents were never able to speak with a unified voice, expressed concern about MARA Pattani, arguing that it was now in a stronger position to "internationalize" the conflict.[95]

An anonymous BRN leader in a rare interview in the Thai Muslim media organ, ISRA, was very explicit in laying out what the BRN really wanted from the talks: social justice.

> The BRN wants justice, in particular just treatment towards the Malay people by state authorities; education and jobs for the people in the restive region and a fair allocation of government jobs for Malay people or Thai Muslims. Krue Se and Tak Bai massacres are regarded by the BRN as a symbol of extreme injustice rendered against the Malay people by the government. . . . The Thai Muslims want the demands once made by the late Haji Surong Tohmeena to the Thai government. The demands include government's recognition of the culture and religion of the Thai Muslims, fair allocation of tax revenue for the region and fair sharing of government jobs for the local Thai Muslims. All of

these demands have never been realized. Injustice in various dimensions is the real root cause of the rebellion against the government by the Thai Muslims.[96]

And he made very clear why the BRN had been withholding its support to restart the peace talks: "BRN has refused to join the peace process with the government because the group does not trust the government that it will respond to their demands or honor its words given to the separatist groups."[97]

And he savaged the rest of MARA Pattani's membership, making clear that the grouping was forced on them by Malaysia, not something that the group endorsed. "It is pointless [for the BRN] to join with MARA Pattani that is mainly consisted of groups of people residing in Malaysia. If the government really wants peace it should talk with the people living in Thailand, in the three southernmost provinces not those living in exile abroad."[98]

A leaked Thai army assessment of the talks was surprisingly candid:

> Most operatives in the field don't agree with the peace talks because they don't believe this attempt is sustainable, and talking with military will only cause them to have disadvantages. . . . At present, the most problematic group is BRN. Some of the seniors/older generation agreed with the talks but they are fading out and their roles are not significant anymore. The other side of its military, which has been controlled by Sapaeing Basoe and Doonloh Waemahoh—including the youth—do not agree with the talks [and] believe they have the upper hand over the government in the fight, and the fight is not yet over. Also, their goal is independence, which conflicts with the peace talks.[99]

The junta leaders, however, remained optimistic, with a third round of talks held in Malaysia August 25–27. The government agreed to expand the number of panel members to ten to make MARA Pattani's representation more inclusive. And it made a rare offer of immunity for those members wanted by the Thai government.[100]

Although one of the government's key proposals was "justice for all," it made a total mockery of justice as talks began by deciding not to charge any security officer in a case in which a man was tortured to death while in detention.[101] The government proposed—though did not define—development as a goal. It also proposed the establishment of a "safety zone" in each province where both sides promised to refrain from violence. MARA Pattani rejected this.

For its part, MARA Pattani laid down three very reasonable demands, a radical departure from its previous intransigence: first, that the Thai government make the Deep South a priority on its national agenda; second, that the government recognize MARA Pattani as a legitimate organization and negotiating partner; and third, that the government guarantee immunity for MARA Pattani negotiators.[102]

Following the talks, MARA Pattani met the press for the first time. The group's chairman, Awang Jabat of the BRN, stated the group's objective. [103]

> Our principle is to find a solution through peaceful dialogue. We hope we can bring the conflict to an end and promote a lasting peace. MARA Patani is aimed at a peaceful mean of fighting. As for the current fights with forces and arms, we will need to reach a stage where both sides can stop such violent means, it is up to how we can build mutual understanding and trust. [104]

Awang said the group's main purpose was to "ensure that the rights and interests of the people of Pattani are heard, considered, discussed and fought for, consistently, systematically, and concretely." But he made clear that independence remains the primary objective: "The demand was not expressed in peace talks at this time, but it is the main agenda of our group." [105]

Yet all hope for talks were dashed in early September, when Gen. Prayuth rejected MARA Pattani's three very clear and fair preconditions for formal talks. [106] But at the same time, the government continued to say that it was open to proposals from MARA Pattani. "The peace team is willing to adjust to the demands of MARA Pattani. We can arrive at agreements on the negotiation table," Aksara said. [107] This was simply nonsensical and like all the other Orwellian doublespeak that people had come to expect from the junta.

In October, the BRN publicly denounced the peace process with the government, which it called "insincere " in a written statement.

> BRN is prepared to achieve peace through peaceful means. However, such a peace process must be dignified and sincere in its pursuit of peace. Not a peace process used as a form of political subterfuge in order to deceive and undermine the strategy of the Patani-Malay people's advancement. . . . Thailand has never accepted the fact that the root cause of the Patani problem is occupation and colonisation. For this reason, Thailand rejected the five conditions in its first negotiation with BRN. The Siamese Occupation seeks to assimilate and Siam-ize Malay people through an education system. [108]

Four members of the BRN's Information Department said that they had been authorized by the Dewan Pimpinan Party to meet with a longtime journalist and security analyst, Anth ony Davis. Due to the insincerity of the military government, they demanded international mediation.

> There are many aspects of this process that we see as unsettling and many of these things are caused by the fact the process bears no relation to the earlier peace process of 2013. We welcome Malaysian involvement in any peace process. But for Malaysia to be acting alone is insufficient. There needs to be other international actors involved as, bluntly speaking, we are deeply suspicious of any form of dialogue with the Thai government which does not involve the international community. We do not feel this is in any way a

peculiar position. Wherever there is political dialogue [between belligerents], you will find the involvement of the international community, be it in the shape of other states or international non-governmental organisations. This is normal. Any decline you see in military operations may be temporary and the party is evolving and growing. The proof of this is that after the military coup, this government went all out to pressure us, but we remain active. If anyone in the Thai military imagines this might all be over in a few years, I would simply urge them to wait and see.[109]

Incredulously, the Thai government doubted the authenticity of the public statement and the interview granted to Anthony Davis, stating that there were "inconsistencies."[110] Yet at the same time, they were angered by it. They called on the BRN to return to peace talks. The BRN refused, but the government proceeded, without three of the seven members, including the chairman.[111] The government again submitted its three-point proposal to establish "a safety zone" in each of the provinces, "areas for urgent development," and "an alternative justice process."[112] Yet the government did not elaborate on any of them.

In Thailand, the peace process has backslid as well due to the military's continued hold on politics since the May 2014 coup. The drafting of a new constitution that will restrict the power of parties and elected officials, while putting ultimate power in the hands of the military and nonelected elites, has been the overwhelming priority of Prime Minister Prayuth Chan-ocha and the junta. There are few signs that the military has any intention of surrendering power to democratically elected politicians, especially with the royal succession imminent. The government's strategy, letting the violence drop to acceptable levels such that it could be attributed to criminality, remained in place. Deep South Watch noted a 16 percent drop in violent incidents in 2015 compared with 2014.[113] However, violence increased in each of the first four months of 2016, leading to 230 more casualties.

In January 2016, the umbrella grouping MARA Pattani met with representatives of the Organization of the Islamic Conference (OIC), which reignited government concerns that the rebels were trying to internationalize the conflict rather than garner support for the peace process. The government received assurance from the OIC that the insurgency was a matter of internal affairs, yet the OIC pushed for immunity for MARA Pattani: "With MARA being stable and secure, then the peace process will also be able to expand as well. But if the peace process cannot be expanded . . . it will become brittle."[114]

At the end of January the Thai government sent a technical team to Kuala Lumpur to meet with MARA Pattani. The government agreed to give the group legal immunity and allow it to travel to peace talks.[115] In a rare news conference, The Thai negotiator, Lieutenant General Nakrob Bunbuathong denied setting preconditions that could undermine the negotiations before they start. "We never ask for an ultimatum that, 'You have to do a cease-fire first, then you can have the peace talks.'" But Nakrob stated the government's firm position that MARA Pattani could not raise the issue of political autonomy or that of an independent home state governed by *sharia*.[116] And still the government refused to recognize MARA Pattani as an entity for fear that the umbrella group would become too "institutionalized and internationalized," instead referring to them only as "Party B."[117]

On March 13, insurgents humiliated the government when some fifty militants took over a hospital in Narathiwat Province for several hours. The government ordered stepped-up patrols and presence in urban areas, while the Fourth Army commander called for a "suppression campaign." If the goal was to kill the peace process, it worked, though some analysts highly skeptical of the insurgents' interest in talks viewed the attack as more of an attempt to regroup and recruit.[118] General Aksara claimed the hospital attack was evidence of a power struggle within the movement and displayed the government's continued cognitive dissonance, believing that the Muslim population remained on the government's side; "If not with us then with who? Are there people on the other side?" and rhetorically questioning, "Is there a need for autonomy?"[119]

On April 27, the government met with MARA Pattani in Kuala Lumpur, but after a mere seventy-five minutes, the Thai side announced that Prime Minister Prayuth was "not ready" to agree to a framework for formal peace talks, known as the terms of reference (TOR).

The TOR was a painstakingly negotiated document that had eight articles that basically set the ground rules and the parameters for the resumption of formal peace talks, which had been frozen since 2013:

Article 1 outlined the background of the peace process and what had been agreed to through 2013.

Article 2 identified the dialogue "Party A" (Thailand) and "Party B" (MARA Pattani), as the government would not give formal recognition to the umbrella grouping or the BRN.

Article 3 detailed the role of the Malaysia, which would serve as a facilitator but not a mediator.

Article 4 addressed the formation of the technical working group(s).

Article 5 determined the geographical area that would be covered in the talks.

Article 6 covered administrative arrangements for the talks.

Article 7 dealt with the sensitive issue of "Security Facilitation," protection for "Party B" and their right of free passage.

Article 8 included amendments and modifications.[120]

The Thai government ceded little in this agreement, yet it was too sensitive for the junta's approval. The insurgents made clear their disappointment:

"The TOR endorsement by the Party A is a much awaited signal to reflect party A's sincerity and commitment at this confidence building stage, so that the process can move forward."

But what really concerned MARA Pattani was the sacking of the head of the Thai team, Lieutenant General Nakrob, who was the original negotiator of the TOR. "He was the 'engine' of the Thai team who is knowledgeable and well-versed of the peace process. He headed the Technical Team of Party A," MARA's Abu Hafez said. "His absence was felt and has considerably affected the process," as he was one of the few Thai army officials who had built up some degree of trust with the BRN rebels. [121]

The mercurial prime minister, who had previously complained that the situation in the South had made him "moody," publicly warned the media to not criticize the government over the stalled peace process and that any such criticism could be "illegal." He warned that the government could not negotiate with "lawbreakers" and that the only way forward for talks would be if the violence ceased. [122] On May 7, 2016, the National Security Council convened a cabinet meeting to review and unilaterally redraft the TOR. [123]

Despite all this, senior Thai military officials continued to assert that the talks were "still on" and that the the rebels should deem the government's efforts as sincere. [124] But in the current political context, when the Thai military is trying to centralize political power in Bangkok, neutralizing political parties and elected officials, stifling civil society and the media, committing egregious human rights abuses with no checks on its power, and trying to inculcate "Thai values" and Buddhist nationalism, it is impossible to see any movement on the peace process. The junta is trying to lessen the violence to acceptable levels so that it will have no pressure to make any concessions. And any movement is done to simply go through the motions, more for the sake of assuaging the Malaysian government than making any serious attempt at finding a durable political solution.

4. ASSESSMENT

The Thai position on the talks is condescending and insincere. It needs the appearance of talks without making any meaningful concessions to BRN demands. Thus, it is no surprise that the talks are going nowhere. The insurgents will show up, but only because Malaysia forces them to do so. But no insurgent or CSO affiliate whom I have interviewed believes that there is anything on offer for them in exchange for laying down their arms. Most will sit it out in the hopes that a future democratically elected government will offer them more, although any future democratic government is going to be highly constrained by unelected elites, the military, the judiciary, and independent bodies.

For now, six structural impediments bar any sort of durable political solution.

The Political Situation Is Not Conducive to Peace, nor Will It Be for a Long Time

It is hard to imagine the peace process moving forward under the current political situation. Since the May 2014 coup, the junta, through its installed legislature, has drafted a constitution that concentrates power not only in Bangkok but in the hands of unelected royalist and military elites at the expense of political parties and the electorate. Yet it was deemed so democratic and threatening to the military and ultramonarchists that it was scrapped.

The interim charter lays out nine principles that the permanent constitution must endorse, the first of which is that the kingdom is one and indivisible. The Thai state will be unitary and inviolable, which precludes any type of political autonomy or devolution of powers, however limited. The National Reconciliation Committee's chief was clear: "The new charter must reflect traditional pillars of Thai society," that is, the monarchy, the military, and Buddhism.

The current system is all checks and no balance. The military's "roadmap" to the restoration of "democracy" is set for mid 2017, but few political analysts expect that to occur. The military is determined to hold onto power with the passing of the monarch in order to oversee the royal succession. And even then, what the military defines as "democracy" will have little bearing with a majoritarian form of government in which an electoral mandate assures the right to govern. Politics will remain highly constrained by unelected elites who wield ultimate authority and are able to interfere with or usurp democratic governance when "national security"—undefined—is threatened.

With the military's stranglehold on politics, it is all but impossible to see the military making any meaningful concessions in peace talks. T he junta 's track record since the May 22 coup has been completely uncompromising in every sphere. Why should we expect the NCPO to make any concessions on an issue that the army has thwarted civilian leaders from making over the past ten years? Indeed, in November 2014, then RTA chief Gen. Udomdej announced his willingness to reconsider the BRN's five demands, which he then immediately rejected.

The military refused implementation of most concessions, such as the use of the Malay language as well as other modest reforms. The Thai government will never allow a formal and legal *sharia* court system. It is unlikely to even allow "Malay" to be listed as an ethnic group on the national identification card. The army has refused to implement a general amnesty. Proposed amnesties have been so highly conditioned that few insurgents trust them. The military rejected the BRN's April 2013 demand for a release of everyone detained on security-related charges. [125]

Nor is there any political pressure on the junta to make concessions. With the National Legislative Assembly and all the key ministries responsible for security firmly in the military's hands, it is under no political pressure to make concessions. Democracy is suspended, so even if there were popular pressure for a peace process, it cannot be manifested.

Deep-Seated Prejudices Remain

Thais remain largely prejudiced toward the Malay of the south and still believe that they are the only minority group that has really failed to assimilate into Thai society. They will not accept any responsibility for what the Malay believe to be historical wrongs or the concept of a Pattani "ancestral domain," as was a cornerstone of the 2014 Philippine agreement with the Moro Islamic Liberation Front. The BRN included the recognition of the "rights of the Malayu Pattani peoples to Pattani land" in its April 2013 demands; this was rejected outright by the army. [126] The government is, likewise, unwilling to meet the BRN's demand that it be deemed a "liberation movement" rather than a "secessionist group" as the former suggests that the BRN has legitimate grievances and that the south is under occupation.

And while this is a small example, it is certainly telling. In 2015, ISOC spent twenty million baht making a feel-good movie about the Deep South, *The Sixth Latitude*, the story of a young Malay woman who falls in love with a Thai soldier. The actress playing the Muslim woman is a former Miss Thailand, who is of course Thai, not Malay. [127] On top of that is the whole crisis, deeply felt in the south, of routine sexual harassment by Thai soldiers of local women that has gone totally unrecognized by the government.

There Will Be No Transitional Justice Mechanisms and the Culture of Impunity Is Too Deeply Rooted

Likewise, it seems unreasonable to countenance the establishment of a transitional justice mechanism to investigate human rights abuses committed by the military, which has operated under a culture of impunity since 2004. The government has rarely waived immunity for its troops except in the most egregious cases and done little to investigate allegations of abuse, including the National Human Rights Commission's findings that 75 percent of torture complaints were filed in the south between 2007 and 2013. [128] Security forces have no accountability, and the government has not countenanced any type of transitional justice mechanism. As the Asia Foundation lamented in a 2015 op-ed:

With the ongoing conflict in the deep South, it is hard to see how transitional justice will change local views towards the state. Providing reparations, with 7.5 million baht now given per victim, is seen by many as an attempt to co-opt dissidents. The government's security approach since the May 2014 coup, where the military outsources security work to local villagers and hunts down militants, has lessened violence, with recorded incidents plunging from 1,298 in 2013 to 793 in 2014. But it provides little room for transitional justice. [129]

The role of civil society and journalists has been hampered, especially since the 2014 coup but even before, with extrajudicial killings (EJKs) and disappearances of activists. Malay Muslim civil society activists whom I have interviewed have all experienced routine harassment, threats, raids, and arrests.

Indeed, in a single month, December 2015, four major legal cases and or court rulings reinforced the sense that the Thai state acts with total impunity and that the rights and interests of the Malay are barely a consideration of the government. All four cases set a bleak precedent for the peace process and reinforce the sense that there can never be justice for the Malay community.

On December 4, 2015, a forty-two-year-old Malay man became the fifth suspected insurgent to die in military custody since 2004. Abdullayi Dorloh had been arrested on November 11 and was thought to be a fairly senior commander. Although an inquest found no signs of physical trauma, it found unexplained blood drops. [130] No charges have ever been filed against any of the military interrogators.

On December 19, a civil court in Bangkok ruled in favor of the Anti-Money Laundering Office and ordered the transfer to the state of the fourteen-*rai* plot owned by a family who ran a small *pondok*, the Jihad Witaya School, in Pattani's Muang District. The government shut down the school in May 2005 after the government alleged the Islamic school was a training ground for insurgents. [131]

On December 29, the Supreme Court upheld the acquittals of five policeman linked to the 2004 disappearance of Muslim human rights lawyer Somchai Neelapaijit, who headed the Muslim Attorney Centre, which provided pro bono legal assistance to suspected insurgents. [132] In 2006, one policeman was found guilty of a minor charge of "coercion"; the other four were acquitted. In 2011, an appeals court acquitted all five. The Supreme Court ruled that the testimony of witnesses was contradictory, but more importantly, it ruled that the cell phone logs that tied the police to one another (seventy-five calls the day of Somchai's disappearance but none before or after) as well as calls to the prime minister's office were not admissible. The court, adding insult to injury, ruled that Somchai's family could not even file a case on his behalf because there is no proof that he is actually dead; this is despite prime minister Thaksin Shinawatra's 2006 admission that Somchai had been killed.

That same day, the Supreme Court overturned two lower court rulings that had acquitted five suspected insurgents in the 2006 killing of a policeman in Pattani, sentencing one to life in prison and the other four to between thirteen and thirty-three years in prison.[133]

Three human rights groups issued a report in January 2016, which states that the incidences of torture of insurgent suspects by Thai security forces has doubled since the May 2014 coup. And while complaints were filed against forty-eight military officers and thirteen police officers for allegedly committing torture and ill treating suspects, no one has been held accountable.[134]

The Thai army denounced the report as a "publicity stunt" ahead of the visit by the OIC head. "Our legal team is verifying the allegations and will discuss the matter with the NGOs. They should have consulted us first. The timing is dubious, given that they have raised unfounded allegations at an international forum before," said Col. Pramote Prom-in, spokesman for the Internal Security Operations Command in the south. And sadly, the spokesman seems to at least acknowledge that mistreatment has happened in the

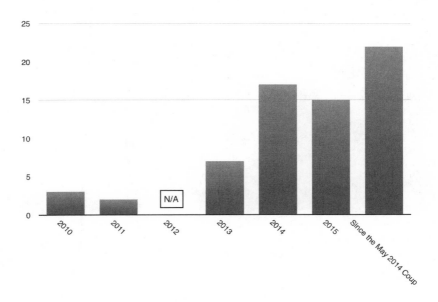

Figure 4.6.   Incidents of Alleged Torture by Government Security Forces of Suspected Malay Insurgents. Source: Cross Cultural Foundation, the Patani Human Rights Network, and Duay Jai, via Prachathai, at http://prachatai.com/english/node/5754

past: "But these [torture] allegations are old stories, we've adjusted ourselves over the years."[135]

No Third-Party Involvement Will Be Accepted

The military-controlled government will countenance no third-party involvement. It cannot accept anything that infringes upon its sovereignty, though no peace process has been successful without some degree of third-party involvement. The junta largely mistrusts foreign NGOs and gives them no space to operate, run back channels, or means of conducting Track II diplomacy.

The government has repeatedly shunted aside calls for the OIC to play a greater role in mediating the peace process. The government believes that giving the OIC a role would be to play into the insurgents' hands by "internationalizing" the conflict. The government has tried to interfere to prevent any such meetings. The irony, of course, is that the OIC has already given in to Thailand's demands that this is an "internal" matter.[136] Moreover, the OIC's perceived lack of support for the militants has been a real irritant. Indeed, the OIC has made three missions to the Deep South in 2007, 2012, and January 2016. And in 2012, militants increased the violence during the OIC mission after the fifty-seven-member group condemned the militancy's targeting and gave the government its support.[137] Once the peace talks resumed, the BRN demanded that the OIC be an official observer, but the Thai government never accepted that, nor did the OIC push for it.[138] Although the Thai government failed to prevent a meeting between the OIC and MARA Pattani in January 2015, after lobbying the Malaysian government, Gen. Aksara brushed aside any threat posed by the OIC mission: "OIC has supported us in the peace talk process and understood that it is an internal affair in which the OIC will not intrude."[139]

The Malaysian role in southern Thailand has obviously been complex. On the one hand, Malaysia accepts the territorial integrity and sovereignty of Thailand. But on the other hand, it feels some degree of obligation for the treatment of the ethnic Malay. As Malaysia has become more Islamically oriented and political, Islam has become a major factor in national politics, so it is now politically costly to be seen as not doing enough for the Malays in southern Thailand. Yet the Malaysian government garners far more benefits from having a cooperative relationship with Bangkok. Malaysian security officials have long kept tabs on the separatists who operate and live in Malaysia, including keeping many of the top leaders on their payroll. The Malaysian External Intelligence Organization, which reports directly to the prime minister's office, has been the key facilitator for almost every round of peace talks. Malaysian authorities have arrested Thai insurgents but are clearly fearful of cracking down on their operations.

Thai authorities, especially under the government of prime minister Thaksin, routinely accused Malaysia of allowing the insurgents to use its territory for training and sanctuary, although no sufficient evidence of large training camps in Malaysia has ever existed. But insurgents routinely cross the border for work, coordination and meetings, and to lie low. Indeed, the ongoing dispute over dual citizenship is the biggest irritant in the relationship between the two countries, the Thai government calling on Malaysia to end its practice of recognizing dual nationality.

Thai authorities believe that Malaysia turns a blind eye to insurgents' use of their country for sanctuary. Malaysian authorities certainly could crack down more, but they do have "red lines." They countenance no trade in illegal narcotics by the insurgents, and when they have active intelligence about bomb making or other caches of weaponry, they conduct raids and make arrests. But there are limits to what they will do. Malaysian authorities are clearly concerned about the potential for any blowback should they crack down on insurgents in their territory severely enough to satisfy the Thai government.

The Thai government has allowed Malaysia to serve as a facilitator for the talks but has made very clear its complete opposition to anything beyond that role. Malaysia has no chance of serving as a mediator, though third-party training sessions for the insurgents are quietly held in Malaysian territory. The reality is that Malaysia is a stakeholder, not a neutral broker. With so many militants living and meeting in Malaysia, the Thai government finds it difficult to view Malaysia as impartial. Malaysia shares Bangkok's interest in the insurgency's not expanding, but as long as it stays low level and concentrated and poses no threat to Malaysia, Putrajaya will not be willing to expend the requisite political and diplomatic capital.

No Legal Off-Ramp for the Militants Is Available

The government's and military's fundamental mistrust of the Malay community has circumscribed the development of their civil society and political arms. Very simply, the military views any Muslim civil society arm or political organization to be a de facto arm of the insurgency. Extensive author interviews with members of fourteen Muslim Malay civil society organizations in October and November 2014 made this abundantly clear. All respondents found the government to assume that they were an arm of the insurgency. All denied it, either citing their dislike of violence or the limitations of force. Others spoke of the danger posed by being affiliated with the insurgency: "The state believes that this is very coordinated. The state looks for the links. We can't afford to show that there is any link [between us and the insurgents], because the state isn't open minded." But many simply were angered at the insurgents' underdeveloped political arm and political operations. These CSO leaders argued that even with government constraints, threats, and coercion, they were far better able to achieve tangible goals for the Malay community. But the military government believes that its continued repression and restrictions on civil society has been able to limit the insurgency from becoming more broad-based.

And while many were angry at the insurgents' lack of a political platform, they understood that the real cause for this was the the refusal of the Thai state to give them any political space: "It's going to be a big challenge for the Thai state to accept the BRN as a legitimate political actor." In short, the government offers no legal off-ramp for the militants or their supporters. Civil society is highly curtailed and restricted, and the possibility that the BRN would be allowed to transform itself into a legal political movement to articulate the interests of the Malay community is unlikely to happen in the near term.

The Decline in Violence Reinforces the Government's Belief That No Concessions Are Really Necessary

Finally, the military really feels that it does not need to make any concessions as the level of violence in 2015 was the lowest in twelve years of conflict. According to Deep South Watch, 2015 saw only 674 incidents of violence, a 16 percent drop from 2014. According to the organization's data set, only 246 people were killed in 2015, a sharp drop from 341 the previous year.[140] SBPAC asserts that the number of "red" villages—plagued by violence—has fallen from 319 in 2014 to 136 in 2015. In that same period of time, the number of "yellow" villages has fallen from 517 to 283, and the number of "green" villages, which have experienced no violence, has climbed from 1,160 to 1,600.[141]

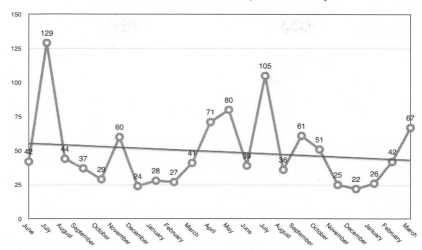

Figure 4.7.   Total Monthly Casualties since the 22 May 2014 Coup d'Etat.
Source: **Author's open source dataset.**

This has given the military the luxury to pursue its agenda, which has always been to minimize the level of violence to the point that it can ascribe it to routine criminality, without having had to make any concession. As one civil society activist put it: "They still think in terms of conflict management rather than conflict resolution."[142]

In sum, the Thai side is hoping to enter any future talks from such a position of strength that any concessions are completely unnecessary. Its conception of peace talks is that the militants show up and surrender, with no political solution reached or concessions made.

A political solution is unlikely to be reached until at least ten years after King Bhumipol dies. It will take that long to accomplish a political transformation that will allow democracy to take root and a peace process to move forward. Democracy can in no way withstand the power of two conservative and antidemocratic political institutions, the crown and the military. Only when the monarchy is fundamentally weakened and discredited will civilian governance have a fighting chance. At the same time, Thai ethnochauvinism is skyrocketing, with the junta's inculcation of twelve core Thai values and slavish obeisance to the monarchy enforced through the draconian *lèse-majesté* provisions (Article 112 of the penal code). Buddhist fascism, similar to what emerged in Myanmar and was a leading force in the anti-Rohingya and Muslim pogroms in 2014–2015, is starting to take root in Thailand. While the junta fortunately quickly silenced one radical monk under royal patronage who called for arson to a mosque for every monk killed by insurgents, one prominent commentator warned, "We should be worried . . . of mainstream clergy's descent deeper into bigotry and ultra-nationalism."[143] In that context, it is impossible for me to see how a lasting peace process that addresses the needs and aspirations of the Malay community could take root. If anything, there is instead a growing sense of alienation.

NOTES

1. This section is drawn from Zachary Abuza, *Conspiracy of Silence: The Insurgency in Southern Thailand* (Washington, DC: US Institute of Peace, 2008).
2. Wan Kadir Che Man, *Muslim Separatism: The Moros of the Southern Philippines and the Malays of Southern Thailand* (Singapore: Oxford University Press, 1990), 34.
3. For more, see Thongchai Winichakul, *Siam Mapped* (Bangkok: Silkworm, 1997).
4. Barbara Watson Andaya and Leonard Y. Andaya, *A History of Malaysia*, 2nd ed. (Honolulu: University of Hawaii Press, 2001), 110–12.
5. Andaya and Andaya, *A History of Malaysia*, 111.
6. The 1921 Compulsory Primary Education Act. See Wan Kadir, *Muslim Separatism*, 64.
7. Wan Kadir, *Muslim Separatism*, 64.
8. Nantawan Haemindra, "The Problem of Muslims in the Four Southern Provinces of Thailand," *Journal of Southeast Asian Studies* 7, no. 2 (1976): 208–25; Pasuk Phongpaichit and Chris Baker, *Thailand: Economy and Politics* (New York: Oxford University Press, 1995), 270.
9. A petition signed by half the adult Muslim population was submitted to the United Nations requesting inclusion in the new Federation of Malaya. See Duncan McCargo, "Southern Thai Politics: Some Preliminary Observations," (Polis Working Paper No. 3, University of Leeds, 2004), 6; Wan Kadir, *Muslim Separatism*, 65–66.
10. S. Dorloh, "Enforcement of Shar'iah in Thailand: Islamic Family and Inheritance Laws in Southern Provinces," in *Proceedings of the International Seminar on "Islam and Democracy: The Southeast Asian Experience*, ed. Hussin Mutalib (Singapore: Konrad Adenaur Foundation, 2004), 58.
11. For more, see International Crisis Group, "Southern Thailand: Insurgency, Not Jihad" (Asia Report no. 98, May 18, 2005), 5–6; Thanet Aphornsuwan, "Origins of Malay-Muslim 'Separatism' in Southern Thailand" (Working Paper Series No. 32, Asia Research Institute, Singapore, 2004).
12. Phongpaichit and Baker, *Thailand: Economy and Politics*, 292.
13. Chaiwat Satha-Anand, *Islam and Violence: A Case Study of Violent Events in the Four Southern Provinces, Thailand, 1976–1981* (USF Monographs in Religion and Public Policy No. 2, University of Southern Florida, Tampa, 1987), 13.
14. Phongpaichit and Baker, *Thailand: Economy and Politics*, 292. Also see Astri Suhrke, "Irredentism Contained: The Thai Muslim Case," *Comparative Politics* 7, no.2 (1975): 187–203; Suhrke, "Loyalists and Separatists: The Muslims in Southern Thailand," *Asian Survey* 57 (1977): 237–50; Surin Pitsuwan, "Elites, Conflicts and Violence: Conditions in the Southern Border Provinces," *Asian Review* 1 (1987): 83–96.
15. Chaiwat, *Islam and Violence*, 14.
16. See Wan Kadir, *Muslim Separatism*; Syed Serajul Islam, "The Islamic Independence Movements in Pattani in Thailand and Mindanao of the Philippines," *Asian Survey* 38, no. 5 (May 1998): 441–56.
17. Joseph Liow, "The Security Situation in Southern Thailand: Toward an Understanding of Domestic and International Dimensions," *Studies in Conflict and Terrorism* 27, no. 6 (2004): 541.
18. PULO, "The Year of National Reorganization (1998–1999)," http://www.pulo.org/reorg.html.
19. Liow, "The Security Situation in Southern Thailand," 534.

20. Muhamad Ayub Pathan, "Insurgency Claimed 6,543 Lives in Last 12 Years," *Bangkok Post*, January 4, 2016, http://www.bangkokpost.com/news/security/815372/insurgency-claimed-6543-lives-in-last-12-years.

21. "Interesting Facts and Figures about the Deep South for the Past 12 Years," IsraNews, January 4, 2016, http://linkis.com/www.isranews.org/sou/uLRBg.

22. "Army Chief Will End Southern Violence with Peacefu Solutions," MCOT.net, October 15, 2014, http://www.mcot.net/site/content?id=543e279cbe0470764e8b456c#.VD7yGEvcqlI.

23. "Turning Back the Clock: Thailand's 2015 Constitution," Prachatai, http://prachatai.org/english/node/4825?utm_source=dlvr.it.

24. CSO activist interviewed by the author, Pattani City, February 12, 2015.

25. Robert B. Albritton, "The Muslim South in the Context of the Thai Nation" (unpublished manuscript, November 2007), 15.

26. Alan Dawson, "The Big Issue: Cleansing the Deep South," *Bangkok Post*, April 13, 2014, http://www.bangkokpost.com/news/security/404789/the-big-issue-cleansing-the-deep-south.

27. "Widow Holds Out in War-Torn Village," *Bangkok Post*, October 8, 2013, http://www.bangkokpost.com/news/local/373661/lone-buddhist-widow-holds-out-in-war-torn-thai-village.

28. Gen. Aksara Kerdphol, Chief of Staff and Secretary of the Internal Security Operations Command, National Council for Peace and Order, "Resolving the Problems in the Southernmost Provinces in Thailand: Policies of General Prayut Chan-o-cha Head of National Council of Peace and Order," September 2014.

29. World Population Review's data on Thailand, http://worldpopulationreview.com/countries/thailand-population/; "Thailand," in *The World Factbook* (Washington, DC: CIA, continually updated), https://www.cia.gov/library/publications/the-world-factbook/geos/th.html.

30. "Malaysian, Thai Leaders Discuss Border Unrest," *Bangkok Post*, February 21, 2012, http://m.bangkokpost.com/news/280756.

31. "Govt Quietly Studies South," *Bangkok Post*, March 8, 2012, http://www.bangkokpost.com/opinion/opinion/283367/govt-quietly-studies-south.

32. King-oua Laohong, "Deep South Governance Bill Criticised," *Bangkok Post*, March 19, 2012, http://www.bangkokpost.com/news/security/284927/deep-south-governance-bill-criticised.

33. King-oua Laohong, "SBPAC Denies Talks with Rebels, *Bangkok Post*, April 4, 2012, http://www.bangkokpost.com/news/local/287326/sbpac-denies-talks-with-rebels.

34. "Talks On with Insurgent Groups: Yuthasak," *The Nation* (Thailand), August 17, 2012, http://www.nationmultimedia.com/politics/Talks-on-with-insurgent-groups-Yuthasak-30188524.html.

35. "Text of the Agreement between Thailand and the BRN," *Bangkok Post*, February 28, 2013, http://www.bangkokpost.com/news/security/338175/general-consensus-on-peace-dialogue-process.

36. Wassana Nanuam, "NSC Reveals Talk with BRN," *Bangkok Post*, March 6, 2013, http://www.bangkokpost.com/news/security/339124/nsc-reveals-talk-with-brn.

37. "Prayuth: Insurgents Must Stop Violence First," *Bangkok Post*, March 14, 2013, http://www.bangkokpost.com/news/local/340498/army-chief-prayuth-insurgents-must-show-sincerity.

38. Nakarin Chinnawornkomol, "BRN Wants Troops out of Far South," *The Nation* (Thailand), March 27, 2013, http://www.nationmultimedia.com/national/BRN-wants-troops-out-of-far-South-30202810.html.

39. Wassana Nanuam, "BRN Demands Release of All Prisoners," *Bangkok Post*, March 29, 2013, http://www.bangkokpost.com/news/local/342861/brn-demands-release-of-all-prisoners.

40. Wassana Nanuam and Muhammad Ayub Pathan, "Paradorn to Endorse Pact with BRN on Talks," *Bangkok Post*, March 6, 2013, http://www.bangkokpost.com/news/security/338980/paradorn-to-endorse-pact-with-brn-on-talks.

41. "Missing Cop Acquitted in Somchai Case," *Bangkok Post*, March 11, 2013, http://www.bangkokpost.com/breakingnews/339883/missing-cop-acquitted-in-somchai-case. In De-

cember 2015, the Thai Supreme Court upheld the verdict. No one has ever been brought to justice for Somchai's disappearance.

42. "Security Chief: Still Too Early for Dialogue to Stop Southern Violence," MCOT.net, March 30, 2013, http://www.mcot.net/site/content?id=51565d76150ba0842b0000f4#. UVgfAb9kLWE.

43. "Deputy Governor, Senior Official Killed in Yala Blast," *The Nation* (Thailand), April 5, 2013, http://www.nationmultimedia.com/national/Deputy-governor-senior-official-killed-in-Yala-bla-30203493.html.

44. "NSC: Peace Talks Not Derailed by Yala Officials' Deaths," *Bangkok Post*, April 5, 2013, http://www.bangkokpost.com/news/local/344130/yala-officials-deaths-won-t-stop-peace-talks.

45. Achara Ashayagachat, Residents Back Peace Talks in Poll," *Bangkok Post*, April 18, 2013, http://www.bangkokpost.com/news/security/345788/residentsback-peace-talks-in-poll.

46. "Pengistiharan Barisan Revolusi Nasional Melayu Patani," YouTube video, 3:44, posted by "Muhammad Abdullah," April 26, 2013, http://www.youtube.com/watch?v=3XzxHyvRu1U&feature=player_embedded.

47. Wassana Nanuam, "BRN YouTube Clip Threatens Talks," *Bangkok Post*, April 29, 2013, http://www.bangkokpost.com/news/security/347469/brn-demands-hard-to-believe.

48. Nanuam, "BRN YouTube Clip."

49. Pakorn Puengnetr, "Little Real Progress Seen in BRN Talks," *The Nation* (Thailand), May 1, 2013, http://www.nationmultimedia.com/national/Little-real-progress-seen-in-BRN-talks-30205187.html; Abdulloh Benjakat and Wassana Nanuam, "5 People, Baby Slain in Pattani Shooting," *Bangkok Post*, May 2, 2013, http://www.bangkokpost.com/breakingnews/347975/5-people-baby-slain-in-pattani-shooting.

50. "Pengistiharan Barisan Revolusi Nasional Melayu Patani."

51. Nanuam, "BRN YouTube Clip."

52. Veera Prateepchaikul, "BRN's Latest Video Clip Provocative," *Bangkok Post*, May 31, 2013, http://www.bangkokpost.com/opinion/opinion/352795/brn-latest-video-clip-provocative; "Talks to Go Ahead Despite BRN YouTube Video," *The Nation* (Thailand), May 27, 2013, http://www.nationmultimedia.com/national/Talks-to-go-ahead-despite-BRN-YouTube-video-30206954.html.

53. "Peace Talks 'behind Surge in Violence,'" *The Nation* (Thailand), May 28, 2013, http://www.nationmultimedia.com/national/Peace-talks-behind-surge-in-violence-30207086.html.

54. Waedao Harai, "Southern Imams Demand 'Peaceful Ramadan,'" *Bangkok Post*, June 9, 2013, http://www.bangkokpost.com/archive/southern-imams-demand-peaceful-ramadan/354223.

55. "Insurgents Agree to Suspend Violence during Ramadan," *The Nation* (Thailand), June 14, 2013, http://www.nationmultimedia.com/national/Insurgents-agree-to-suspend-violence-during-Ramada-30208298.html; Wassana Nanuam, "BRN to Reduce Violence for Ramadan," *Bangkok Post*, June 13, 2013, http://www.bangkokpost.com/breakingnews/354966/brn-to-end-violence-during-ramadan-with-conditions-in-exchange.

56. "Security Chief: BRN Can Alleviate Violence during Holy Month," MCOT.net, June 14, 2013, http://www.mcot.net/site/content?id=51baf72e150ba0a602000292#.UbsWZJU5R94.

57. Achara Ashayagachat, "BRN Negotiator Gives First Media Interview," *Bangkok Post*, June 19, 2013, http://www.bangkokpost.com/news/local/355906/five-demands-remain-focus-of-peace-talks-says-brn-negotiator-hassan-taib.

58. Ashayagachat, "BRN Negotiator Gives First Media Interview."

59. "BRN Demands Troop Withdrawal as Condition for Ramadan Ceasefire," *Bangkok Post*, June 25, 2013, http://www.bangkokpost.com/news/local/356831/troops-out-alcohol-ban-for-ramadan-among-new-conditions-set-for-peace-talks.

60. Wassana Nanuam, "The BRN's Giant Bluff," *Bangkok Post*, June 26, 2013, http://www.bangkokpost.com/news/security/356911/the-brn-giant-bluff.

61. Wassana Nanuam, "Ramadan Ceasefire Hopes Fade," *Bangkok Post*, June 25, 2013, http://www.bangkokpost.com/news/security/356896/ramadan-ceasefire-unlikely-after-unacceptable-brn-demands.

62. Nanuam, "Ramadan Ceasefire Hopes Fade."

63. "Ramadan Peace Initiative 2013," *Bangkok Post*, July 12, 2013, http://www. bangkokpost.com/news/security/359594/ramadan-peace-initiative-2013; "South Ceasefire in Place," *Bangkok Post*, July 13, 2013, http://www.bangkokpost.com/news/security/359625/ south-ceasefire-in-place; "Ramadan Truce Hailed as a Positive Step for Peace Dialogue," *The Nation* (Thailand), July 14, 2013, http://www.nationmultimedia.com/national/Ramadan-truce-hailed-as-a-positive-step-for-peace--30210359.html.

64. The text of the agreement can be found at "Ramadan Peace Initiative 2013," *Bangkok Post*, July 12, 2013, http://www.bangkokpost.com/news/security/359594/ramadan-peace-initiative-2013.

65. "Govt Not Breaching South Ceasefire Pact: Paradorn," *Bangkok Post*, July 21, 2013, http://www.bangkokpost.com/news/security/360840/govt-not-breaching-south-ceasefire-pact-paradorn.

66. "Paradorn Downplays Truce Violence," *Bangkok Post*, July 26, 2013, http://www. bangkokpost.com/breakingnews/361576/paradorn-downplays-truce-violence.

67. "NSC: South Talks Will Continue," *Bangkok Post*, August 10, 2013, http://www. bangkokpost.com/breakingnews/364014/southern-peace-talks-not-derailed-insists-nsc.

68. "Panel to Vet BRN Demands," *Bangkok Post*, August 13, 2013, http://www. bangkokpost.com/news/local/364298/government-rethinks-brn-demands.

69. "Panel to Vet BRN Demands."

70. "Prayuth Calls BRN Terms Unacceptable," *Bangkok Post*, August 20, 2013, http:// www.bangkokpost.com/news/security/365425/prayuth-calls-brn-terms-unacceptable.

71. http://www.nst.com.my/latest/malaysia-and-thailand-renew-commitment-for-co-operation-dpm-1.342344?cache=03%2F7.202804%2F7.221245%2F7.280225%2F7. 288063%2F7.330034%2F7.330034%2F7.330034%3Fpage%3D0.

72. Wassana Nanuam and Waedao Harai, "Government to Discuss BRN's Demands," *Bangkok Post* , August 24, 2013, http://www.bangkokpost.com/news/security/366121/ government-mulls-brn-demands.

73. "BRN Rebels Blamed for Yala School Bomb," *Bangkok Post*, September 10, 2013, http://www.bangkokpost.com/news/security/369021/yala-bomb-kills-two-soldiers-and-wounds-young-student.

74. "Fierce Battle Leaves Six Dead in South," *Bangkok Post*, October 6, 2013, http://www. bangkokpost.com/news/local/373185/fierce-battle-leaves-six-dead-in-south.

75. Jeerapong Prasertponkrung, Supitcha Rattana, and Nakharin Chinnavornkomon, "Two More Groups to Join Peace Talks This Month: NSC," *The Nation* (Thailand), October 2, 2013, http://www.nationmultimedia.com/national/Two-more-groups-to-join-peace-talks-this-month-NSC-30216087.html.

76. Wassana Nanuam and Achara Ashayagachat, "NSC Postpones Peace Talks Indefinitely," *Bangkok Post*, October 11, 2013, http://www.bangkokpost.com/news/security/374085/nsc-postpones-peace-talks-indefinitely.

77. "Peace Talks on Thailand's Southern Unrest Postponed Indefinitely," MCOT.net, October 11, 2013, http://mcot-web.mcot.net/mcot-testing /site/content?id=525759bd150ba0a47c000050#. UlfwMhY5R94.

78. Wassana Nanuam, "NSC Speaking to the 'Wrong' Insurgents," *Bangkok Post*, November 29, 2013, http://www.bangkokpost.com/news/security/382198/nsc-speaking-to-the-wrong-insurgents-says-former-bersatu-leader.

79. Kultida Samabuddhi, "Hassan Sets New Demands on Peace Talks," *Bangkok Post*, December 2, 2013, http://www.bangkokpost.com/news/security/382618/hassan-sets-new-demands-on-peace-talks.

80. Indeed, on February 28, Thai National Security Council chief Lt. Gen. Paradorn said, "Credit should be given to former prime minister Pol. Lt. Col. Thaksin Shinawatra. Without his private talks with Malaysian Prime Minister Najib Razak, Malaysia would not help us to make today happen." Wassana Nanuam, "NSC: Talks with Separatists in 2 Weeks," *Bangkok Post*, February 28, 2013," http://www.bangkokpost.com/news/security/338137/nsc-chief-says-talks-with-separatists-start-in-2-weeks.

81. "Talks with Insurgents to Continue," Bangkok Post, July 2, 2014, http://www. bangkokpost.com/most-recent/418507/peace-talks-process-witjh-insurgents-will-be-changed-

says-ncpo; "Shed Light on South Policy," *Bangkok Post*, July 2, 2014, http://www.bangkokpost.com/opinion/opinion/418445/shed-light-on-south-policy.

82. "Special Team to Malaysia to Discuss Resumption of Peace Dialogue," IsraNews, August 26, 2014, http://www.isranews.org/south-news/english-article/item/32394-peacetalk_32394.html; Wassana Nanuam, Aksara Heads Southern Talks Team, *Bangkok Post*, October 24, 2014, http://www.bangkokpost.com/news/security/439430/aksara-heads-southern-talks-team.

83. Achara Ashayagachat, "Separatists Pan Head of South Talks," *Bangkok Post*, September 8, 2014, http://www.bangkokpost.com/news/security/431016/separatists-pan-head-of-south-talks.

84. "'Period of Non-violence Must for Peace' in South," *The Nation* (Thailand), December 2, 2014, http://www.nationmultimedia.com/politics/Period-of-non-violence-must-for-peace-in-South-30248986.html; "Thailand Recognises Malaysia's Role in Southern Thailand Peace Process—Najib," Bernama, December 1, 2014, http://www.bernama.com/bernama/v7/newsindex.php?id=1089807; Achara Ashayagachat, "Prayuth Talks Peace amid Protests," *Bangkok Post*, December 1, 2014, http://www.bangkokpost.com/news/security/446472/Prayuth-talks-peace-amid-protests; "Gimmicks Won't Work in the South," *The Nation* (Thailand), December 5, 2014, http://www.nationmultimedia.com/opinion/Gimmicks-wont-work-in-the-South-30249138.html.

85. "'Period of Non-violence Must for Peace' in South"; "Thailand Recognises Malaysia's Role in Southern Thailand Peace Process—Najib."

86. Wassana Nanuam, "Malaysia Asked to Track Dual Citizens," *Bangkok Post*, December 2, 2014, http://www.bangkokpost.com/news/security/446712/malaysia-asked-to-track-dual-citizens.

87. Wassana Nanuam and Waedao Harai, "Negotiators Ask Malaysia to Find Rebels," *Bangkok Post*, December 17, 2014, http://www.bangkokpost.com/news/security/450273/negotiators-ask-malaysia-to-find-rebels.

88. Patsara Jikkham, "PM Oulines Steps for South Talks," *Bangkok Post*, January 28, 2015, http://www.bangkokpost.com/news/security/461196/pm-outlines-steps-for-south-talks.

89. Patsara Jikkham, "NSC: South Peace Talks 'Underway,'" *Bangkok Post*, April 28, 2015, http://www.bangkokpost.com/news/security/544327/nsc-south-peace-talks-underway.

90. "Southern Thailand Rebel Groups Set Up Umbrella Group for Peace Talks," *BenarNews*, May 13, 2015, http://www.benarnews.org/english/news/thai/deep-south-peace-talks-05132015180353.html; "Govt Restarting Peace Talks in the Far South," *The Nation* (Thailand), May 13, 2015, http://www.nationmultimedia.com/politics/Govt-restarting-peace-talks-in-the-far-South-30259957.html.

91. "Southern Thailand Rebel Groups Set Up Umbrella Group for Peace Talks"; "Govt Restarting Peace Talks in the Far South."

92. "Six Separatist Groups Formed Organization to Hold Peace Dialogue," IsraNews, May 25, 2015, http://www.isranews.org/south-news/english-article/item/38829-pulo_38829.html#.VWPFmfb5XJ4.twitter; Thaweenporn Kummetha, "Srisompob Jitpiromsri on the Latest Round of Deep South Peace Talks," Prachatai, June 18, 2015, http://prachatai.org/english/node/5168?utm_source=dlvr.it&utm_medium=twitter; Wassana Nanuam, "'Secret' Talks with Insurgent Groups Under Way," *Bangkok Post*, June 25, 2015, http://www.bangkokpost.com/news/security/604116/secret-talks-with-insurgent-groups-under-way.

93. Achara Ashayagachat, "Govt Optimistic on Peace Declaration," *Bangkok Post*, June 27, 2015, http://www.bangkokpost.com/news/general/605492/govt-optimistic-on-peace-declaration; Pimuk Rakkanam, "Malaysia 'Glue' to Solving Thailand's Southern Conflict, Official Says," *BenarNews*, June 26, 2015, http://www.benarnews.org/english/news/thai/nakrob-boontbuathong-06262015182342.html.

94. "Deep South Bombing Spree Continues, Killing One Ranger," *Khaosod English*, July 14, 2015, http://www.khaosodenglish.com/detail.php?newsid=1436866778&typecate=06&section=.

95. Don Pathan, "Bangkok Lacks THE WILL to Make Peace in Deep South," *The Nation* (Thailand), June 27, 2015, http://www.nationmultimedia.com/opinion/Bangkok-lacks-THE-WILL-to-make-peace-in-deep-South-30263252.html.

96. "BRN Was Not Represented in Previous Peace Talks," IsraNews, June 29, 2015, http://linkis.com/www.isranews.org/sou/xxYDA.

97. "BRN Was Not Represented in Previous Peace Talks."

98. "BRN Was Not Represented in Previous Peace Talks."

99. "Thailand: Southern Insurgents Cool toward Peace-Talk Prospects, Report Says," *BenarNews*, July 13, 2015, http://www.benarnews.org/english/news/thai/peace-talks-07132015183506.html.

100. "Thailand: Southern Insurgents Cool toward Peace-Talk Prospects, Report Says."

101. "Compensation but No Prosecution over Death of Deep South Torture Victim," Prachatai, August 22, 2015, http://prachatai.com/english/node/5408; Max Constant, "Rights Group Wants Thai Military Prosecuted for Torture," Video News, August 25, 2015, http://news.videonews.us/rights-group-wants-thai-military-prosecuted-for-torture-2531198.html.

102. Rapee Mama and Hata Wahari, "Independence Still Primary Goal of Southern Thailand Rebels: Negotiator," *BenarNews*, August 27, 2015, http://www.benarnews.org/english/news/thai/mara-pattani-08272015134159.html; "Mara Patani Calls for Revived Peace Talks," *Bangkok Post*, August 27, 2015, http://www.bangkokpost.com/news/security/671284/mara-patani-calls-for-revived-peace-talks; "Thai Negotiator Declares Meeting with Southern Separatists a 'Success,'" *Khaosod English*, August 28, 2015, http://t.co/L2ME0XhOIS; Wassana Nanuam, Achara Ashayagachat, and Waedao Harai, "'Mara Patani' Heralds Fresh Hope for Peace," *Bangkok Post*, August 28, 2015, http://t.co/V9se1KpcWC.

103. Other members included Sukree Haree (BRN), the lead negotiator, Ahmad Chuwo (BRN), Abu Hafez al-Hakim (BIPP and MARA Secretariat), Jekhumae Kuteh (GMIP), Kasturi Mahkota (Pertubuhan Pembebasan Patani Persatu-MKB), and Abu Nathan from Pertubuhan Pembebasan Patani Persatu-DSPP).

104. Mama and Wahari, "Independence Still Primary Goal"; "Mara Patani Calls for Revived Peace Talks"; "Thai Negotiator Declares Meeting with Southern Separatists a 'Success'"; Nanuam, Ashayagachat, and Harai, "'Mara Patani' Heralds Fresh Hope for Peace."

105. Mama and Wahari, "Independence Still Primary Goal"; "Mara Patani Calls for Revived Peace Talks"; "Thai Negotiator Declares Meeting with Southern Separatists a 'Success'"; Nanuam, Ashayagachat, and Harai, "'Mara Patani' Heralds Fresh Hope for Peace."

106. "Stumbling at the Very Outset," *The Nation* (Thailand), September 13, 2015, http://www.nationmultimedia.com/opinion/Stumbling-at-the-very-outset-30268680.html.

107. "Authorities Open to Offers from South's Mara Patani," *The Nation* (Thailand), September 23, 2015, http://www.nationmultimedia.com/national/Authorities-open-to-offers-from-Souths-Mara-Patani-30269347.html.

108. "Deep South's Most Active Insurgent Group Denounces Peace Talks," Prachatai, October 12, 2015, http://prachatai.org/english/node/5535?utm_source=dlvr.it&utm_medium=twitter.

109. Anthony Davis, "Rebels Reject Peace Talks in Deep South," *Bangkok Post*, October 12, 2015, http://www.bangkokpost.com/news/security/726792/rebels-reject-peace-talks-in-deep-south.

110. "ISOC Doubts BRN's Latest Statement," Thai PBS, October 13, 2015, http://englishnews.thaipbs.or.th/isoc-doubts-brns-latest-statement.

111. "Thailand May Reopen Peace Talks with Southern Rebels in November: Official," *BenarNews*, October 12, 2015, http://www.benarnews.org/english/news/thai/peace-talks-10122015185723.html.

112. Wassana Nanuam, "Peace Proposal Sent to Mara Patani," *Bangkok Post*, November 12, 2015, http://www.bangkokpost.com/news/security/762912/peace-proposal-sent-to-mara-patani.

113. "Thai PM Boosts Security in Muslim South after Attacks," Reuters, March 14, 2016, http://uk.mobile.reuters.com/article/idUKKCN0WG0JK?irpc=932.

114. Thaweeporn Kummetha, "Interview: What Is Being Discussed by OIC, Patani Independence Group in KL?" *Prachathai*, January 13, 2016, http://prachatai.org/english/node/5763?utm_source=dlvr.it&utm_medium=twitter.

115. Editorial, "A Peace Process That's Going Nowhere," *Nation* (Thailand), March 13, 2016, http://www.nationmultimedia.com/opinion/A-peace-process-thats-going-nowhere-30281417.html.

116. Richard Ehrlich, "Thailand Gives Islamist Rebels Immunity for Talks to End 12 Years of Bloody Conflict," *Washington Times*, March 3, 2016, http://www.washingtontimes.com/news/2016/mar/3/thailand-gives-islamist-rebels-immunity-for-peace-/.

117. Rungrawee Chalermsripinyorat, "Regime's Stance Hurts South Peace Talks," *Prachathai*, May 9, 2016, http://prachatai.org/english/node/6130?utm_source=dlvr.it&utm_medium.

118. "Latest Attacks Show BRN's New Strategy," *Bangkok Post*, March 29, 2016, http://www.bangkokpost.com/opinion/opinion/913617/latest-attacks-show-brns-new-strategy.

119. Interview with with General Aksara Kerdphol, "Hospital Siege Shows Disunity among Deep South Separatists: Authorities," *Prachathai*, April 7, 2016, http://prachatai.org/english/node/6017?utm_source=dlvr.it&utm_medium=twitter.

120. Abu Hafez Al-Hakim, "Dissecting the T-O-R," *Prachatai*, May 19, 2016, http://prachatai.org/english/node/6175?utm_source=dlvr.it&utm_medium=twitter.

121. Razlan Rashid and Pimuk Rakkanam, "Thailand 'Not Ready' to Accept Reference Terms for Peace: Southern Rebels," *Benar News*, April 28, 2016, http://www.benarnews.org/english/news/thai/Deep-South-peace-04282016070504.html.

122. "Junta Leader Warns Media about Criticising Govt as Deep South Peace Talks Stalled," *Prachatai*, May 2, 2016, http://prachatai.com/english/node/6107.

123. "Thailand to Unilaterally Review TOR of Deep South Peace Talks," *Prachatai*, May 9, 2016, http://prachatai.org/english/node/6132?utm_source=dlvr.it&utm_medium=twitter.

124. Wassana Nanuam, "Peace Talks Still Going, Army Insists," *Bangkok Post*, May 13, 2016, http://www.bangkokpost.com/news/security/970561/peace-talks-still-going-army-insists.

125. "BRN Sets Peace Talk Conditions," *Bangkok Post*, April 28, 2013, http://www.bangkokpost.com/news/local/347425/brn-vows-to-fight-and-talk-in-south; "Pengistiharan Barisan Revolusi Nasional Melayu Patani" ; Pakorn Puengnetr and Don Pathan, "NSC Rebuts BRN Demands," *The Nation* (Thailand), April 29, 2013, http://www.nationmultimedia.com/national/NSC-rebuts-BRN-demands-30205006.html.

126. Benjakat and Nanuam, "5 People, Baby Slain in Pattani Shooting." The RTA also rejected the BRN's seven conditions for a 2013 Ramadan cease-fire: Nanuam, "Ramadan Ceasefire Hopes Fade."

127. Wassana Nanuam, "Actor's Marital Scandal Prompts Boycott of Isoc South Film," *Bangkok Post*, July 14, 2015, http://www.bangkokpost.com/news/security/622352/actor-marital-scandal-prompts-boycott-of-isoc-south-film.

128. Waedao Harai, "Ranger Faces Boy Murder Cover-up Rap," *Bangkok Post*, September 6, 2014, www.bangkokpost.com/news/security/430752/ranger-faces-boy-murder-cover-up-rap; Achara Asha yagachat, "UN to Probe Thai Torture," *Bangkok Post* , April 25, 2014, www.bangkokpost.com/breakingnews/406511/un-to-probe-thai-torture.

129. "Deep South Peace Requires Justice First," *Bangkok Post*, February 19, 2015, http://m.bangkokpost.com/opinion/478749.

130. Abdulloh Benjakat, "Insurgency Suspect Dies in Military Custody in Pattani," *Bangkok Post*, December 4, 2015, http://www.bangkokpost.com/news/security/785153/insurgency-suspect-dies-in-military-custody-in-pattani; Abdulloh Benjakat, "Widow Asks Why Husband Died in Custody," *Bangkok Post*, December 5, 2015, http://www.bangkokpost.com/news/security/785789/widow-wants-answers.

131. Abdulloh Benjakat, "Family Fights State Seizure of Pattani Ponoh Land," *Bangkok Post*, December 19, 2015, http://www.bangkokpost.com/news/general/799852/pattani-family-fights-seizure; Don Pathan, "Southern Insurgency: Islamic Schools Next in Firing Line?," *The Nation* (Thailand), December 30, 2015, http://www.nationmultimedia.com/opinion/Southern-insurgency-Islamic-schools-next-in-firing-30275889.html.

132. "Supreme Court Rules No One Guilty for Somchai's Enforced Disappearance," *Prachatai*, December 29, 2015, http://prachatai.com/english/node/5735; Achara Ashayagachat, "Court Upholds Acquittals in Missing Lawyer Somchai Case," *Bangkok Post* , December 29, 2015, http://www.bangkokpost.com/news/general/810152/court-upholds-acquittals-in-missing-lawyer-somchai-case.

133. "Separatist Given Life Term for 2004 Murder of Pattani Policeman," *Bangkok Post*, December 29, 2015, http://www.bangkokpost.com/news/crime/810376/separatist-given-life-term-for-2004-murder-of-pattani-policeman.

134. "Allegations of Torture against Malay Muslims in Deep South Double after Coup," Prachatai," January 9, 2016, http://prachatai.com/english/node/5754.

135. Achara Ashayagachat, "Army Slams 'Dubious' Torture Claims," *Bangkok Post*, January 11, 2016, http://www.bangkokpost.com/news/politics/821804/army-slams-dubious-torture-claims.

136. Suhana Osman, "Thai Rebels to Meet in Malaysia with Head of World Islamic Body," January 8, 2016, http://www.benarnews.org/english/news/malaysian/thai-rebels-01082016141549.html.

137. Thanida Tansubhapol, "Political Will Needed for Peace in the South," *Bangkok Post*, May 15, 2012, http://www.bangkokpost.com/news/local/293317/political-will-needed-for-peace-in-the-south; Rungwaree Chalermsripinyorat, "Govt Must Now Take Lead in Peace Dialogue," *Bangkok Post*, May 22, 2012, http://www.bangkokpost.com/news/local/294480/govt-must-now-take-lead-in-peace-dialogue.

138. Achara Ashayagachat, "OIC Pledges to Help Boost Peace Efforts," *Bangkok Post*, July 9, 2013, http://www.bangkokpost.com/news/security/358950/oic-pledges-to-help-boost-peace-efforts; "Thailand Due for Upbraiding on the South," *The Nation* (Thailand), January 8, 2016, http://www.nationmultimedia.com/opinion/Thailand-due-for-upbraiding-on-the-South-30276358.html.

139. Osman, "Thai Rebels to Meet."

140. Tan Hui Yee, "Less Violence in Thai South but Bigger Issue Remains, *Straits Times*, January 7, 2016, http://www.straitstimes.com/asia/se-asia/less-violence-in-thai-south-but-bigger-issue-remains; Muhamad Ayub Pathan, "Insurgency Claimed 6,543 Lives in Last 12 Years," *Bangkok Post*, January 4, 2016, http://www.bangkokpost.com/news/security/815372/insurgency-claimed-6543-lives-in-last-12-years.

141. "Interesting Facts and Figures."

142. Achara Ashayagachat, "Fall in Violence Spurs Hope for Peace in South, *Bangkok Post*, January 4, 2016, http://m.bangkokpost.com/news/814668.

143. Venerable Aphichat Promjan, chief lecturer monk at Benjamabophit Temple, a Bangkok temple under royal patronage in Bangkok, called on his followers to set fire to a mosque for each monk who is killed in the Deep South in a posting on his Facebook page. He said there should be "no mercy" for "Malayu bandits" who have targeted the Buddhist community. "If a [Buddhist] monk in the three southern border provinces dies from an explosion or being shot at the hands of the 'Malayu bandits,' a mosque should be burned, starting from the northern part of Thailand southwards." "Monk Urges Authorities to Burn 1 Mosque for Each Buddhist Monk Killed in Deep South," Prachatai, October 30, 2015, http://prachatai.org/english/node/5577?utm_source=dlvr.it&utm_medium=twitter. The government quickly silenced the monk. Jitraporn Senawong, "Govt to Speak to Monk over FB Posts Calling for Revenge in Deep South," *The Nation* (Thailand), November 5, 2015, https://t.co/cd94JylaVQ; Max Constant, "Thai Monk Brought to Heel after Anti-Muslim Comments," Anadolu Agency (Turkey), June 11, 2015, http://aa.com.tr/en/politics/thai-monk-brought-to-heel-after-anti-muslim-comments/468254 ; Sanitsuda Ekachai, "Supreme Patriarch Row Won't Help Clergy," *Bangkok Post*, January 6, 2016, http://www.bangkokpost.com/opinion/opinion/817320/supreme-patriarch-row-won-t-help-clergy.

Chapter Five

Conclusion

What Makes a Peace Process More Likely to Succeed?

Nothing is harder than a peace process. Peace processes are enormously complex, multifaceted agreements that touch on core principles, red lines, emotions, dogmas, and lost blood and treasure.

Every insurgency, *ergo* every peace process, is *sui generis*. Yet they all have some important requisites. Though they do not guarantee success, their absence ensures failure. This chapter seeks to look at what made the peace process in Aceh the most successful peace process in the region and one of the most successful in the world in recent memory. The Philippines peace process came enormously close to fruition but has hit a significant setback since the January 2015 Mamasapano incident. The Philippine Congress gutted key provisions of its implementing legislation, and amid a hotly contested presidential campaign, no one saw votes in defending the peace process. So while there are many "successes" in the Philippine case, to date they are on paper only, with implementation stalled or significantly less promising than the 2012 and 2013 agreements. Nonetheless, both the agreement and the mechanisms that were established to reach and implement it are important and worthy of study. Indeed, the durability of these mechanisms is what has kept the peace processs alive.

At the same time, the absence of almost all of these requisites in Thailand ensures that a durable political solution is highly unlikely to be achieved anytime soon, unless some fundamental changes occur in the mindsets of Thailand's ruling elites, which is highly unlikely.

So what are the takeaways? What do you need for a peace process to be successful? I posit twenty key variables. These are necessary but alone insufficient to deliver peace. They are not guarantors of a successful peace process, but their absence—demonstrated clearly in the case of Thailand—almost guarantees a failed peace process and protracted conflict.

They are a useful checklist for studying and analyzing peace processes around the world and a useful indicator of how durable a political settlement will be.

1. GIVE WAR A CHANCE

First, the elites from both the government and the rebels must come to a realization that nothing more can be gained from fighting. The battlefield must be at a stalemate, and all sides must recognize that the marginal utility of additional casualties is declining. As long as one side believes that something can be gained from continued combat, a peace process is impossible. Cease-fires might be reached and talks begun, but they are only tactical lulls if one side still believes it can improve its negotiating position through gains or by weakening its adversary's position on the battlefield. Sometimes you just have to give war a chance. You cannot rush or force a peace process. In the parlance of negotiators, there can be no "BATNA" (better alternative than a negotiated agreement). As long as there is, or there is perceived to be, a BATNA, then any attempt at peace will fail. Rebels do not have to win; they only have to hold out and deny the government a clear-cut military victory or even an exit strategy.

We saw this in the case of Aceh most clearly. Nearly thirty years of war led neither side to its stated objectives. The GAM was no closer to independence than when it started, while its aging and exiled leadership was increasingly out of touch with the movement's rank and file as well as the general population. In October 2004 when a career military officer, SBY, ascended to the presidency, he understood that a military defeat of the GAM wasn't possible; it had too much legitimacy, too many outstanding grievances, and too much mistrust toward the central government. Or if a military defeat was possible, it would require an escalation of the conflict and tactics that were anathema to the country's democratic transition and greater commitment to human rights. It would also require a substantial increase in budget and resources that the country, still reeling from the impact of the 1998 Asian economic crisis, could ill afford. SBY was able to use his influence over the military to make concessions that no weak civilian leader ever could. As soon as he entered office, he instructed senior officers to quietly reach out to GAM field commanders, bypassing the intransigent exiled leadership. The popular narrative in the media is that it was the tsunami in December 2004 that brought GAM to the negotiating table. The reality is that GAM was the least affected group in Aceh; its fighters were in the mountainous hinterlands. While their families and supporters were devastated, they emerged intact. What made negotiations possible at that time was not the tsunami but the realization that nothing more could be gained from fighting. This was strongly felt throughout the movement with the exception of the exiled leadership, who was out of touch and unrealistic. The international community's involvement in Aceh's rehabilitation provided an unparalleled opportunity.

In the Philippines, conflict had raged for over thirty years. But the tides changed significantly. The MILF had become a shadow of its former self. Whereas in 1999 and 2000 it controlled swaths of Mindanao, with much of the territory ruled as a de facto state and recognized as absolutely no-go zones for the government, that simply was not the case by 2012. After 2003 the MILF lost territory in every military engagement with the Philippine Armed Forces. The government's 2003 military offensive opened up the highway between Cotabato and Davao. Trade and commerce flowed across the island, and cell phone towers broke the MILF's monopoly on information. Its control over the population weakened. As rudimentary as government social services such as health and education were, they still exceeded what the MILF had provided. Hard-liners within the movement were very concerned that the protracted peace process would lead to the loss of military effectiveness: the loss of urgency would lead to declines in recruitment, training, and morale. It would dry up the black market for arms and ammunition. And they were correct. When the Arroyo administration rejected the draft peace agreement in 2007 and the Supreme Court ruled against it 2008, MILF had every reason to go back to war. Yet it could barely sustain less than a month's worth of hostilities; it simply did not have the military capabilities to continue fighting. To do so would have resulted in the further loss of territory and popular support. Weakened, it ceased combat operations, though it did not return to the table until the end of President Arroyo's term in 2010. But the imperative to negotiate was there. At every junction, the government was able to offer the MILF less. US assistance to the AFP was important. Though it still remains militarily weak and the Americans are palpably frustrated that their counterparts have done so little with so much assistance, the reality was that the AFP had started to change the balance of power on the battlefield. The international context had changed, and illicit arms networks had started to dry up. Despite these improvements, the AFP would never be strong enough to defeat the MILF, which continued to enjoy popular legitimacy.

In Thailand that recognition has never happened, either by the military or the insurgents. The Thai military believes that the insurgents can be significantly degraded to the point of irrelevance, that it can bring down the level of violence to the point that it can be attributed to mere criminality rather than a recognition that the violence has been perpetrated by a group with legitimate political grievances that must be addressed. The insurgents recognize that their operating environment is more difficult. After twelve years, the government forces have improved their capabilities. The combination of effective checkpoints, the introduction of forensics, and improved intelligence has limited the insurgents' ability to operate at will. Yet the government cannot defeat them. Violence has plateaued. A steady amount of violence accrues month to month no matter what measures the government puts in place. Although the number of monthly casualties has come down since 2009, still over twenty people are killed every month. And at the same time, the number of shootings and IED attacks have actually gone up in that period. With the military government committed to centralizing control, and with no devolution of power, the insurgency has absolutely no reason to come to the table. The military believes that with a little more time, greater resources, more locally based personnel, greater intelligence, and more resources for forensic analysis, the militants can be defeated or degraded to the point of irrelevancy, which will erode their popular support. The Thai government is exceptionally arrogant and completely underestimates the degree of popular support for the militants. To the government, negotiation and making meaningful concessions that would satisfy the majority of the Malay insurgents is simply unacceptable. For the Thai state, especially the military rulers since the May 2014 coup, there is a BATNA. Negotiations are perceived to be more costly to the Thai state than continued war.

2. WAR WARINESS: DON'T TAKE POPULAR SUPPORT FOR GRANTED

The second factor is the war wariness of a population. Just as governments have a tendency to underestimate popular support for the insurgents, the insurgents themselves have a tendency to overestimate their popular support. Insurgent groups invariably view themselves as a vanguard and the natural leaders of their constituents. These movements are elitist and patronizing. For years, if not decades, they have represented the people's interests. They have positioned themselves as the defenders of the community's culture, if not survival. But insurgencies always overestimate their popular support, especially in protracted conflicts. They provide far fewer social services than they claim, their governance is sketchy, and they rule through fear, exacting harsh retribution against dissidents within their community. But most of all, they must contend with the costs of a protracted conflict, which make the poorest parts of a poor country even poorer. The regions that are affected by protracted conflicts tend to lag in almost every measure of human development. So it's critical, especially on the part of the insurgents, not to take popular support for granted. Moreover, support for continued conflict, when there is a palpable hope for peace, dissipates rapidly. And support for war really erodes when the population sees a peace dividend, or at least when the initial peace dividends are so apparent. After protracted conflicts, people latch onto hopes for peace and a better life for their children. Thus insurgent groups make a calculation that in order to hold onto power, they need to negotiate.

In Aceh, the population was already war wary before the December 2004 tsunami that killed over 179,000 Acehnese and devastated their already decrepit and underdeveloped infrastructure and economic base. When the promise of massive international assistance was on offer—far greater than anything that the Indonesian government had, to date, ever done for the local population—they certainly were not going to countenance a return to war. The tsunami's devastation was so all-encompassing that the people of the region were in a state of shell shock. They would support absolutely nothing that led to further poverty and underdevelopment. If GAM called for a return to war, no one in the population would have supported it. Its popular legitimacy would have evaporated overnight. To maintain its legitimacy, GAM had to be seen as leading reconstruction and rehabilitation, which it could do only through a peace process; it certainly could not afford to allow the Indonesian government to take the lead on the post-tsunami rehabilitation.

In the Philippines, the population too was thoroughly war wary. Even though Mindanao is quite large, the lack of infrastructure, especially roads, means that the population tends to be quite concentrated. When conflicts erupt, they immediately create floods of displaced persons. An intense conflict can create tens of thousands of IDPs in no time. While the death toll in Mindanao is not nearly as high as some public estimates, the number of IDPs that are regularly created is a serious problem. Mindanao is enormously wealthy in terms of raw materials. It could be a major source of food and raw materials not only for the Philippines but also for the rest of Southeast Asia and China. The potential is there, and everyone knows it. Yet forty years of conflict have left the region the poorest part of a poor country. Since 2003, when the peace process with the MILF got under way, places like Cotabato experienced a building boom. Peace, even periods of peace, were tremendous for the local economy. Investment, not necessarily foreign investment but local, flooded back in. Wealth that had been going to Manila and Makati for decades was now returning. The MILF would have lost leadership of the population had it returned to war in 2007–2008 or even after the Congress's gutting of the BBL in 2015.

In Thailand, there really isn't a sense of war wariness. What strikes me about southern Thailand is that the level of violence, which has remained very steady between 2009 and 2015, has been accepted as the "new normal." The level of violence seems highly calibrated, enough to achieve the insurgents' goals, such as maintaining leadership, eliminating rivals within the Muslim community, and targeting the "occupation force," without alienating the general population. There is no public backlash against the insurgents.

Though sometimes what they do is considered beyond the pale, they do respond to public pressure. While the violence has deterred some investment, the reality is that southern Thailand is not the poorest part of the country, and indeed, things that the Thai government wants to do to develop the economy are often rejected by the local community as things that might erode their culture. In short, despite twelve years of conflict, there is no widespread public pressure on the government and insurgents to negotiate. Public opinion polling shows support for talks in a general sense but neither urgency nor confidence in the outcome of such talks.

3. ELIMINATING THE TRUST DEFICIT

The third factor is about developing trust between the governments and insurgents. How do you build trust between warring parties who have been in a nasty intergenerational struggle, between parties that have Manichean worldviews and zero-sum perceptions? Peace processes are long-term processes that are filled with setbacks and enormous challenges. The issues are enormously complex; otherwise, these conflicts wouldn't be so intractable. Hardliners and those who seek to sabotage the peace process exist on both sides. Cease-fires are broken, and deals are undermined by politicians or thwarted by hard-liners in the military or government. Often these actions are perceived to be an intentional and calculated ploy, when all too often negotiators are hung out to dry by senior leaders who get cold feet or feel they are losing the support or confidence of their militaries and security services. Successful peace processes require high levels of trust in order to overcome these setbacks. And that is very different from co-option or trying to buy off your adversary, which is a common tactic. Personal rapport is important. Knowing that your interlocutor has the ear or support of the leader is even more important. Trust must be based on an honest discussion and acceptance of the other side's red lines. Each side has to truly acknowledge that there are certain things their opponents simply cannot do, that doing those things is either political suicide or deemed illegitimate and doomed to failure. Finally, trust has to be more than personal rapport. It is made possible through the establishment of durable institutions that work together day in and day out.

In Aceh, there was trust between the government and the GAM negotiators, but that was achieved only after years of mistrust and failed negotiations. So in 2004–2005, where did that trust come from? In part it was SBY and Vice President Jusuf Kalla's commitment to the peace process. They began reaching out to GAM combatants as soon as they entered office. Resolving the conflict was a priority for them. Their recognition that the war could not be won militarily and was a financial drain on the economy was essential. Most importantly, there was confidence that SBY had enough sway over the TNI that he could impose a peace settlement on it in a way that no weak and ineffective civilian leader would ever have the temerity to attempt. Besides being a former general and the minister for political-security coordinating affairs, SBY was the first directly elected president. He had a national mandate. Kalla's sway over Golkar, the largest party in parliament, also assured GAM that any agreement would be ratified. SBY and Kalla were always available to their negotiators and gave them the requisite political cover. But part of the confidence was also derived from the fact that after the tsunami, the international community was physically there. Until the tsunami, the Indonesian government had effectively kept all foreigners out of Aceh. Though the peace process was not formally part of the rehabilitation effort, it was widely seen as being connected, and the international community's presence made cheating or cease-fire violations less likely. But the Acehnese peace process also benefited from the fact that very few things truly challenged it. Cease-fire violations happened, but they were quickly minimized. Indonesian security forces still did some abusive things, but far less than before.

In the Philippines, trust was always much harder to come by. For one thing, the MILF had assiduously studied the government's behavior and negotiation strategy with the MNLF. It was all too aware of the ways that the government had either not implemented or had undermined the 1996 accord. So the MILF worked to ensure that those things could not happen again. And for their part, Philippine negotiators understood that the government's track record in implementing the 1996 accord was patchy at best. Other things helped shore up or undermine confidence. In the negotiations for the 1996 accord with the MNLF, the government's top negotiator had twenty-four-hour access to the president, who gave him full political cover. Ramos was committed to peace, and the MNLF believed him. President Arroyo was never seen as committed to peace, and there was no confidence that she had control over her armed forces. In 2003, on the eve of talks in Kuala Lumpur, the military launched a major offensive. While it was successful in penetrating the MILF's homeland and weakening the MILF, it was a poison pill. The MILF could not trust the government. In 2007, after four years of fraught negotiations, President Arroyo rejected the draft agreement due to opposition from the military and hard-liners. The January 2015 Mamasapano incident, in which forty-four SAF troops were killed in a botched raid, should have effectively killed the peace process. Congress was vociferous in its criticism of the peace process and has gradually sabotaged it. But the government's peace panel and the MILF have been steadfast in their commitment to it. There is simply a reservoir of trust in each other and in both sides' commitment to peace. The government's peace negotiator and OPOPP chief were personally savaged by members of Congress for their continued commitment to the peace process and willingness to trust the MILF's sincerity. They were personally accused by some members of Congress of being treasonous, and calls for their firing were widespread because they accepted the MILF's position that Mamasapano was a tragic misencounter whose blame largely rested at the feet of the SAF for failing to abide by proper cease-fire coordinating mechanisms. In the end, trust has been maintained in the southern Philippines because the myriad of institutions, such as the CCCH and the AHJAG, have been long-standing and fairly effective in dealing with situations as they arise.

In Thailand, there is simply no trust. On the government's side, the lack of trust derives from the belief that the people who say they're in charge really have no authority or command and control over the militants. So, for example, in 2013, after the BRN came out of the shadows and began the formal peace process with the government, two things happened. The first is that the BRN then issued five preconditions post facto. It made them look completely amateurish and incompetent, but it also raised legitimate concerns within the government that they really were not the leaders of the movement but were having terms and preconditions dictated to them. Second, the government demanded a total cease-fire as both a sign of goodwill and a demonstration of effective command and control. The BRN refused, arguing that Thai security forces were an occupying force and thus a legitimate target. For several months the BRN drastically reduced—though it did not stop—attacks on civilians, but it escalated attacks on security forces. The government understood this, but the RTA leadership was incensed, arguing it was both a lack of goodwill and proof of a lack of command and control. Insurgents made clear to me that their attacks mostly on security forces and not civilians was a very clear sign of command and control. But there was such mistrust on the part of the RTA that it could not see that. In 2015, the military government announced that it wanted to resume peace talks with the BRN. But it was never a priority for the government, and indeed it was the same military that killed the peace talks in 2013, not popular unrest against the government of Yingluck Shinawatra, as the military government's narrative goes. There was no illusion that the primary concern of the military government was consolidating military and royalist elites' control over Thai politics, holding onto power during the royal succession period while diminishing the power and authority of democratically elected politicians and parties. The BRN views the military as being unwilling to make even the most basic concessions, let alone implement devolution of political powers. In October 2015, the BRN formally quit the nascent peace process, citing the government's lack of honesty and commitment to the peace. In May 2016, the RTA sacked its chief negotiator, who had drafted the terms of reference with the BRN to restart talks, for fear that he was too empathetic. There is no trust on either side of the equation.

4. NOT JUST LEADERSHIP BUT STATESMANSHIP

The fourth requisite is that a peace process needs more than leadership; it requires true statesmanship. Bold and courageous leadership is required on the part of both the rebels and the government. They need to look beyond their short-term political horizon and always focus on the long game. Usually peace processes are nearly as protracted as the conflict. They have failed or been set back on multiple occasions, and they have outlasted political leaders on both sides. Leaders have to be bold and creative, willing to reject old and failed paradigms. Successful peace processes require leaders who can empathize with their adversary and convey that empathy to their own supporters. But most of all, they have to break out of the Manichean worldviews and zero-sum perceptions that have been accepted as dogma. They have to have enough political capital and be willing to spend it to achieve long-term goals of peace and reconciliation. And leaders have to be willing to take personal risks: they will be challenged by hard-liners, from political challenges to attempts on their lives. But at the end of the day, the leaders have to be willing to make very painful concessions, including concessions on issues that heretofore had been politically impossible. They are going to have to make concessions on issues that are core to their worldview, whether it be challenging the unitary nature of the state, accepting autonomy or devolution of powers, the secular nature of the government, or the right to independence and the establishment of a homeland. The stark reality is that leaders have to be able to explain to mothers and widows why their children or husbands died for a compromise. As they shift from maximalist demands, leaders have to be expert at managing the expectations of the public that has borne the brunt of the conflict.

SBY confronted a military leadership stung by the loss of East Timor and that had effectively vetoed any meaningful concessions to GAM during either Abdurrahman Wahid's or Megawati Sukarnoputri's terms in office. Neither was able or willing to challenge the TNI on Aceh; indeed, both caved in to TNI demands. That the international community played such a key role in East Timor's referendum and independence made the TNI all the more suspicious. SBY used his personal relations and influence over the TNI to win over its support. Though SBY was a democratically elected president, democracy was still very young and fragile; its gains were not irreversible. And while the TNI had withdrawn from direct interference in civilian governance, such as ending the policy of *dwi fungsi*, it remained the kingmaker in Indonesian politics. The military had withdrawn support from B. J. Habibie and Wahid, making their continued rule impossible. SBY made the resolution of Aceh a top priority, he delegated day-to-day responsibility to Vice President Kalla, and thus the issue remained as a top administration priority. When hard decisions and concessions needed to be made, SBY made them. After the peace process, SBY moved the implementing legislation through parliament. SBY and Kalla used their influence, democratic mandate, and patronage networks.

For GAM, the situation was slightly different. Because Indonesian officials so effectively began behind-the-scenes negotiations with GAM's field commanders, the exiled leaders who had been so hard-line and intransigent panicked. They realized that the peace process was happening without them. Thus, if they were to maintain their influence, command, and control, as well as make sure that the spoils of peace fell their way, they had to jump on board the peace process. They abandoned their demand for *merdeka*, accepting considerable political, legal, cultural, and economic autonomy.

In the Philippines, President Arroyo completely caved into the demands of her military and hard-liners within her own cabinet. She had no political will to push through an agreement in her own cabinet, let alone Congress. Arroyo seemed far more concerned about personal enrichment than building her political legacy. President Aquino began very quietly. In his first year and a half in office, he barely mentioned Mindanao or the peace process. Not until November 2011 did he and MILF chairman Murad meet in Tokyo and discuss the broad contours of an agreement. Once that happened, he made the peace process a top priority. He was creative and sought to avoid all of the legal and constitutional challenges that befell the 2007 draft peace agreement. He was magnanimous and treated the MILF chairman as an equal partner. But the BBL was creative, out-of-the-box thinking. The government made enormously generous concessions on mineral rights and fiscal autonomy. The establishment of a parliamentary system of government was a creative way to try to win over support from the MNLF that was still smarting from having its 1996 accord superseded. Arguably Aquino's leadership fell flat after the Mamasapano incident. But at that point, the BBL had already been negotiated and was being deliberated by Congress. It was legally out of his hands. He should have done more to cool the congressional hotheads and not let key deadlines pass. But the reality was that members of Congress, and in particular the Senate, were already in full-on campaign mode, while Aquino was entering lame duck status. His political capital had dramatically diminished, while members of Congress were trying to figure out how to best leverage the BBL and Mamasapano hearings for political gain. One only need look at the effectiveness of Senator Grace Poe, who used the Mamasapano hearings to jump to the top of the presidential polls despite her neophyte status in the Senate. Senator Marcos rewrote the entire BBL, producing a drastically diluted version, in his attempt to move up and out of single digits in the polls. Aquino's legacy is, of course, not delivering a lasting peace, but he came closer than any other president.

On the part of the MILF, Ebrahim Murad also showed real leadership. Under Salamat Hashim, the group was unwilling to countenance autonomy.

It demanded not only independence, but an independent Islamic state. Its demands were maximalist, but the MILF was also militarily stronger. When Murad took over in 2003, it was already the beginning of the end for the MILF militarily. Murad, as a former field commander and not an *ustadz*, understood the battlefield realities, that the MILF was steadily losing territory and the military initiative. He understood the imperative to negotiate a durable solution, understanding the pitfalls and weaknesses of previous government agreements with Moro groups. Under Murad, the MILF rejected its bid for independence, accepting autonomy, which heretofore was an absolutely poisonous term in Mindanao. Murad oversaw the formal decommissioning of arms, an incredibly emotional event for the rebels, who were now formally renouncing war as an instrument of statecraft. Murad did all this at enormous personal risk. Hard-liners, including Salamat Hashim and Ustadz Ameril Umbra Kato, challenged Murad repeatedly for the leadership of the movement. We know of at least several attempts on his life. But Murad also displayed leadership when thinking about the postconflict environment. The BBL would establish a democratically elected government; it did not necessarily hand over power to the MILF. Indeed, MILF stood to lose significantly at the polls to its MNLF rivals in Sulu, Tawi-Tawi, Basilan, and Zamboanga. Yet that was going to be the cost of trying to get the MNLF to endorse the peace process and get on board. That was real leadership. But perhaps at no time did Murad display more leadership than after the Mamasapano incident. When the Philippine Congress held hearing after hearing calling the MILF's interpretation of events deeply flawed, challenging their commitment to the peace process, and gutting the BBL (the peace process's implementing legislation), the MILF never lost hope. More importantly, it continued to renounce war as a recourse. It remained committed to peace while Philippine legislators were trying to maximize the tragedy for political gain. Murad maintained the long view and the morale of his rank and file, who were all too familiar with seeing national politics lead to the Moros being dealt with badly. Maintaining that long view is the hallmark of leadership. Aquino maintained it, but he didn't expend the requisite political capital to push it through.

In Thailand, leadership has been in extremely short supply due to the country's tumultuous politics and constant military interference. Thaksin did try to have back-channel talks with the rebels, but he simply assumed that they could be bought off. The military junta that replaced him in 1996 abolished the 1997 constitution that would have begun to devolve political powers. The successive democratic governments between 2008 and 2014 were too wary of another coup to provoke military anger at making concessions to the rebels. Indeed, the trend since 2007 has been to acquiesce to the military's consolidation of political power. Following the 2014 coup, the military sought to enhance its power—under the cloak of defending the monarchy and the unitary Thai state at the expense of democratic politics and institutions. No one was willing to make a bold move in an attempt to forge a peace. Prime minister after prime minister was terrified of doing anything that would run afoul of the military, and the insurgency, which had remained highly contained in the Deep South, was a low political priority. For example, during his two years in office, Prime Minister Abhisit made two one-day trips to the south. Yingluck was no better; and this is a mere hour and a half's flight away from Bangkok. No political leader was even willing to make a modicum of concessions on language, cultural rights, or holding the military accountable for human rights abuses, including EJKs and forced disappearances. The civilian governments were obsessed with staving off another coup, while the military was busy staving off a return to electoral democracy. Ending the insurgency was nothing more than a token response.

Likewise, the insurgents showed no leadership. The movement remained faceless. It was a thoroughly horizontal insurgency, with some groups stronger than others but no one in charge. The insurgents were constantly negotiating among themselves and could rarely come up with a common platform. No one was willing to step up and assume the mantle of leadership. In part, this is a cultural phenomenon. But it also reflected a real concern over personal security. The insurgents had little confidence that should the BRN leaders identify themselves, they would not be the victim of targeted assassination by Thai security forces. The loose collective leadership really prevented bold decision making and allowed for dissenting factions to undermine the process.

5. *BELLUM SE IPSUM ALET*

Any peace process will always have hard-line spoilers. For the most part, their dissent is based on ideological grounds: maintaining a commitment to the original goals of the movement or not dissipating state power. They see compromise as weakness, and they portray those who seek a negotiated settlement as betraying the martyrs of the movement and their families, as selling out the goals and ideals.

But beyond these ideological motivations are often pecuniary ones. War creates vested interests and constituencies who stand to lose from peace. Given this, all parties must acknowledge the concept of *bellum se ipsum alet*, "war feeds itself," and identify those constituencies. Leaders must demonstrate an ability and willingness to take on vested interests within their own constituency, including having the will and capability to neutralize hard-line spoilers. Importantly, military commanders who fear that the peace process will lead to cuts in budgets must be assuaged and given new roles and missions, with new hardware and requisite funding. Militaries have a vested interest in maintaining a low level of hostilities: it's job security, it's avenues for promotion, it's political influence, and it's a secure budget. Leaders need to address each of these areas. Other military experience rather than combatting a domestic insurgency must be a consideration for promotion. But most of all, to receive buy-in from the militaries, leaders must assure them that their budgets and prestige will be protected. Leaders must help to transform the mindset of the military from one of internal defense to one of external defense, with new roles, new missions, and new equipment. In Indonesia and the Philippines, two archipelagic nations with no navies to speak of, it was not a terribly hard case to make. And while military budgets go up, the experiences in the Philippines and Indonesia show that the end of hostilities has such a multiplier effect on the overall economy, such as improving investor confidence and lowering political risk, that the net increases in military spending are not a burden on the overall economy.

In Indonesia, the military budget went from 20.8 billion rupiah in 2005 to 30.6 billion rupiah in 2007, a 47 percent increase in only two years. Though the increase is not quite as impressive in US dollars, due to depreciation of the rupiah, it still increased from $2.2 billion to $7 billion, a 227 percent increase. SBY used the end of the insurgency as an opportunity to modernize the TNI. By the end of SBY's term in 2014, the TNI's budget had increased by 300 percent from the 2005 budget, to some 83.3 billion rupiah. Of course, part of the increase was due to the fact that the government has tried to get the military to divest itself of its businesses, both legal and illegal, which previously made up an estimated two-thirds of the budget. But SBY was able to get the military to focus on external defense, especially a much-needed modernization of its maritime forces. Per capita spending on defense, likewise, tripled from $9.60 per person to $27.80. In terms of a percentage of GDP and government spending, the defense budget increases only marginally. But the end of the insurgency had a positive effect on the overall economy, which allowed the military budget to go up 300 percent without being a burden on the economy. SBY framed the end of the insurgency as a window for overall defense modernization, with new missions, roles, and equipment. The value of imports increased 3,556 percent between 2004 and 2013. Even since the postrecession recovery in 2010, the increase has been 1,103 percent.

Indonesia is clearly trying to make up for years of underinvestment as its military also begins to focus more on external defense than internal security and counterinsurgency. Indonesia's ability to protect its maritime domain remains paltry, given the scope of the challenge in defending seventeen thousand islands and ninety-three thousand square kilometers of ocean. The winding down of the insurgency would lead to a decline in human rights abuses, which would reopen opportunities for bilateral defense cooperation. The end of the conflict would also help with Indonesia's democratic transi-

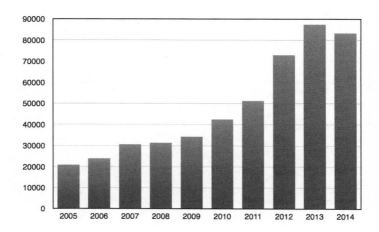

Figure 5.1.   Indonesian Defense Expenditures, 2005 to 2014 in Indonesian Rupiah (billions). *Source*: **Stockholm International Peace Research Institute, Military expenditures data set, at www.sipri.org.**

tion by forcing the military out of local governance in the last bastion of *dwi fungsi*—or dual function. Without the promise of increased budgets, new missions, and a concerted effort to modernize the military, it is very hard to imagine the TNI backing the peace process.

In the Philippines, we see almost the same thing, though on a much smaller scale. The AFP's budget went from 117 billion pesos in 2010 to 136 billion pesos, a 33 percent increase. In US dollars, Philippine defense expenditures have risen marginally, from $1.24 billion in 2004 to $3.3 billion in 2014, or 166 percent. In 2011, President Benigno Aquino announced plans to allocate more resources to upgrading the military by establishing the Armed Forces of the Philippines (AFP) Modernization Act Trust Fund and reaffirmed them in the 2012 Revised Modernization Program. In May 2013, President Aquino announced a $1.8 billion military modernization program; these funds were in addition to the normal defense budget, which largely goes to pay personnel costs. After several increases in funding, some sixty billion pesos were earmarked for new equipment that would help protect the archipelagic country's maritime domain. In 2014, President Aquino requested a 29 percent increase in defense expenditure in the face of growing Chinese assertiveness in the South China Sea.

The Philippines military is still the laggard in Southeast Asia and is dependent on hand-me-downs from the country's partners, including the United States, Japan, Australia, and South Korea. But almost all new military spending and aid has gone toward bolstering the maritime and aerial capabilities of

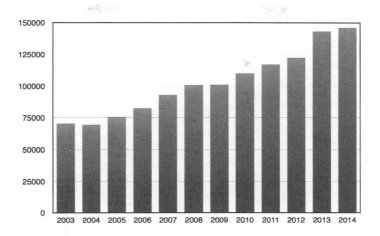

Figure 5.2. Philippine Defense Expenditures, 2003 to 2014 in Philippine Pesos (billions). *Source*: **Stockholm International Peace Research Institute, Military expenditures data set, at www.sipri.org.**

the AFP, which languished during the decades of counterinsurgency. Aquino very clearly was driven by Chinese aggression in the South China Sea and effectively convinced the AFP that the real threat posed to Philippine sovereignty comes not from insurgents who have accepted a degree of autonomy but from China's grabs of features on the Philippine continental shelf and EEZ. And if Aquino was to receive significant amounts of bilateral defense assistance from the United States, Japan, and Australia for its maritime defense, then he had to wind down the insurgency and reprioritize the AFP's missions.

In Thailand, the defense budget has soared but not because of the insurgency or modernization. In 2004, when the insurgency erupted again, the budget was seventy-eight billion baht; it increased by 47.4 percent by 2006, in part due to the insurgency but more to make up after years of low expenditure following the Asian economic crisis. But with the 2006 and 2014 coup d'états by the military, the budget has nearly tripled from $2.4 billion to over $6.3 billion. Thailand has no meaningful external security threats, but it does have a love of prestige items. Unlike the Philippines and Indonesia, it has no maritime or territorial dispute with China in the South China Sea. The increases in the military budget are part of the RTA's expanded role in internal security. Unlike the Philippines and Indonesia, which used the peace process to modernize its military roles, missions, and capabilities, Thailand continues to reward itself with large budget increases but geared for external, not internal, security.

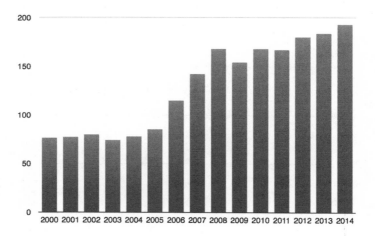

Figure 5.3. Thai Defense Expenditures, 2000 to 2014 in Thai Baht (billions).
Source: **Stockholm International Peace Research Institute, Military expenditures data set, at www.sipri.org.**

6. NEW MECHANISMS AND INSTITUTIONS

Peace requires new mechanisms, processes, and institutions. A peace process is an immensely complex process that requires a host of specialized institutions and organizations with new norms, processes, and procedures. Some will be formal, and others, ad hoc or informal. Some will be at the government/organizational level, and others will comprise civil society organizations. They will have different requirements, from information gathering and sharing to investigations and coordination. These organizations need the requisite resources, funding, and manpower. But most of all they need the autonomy, the independence, and the political backing to do their jobs. They must show creativity and flexibility, establishing new chains of command. These institutions must be durable and outlive the people who negotiated them. They have to be transparent to win the trust of the local community. These include cease-fire organizations, transitional justice mechanisms, development agencies, IDP and refugee resettlement bodies, and organizations to resolve land ownership and other aspects of compensation. I cannot emphasize how important these various bodies were for building trust and working level relationships between the two sides.

Indonesia was a bit of an anomaly because the entire peace process was just so fast. Institutions were not quite as durable as one would expect. Yet the peace panels showed some consistency, especially among the GAM. They built important institutions to help implement key components of the peace process, especially transitional justice and disarmament, disengagement, and rehabilitation. But the institutions they did build had high-level support and resourcing.

In the Philippines, such institutions truly made the peace process possible. During the term of President Arroyo, there was a lot of back channeling and a lot of informality. But that lack of official and formal buy-in made the peace process less durable.

Things became far more established and transparent under Aquino. On the government side was OPAPP, which reported directly to the president. It had its team of lawyers, technical experts, negotiators, and an in-house reservoir of experience. Under Aquino, OPAPP was ably led by Ging Deles and her lead negotiator Miriam Coronel-Ferrer. They were unflappable in the face of the greatest setbacks and indefatigable. And importantly, OPAPP set a very high bar for transparency. Its website, http://www.opapp.gov.ph, was an up-to-date repository of every document, agreement, statement, and speech. Its public outreach, community engagement, and educational activities—in person or through social media—are a model.

The MILF established its own peace panel, with a secretariat in charge of day-to-day operations, a collection of past agreements, and a group of specialized technical committees. There was a long degree of continuity, especially in the MILF peace panel. And even after the agreements were signed, the different peace panels played an incredibly important role in terms of peace education and advocacy, especially after the Mamasapano incident.

But the most important institutions and mechanisms were created on the ground in Mindanao, including the Coordinating Committee for the Cessation of Hostilities (CCCH) and the Ad Hoc Joint Action Group (AHJAG). The CCCH was established in 2003 and staffed by members of the MILF and the government, who did everything in tandem. Every investigation, every cease-fire violation had to be reported by both sides. The Philippine members were mostly members of the AFP, but they were outside the chain of command, in particular the Sixth Infantry Division. They had their own office, mission, budget, and staff. Though headed by an AFP colonel, it was a relatively autonomous organization. And one thing that was important in its success is that it recruited people from Mindanao to be part of it. They had a real personal and long-term interest in peace.

The AHJAG was a law enforcement coordinating body established in 2005. It was a mechanism for which the PNP or AFP could go to their MILF counterparts and ask them to investigate or arrest criminals operating or simply seeking sanctuary within MILF-held territory. Clearly, many were cynical about the AHJAG. Few expected the MILF to actually turn over kidnappers or people wanted in connection with terrorism who were fellow Muslims, tied by family and clan and often members of the MILF itself. But to a degree, it worked. The Pentagon Gang—which many linked directly to the MILF—ceased operations. Kidnaps for ransom in and around MILF territory in central Mindanao dropped precipitously. The AHJAG made the MILF feel like they were equal partners, responsible for maintaining law and order.

The third institution was the Bangsamoro Development Agency (BDA), which was the primary mechanism for the MILF to lead economic and social development projects and partner with the Philippine government as well as with bilateral and multilateral donors. But it also played an important role in developing the human capital of the MILF and its community. As the MILF prepared to administer the region, it was all too aware of exactly how shallow its pool of human capital was. And it was fearful that if it could not rapidly develop its human capital, it would follow the MNLF's path of inept administration and rampant corruption. Bi- and multilateral donors, other NGOs, and the Asian Institute of Management in Manila conducted hundreds of training sessions for MILF cadres, from civil administration to management, economic planning, and revenue collection.

Finally, after the CAB was signed, important institutions with specialized roles came into being. The MILF, with the assistance of the Philippine government and international donors, established the Sajahatra Bangsamoro Foundation to implement and fund disarmament, disengagement, and rehabilitation of combatants.[1] A component of this was creating an educational trust fund for the children of MILF combatants. It enrolled over 22,000 MILF members and their dependents in the national health insurance program. It provided educational and vocational training in Bangsamoro communities. Clearly it was underfunded, but no one doubts the importance of the mission. The peace process established a neutral third-party monitoring team made up of external observers as well as Philippine and MILF members. The IMT played a critical role at key junctures in the negotiations, helping to build trust at impasses in the talks. Finally, an independent monitoring body, which included Philippine government, MILF and international representatives, safeguarded the MILF's decommissioned arms.

In Thailand, the institutions were very weak and nondurable. From 2004 through 2013, neither side had a concerted peace panel. There were different peace panels and back channels, but nothing consistent. From 2005 to 2006, Thaksin sent some back channels out, but they were really out of the loop. They reached out to exiled groups of former insurgents from previous rebellions who couldn't deliver anything but tried to leverage political power anyway. The RTA undermined Thaksin's team. Even the rule of the pro-establishment Democrat Party that came to power through military machinations was thwarted by the military. Abhisit's team had its own team that tried to establish a back channel but was thwarted by the military, which started to begin its own back channeling. The former Malaysian prime minister Mahathir Mohamad tried to begin his own peace initiative, but he had no real influence or backing. It was nothing more than his own actions driven by his own ego. Former militants again leveraged a place at the table, but they had no control over the insurgency. When Yingluck began her peace initiative, she finally brought some organizational structure. The government and BRN formed an organized panel that met a number of times. But much of the initial legwork was being done by her ousted brother, former prime minister Thaksin, who was trying to arrange the peace process in order to help himself return to Thailand and power. Moreover, the BRN side did not have the full backing by the full authority of the leadership and was punished for exceeding its mandate. Unlike in the Philippines or Indonesia, the BRN's top leaders remained out of the picture, fearful that if they revealed themselves they would be assassinated. So the leadership was never vested in the peace process. An attempt was made in 2015 to form a formal organization that represented all of the southern Thai groups, MARA Pattani, but the BRN quit the group soon after because it had no faith in the government's commitment to peace. MARA Pattani tried to keep going, but the BRN held four of seven seats, including the chairmanship of the organization.

In Thailand, multiple and competing groups were always seeking talks, but they accomplished nothing centralized or anything that would last beyond the life of a government. And as previously explained, between 2004 and 2015, a total of nine prime ministers and two military governments had held power. Moreover, there was never a cease-fire committee, never a body to even deal with amnesties or prisoner releases, low-level actions that helped to build trust. The few Thai government interlocutors, such as Thawee Sodsong or Paradorn Pattanatabut, who have been truly trusted by the Malays community and BRN, have all been sacked by the military. The junta sacked its lead negotiator in May 2016 after he negotiated the Terms of Reference to restart talks with the BRN, which prime minister Prayuth also rejected. The combination of weak institutions and the constant rotation of personnel has ensured talks have never gained traction.

8. ACKNOWLEDGMENT OF HISTORICAL RIGHTS AND WRONGS AND THE CREATION OF CULTURAL SPACE

It is a truism that the peace process and its agreements and various annexes have to be fair and equitable. A lopsided peace process, in which one side dictates the terms to the other, is never going to bring a lasting and durable political solution. It will only sow the seeds of future conflict. The public must note a sense of equity for the process to gather broad-based public support. But the peace process and agreements must be more than simply equitable.

Each side has to acknowledge the other's right to exist, its constitutional and cultural rights as well as a degree of sovereignty. An acknowledgment that the insurgents' core grievances are legitimate and that historical wrongs were committed and must be addressed is absolutely critical. Many times, simply acknowledging past injustices, historical wrongs committed by the state such as the taking of land, satisfies many on the insurgents' side. The according of the minority group with "first nation" status is an important step. Not everyone expects historical wrongs to be reversed (though that is an ideal), but they have to at least be acknowledged. It's amazing how much formal apologies or official acknowledgments of misdeeds, abusive policies, and internal colonial practices go in winning over popular support. Yet so often, governments feel that an apology is a sign of weakness and that any such admission sets dangerous legal precedents for other ethnic minorities and regions looking to secede.

And acknowledging historical wrongs and the other group's cultural iden-tity, sovereignty, and right to exist creates a sense of cultural security. There must be a sense that the nation has enough space for multiple cultures, national identities, and values to coexist, that it is not a zero-sum competition or that cultural survival is at stake. The state must convey that it not only welcomes diversity but that diversity makes the country stronger. It's about respect. Does space exist for the minority within the national consciousness and narrative?

The state must protect cultural and minority rights, including language rights. This has to be a cornerstone of any peace process, its agreements, and the postconflict political order. A group's identity must have genuine protec-tions. And what is critical, though so often lacking, is that identity becomes not merely protected but embraced by the country as a whole. For example, my friend often talks about how Native American symbols or names are used in the United States as symbols of warriors, bravery, and resoluteness.

In the case of Aceh, the government made room for a separate historical narrative and cultural identity. It did not merely devolve political power but allowed the autonomous government to set up its own *sharia* courts and religious police in order to protect that identity. The government acknowl-edged wrongdoing by the previous administrations and tried to draw a clear distinction between it and Suharto's regime. But in doing so and establishing the transitional justice mechanism, the government admitted that egregious human rights violations were committed. During the peace process, the government kept reiterating one of the core founding principles of Indonesia: "unity in diversity." There was space within Indonesia for multiple cultures, national identities, and values to coexist.

In the Philippines, the government recognized "Bangsamoro identity" and noted that they were "first nation," original inhabitants. Moreover, the government accepted the concept of the "Bangsamoro," which is a totally artificial construct. There is no singular Moro nation or linguistic group. Yet if that was how they wanted to self-identify, then the government was willing to accept it. Through the negotiations on "ancestral domain," the government acknowledged that the Bangsamoro had historical rights to the land and that they had lost land to Christian settlers who took advantage of different conceptions of property rights. The MILF conceded that it would not have all of these lands restored to it. But the peace agreements acknowledged their historical ownership of the land. Moreover, the government helped to make the Bangsamoro feel like less marginalized communities and part of the greater identity of the Philippine nation. After the Comprehensive Agreement was signed, museum exhibitions celebrated the identity and contributions of the Moro to Philippine history and culture. By acknowledging wrongs and past injustices, space was created for the Moro nation. They had the space and recognition to thrive as a culture. This did not happen overnight. It took a long time and the development of democracy and the rule of law for the MILF to feel that its cultural heritage was no longer under assault and that there was space for it within the construct of the Philippines.

In Thailand, you never had anything of the sort. Thai policies represent over a century of a failed colonial experiment rooted in assimilation to Thai culture, religion, and values. The Malay are the only minority in the country to have steadfastly resisted assimilation for the sake of citizenship, and this drives successive governments crazy. Their policies are all based on assimilation, starting with language and education. The Malay feel they have no space in the construct of the Thai state. They believe Thai government policy remains colonial in nature and based on the inculcation of Thai political and cultural values. They have a deep sense that their language, religion, and culture are disrespected. It would take a profound political shift for a Thai government to ever acknowledge the ancestral domain of the Malay, as that would be tacit acknowledgment of its colonial policy. It is highly unlikely to ever offer an apology for crimes committed. Indeed, successive governments have demonstrated a total unwillingness to hold their forces to any degree of accountability, creating a culture of abuse and impunity. There is nothing like the Indonesian concept of "unity in diversity"; it's always about assimilation.

9. SOME FORM OF TRANSITIONAL JUSTICE

Counterinsurgencies inevitably create egregious human rights abuses. Indonesian, Philippine, and Thai security forces have very poor track records in human rights abuses. Indeed, their crimes against civilian populations, including attacks on civilians, rape, war crimes, torture, and extrajudicial killings, have all been widely documented by human rights organizations.

Not every country is going to be South Africa, with its famed National Truth and Reconciliation Commission. But at least some sort of transitional justice mechanism is necessary, short of formal war crimes tribunals. There cannot be lasting peace without some form of justice. Yet there are limits. No government will agree to its security forces being scapegoated; and if security forces believe that they are being sacrificed for the sake of peace, they will act as spoilers. They have to be confident that the government will protect their interests for what they did in the name of the state. Still, it's important that wrongs by all sides be addressed, as insurgents, who operated in the shadows, were often abusive and terrorized the local population into supporting their struggle and holding some of the civilian population responsible for battlefield losses through citizens' active or passive support for the government.

Both the Philippines and Indonesia had transitional justice mechanisms in their peace processes. These were not exactly thorough or encompassing. In the case of the Philippines, the agreement in the FAB was deliberately vague: the two parties agreed to establish some sort of mechanism to deal with transitional justice and long-standing grievances and human rights violations without providing the specifics. And the reality is that we haven't even gotten to that point. In Indonesia, part two of the MoU established a truth and reconciliation commission charged "with the task of formulating and determining reconciliation measures." To date, none has ever been established.

While the peace process itself may be too fragile to fully implement a transitional justice mechanism, simply having it in the peace agreements may be a showstopper, without which the rebels are unable to sell the agreement to their public. It's inclusion creates a sense of finality and is a key component of the peace agreement that the rebels can point to. It would be difficult to make the case that the peace process brought justice to a war-torn region without at least a nominal transitional justice mechanism or a forum where people could keep their oral histories alive. Local communities will not have confidence in the state and its security forces without a transitional justice mechanism or some other process that holds security forces accountable for their actions.

There has always been a sense in both the Philippines and Indonesia that peace trumps justice. This was most sadly seen in the fiftieth anniversary of the Indonesian government's unwillingness to even acknowledge the extent of the bloodletting that led to the deaths of three hundred thousand to five hundred thousand Parti Kommunis Indonesia (PKI) members and their supporters following the 1965 coup that brought Suharto to power, let alone an official apology.[2]

In Thailand, as mentioned earlier, the culture is one of impunity. In twelve years of conflict, fewer than twenty government forces have been formally charged with crimes, as they continue to operate under the 2005 Emergency Decree, which gives them near-total immunity. Yet in almost all of these cases, charges were quietly dropped after a brief interlude, or the soldiers or police were acquitted. In all cases in which security forces were convicted, they were freed on appeal. So to think that Thailand could ever have an even-handed transitional justice system is far-fetched.

10. AMNESTIES

Essential to any peace process is the release of political prisoners, captured insurgents, and POWs. But in most insurgencies, the government doesn't give insurgents belligerent status for fear that doing so would legitimize their struggle. In practice, most are not simply released at the end of the conflict but only through an act of law. Most governments treat captured insurgents as terrorists, murderers, and other common criminals in their quixotic attempt to delegitimize the insurgents' political struggle. And it is sometimes difficult for governments to put in place the legal mechanisms to free these individuals, but even harder to sell their release to the public, especially outraged victims groups and the politicians who cynically champion them.

And one of the thorniest issues is determining who is indeed an organic member of the insurgency. Some insurgent groups keep records and rolls. But most do not. And even those who do are often afraid to share those roles with their government counterparts, even during the peace process. Should the peace process break down and hostilities resume or even threaten to resume, the fear is that government hitmen could decimate the movement's ranks. But having a general amnesty remains a *sine qua non* of any peace process.

In the case of Aceh, the Indonesian government granted full amnesty to all GAM members and combatants and pledged to release all detainees and political prisoners within fifteen days of the signing of the agreement. In a handful of disputed cases, the government did try to argue that the individuals in question were common criminals and not part of GAM's chain of command, hence ineligible for release. All of these disputed cases were handed over to the international Aceh Monitoring Mission for resolution. Yet any further use of weapons by GAM members or crime, such as extortion, after the MoU was signed was ineligible for the general amnesty. They were very clear that the amnesty could not be abused in any way that would jeopardize the fragile law-and-order situation, especially while the autonomous government and their local police force were being stood up. The government pledged to restore all citizenship rights and privileges to GAM members, including those living in exile. But one of the real stumbling blocks in the amnesty program was the fact that GAM was highly reluctant to turn over its membership rolls to the government for fear that intelligence agents who remained within Aceh would begin a campaign of liquidation so that GAM would be unable to pick up arms ever again should the peace process fail.

In the Philippines, the situation has been more complex. Nowhere in the agreements does it spell out that any MILF combatant had to be released from prison or that there would be a general amnesty, but it was an unstated agreement, part of the decommissioning annex. The problem is that the MILF combatants held by government forces were almost always linked to bombings or other criminal acts, such as kidnapping, and charged in the criminal courts. The situation in the Philippines was further complicated following the January 2015 Mamasapano incident, when Philippine prosecutors under intense political pressure charged over one hundred MILF and BIFF members with murder and issued warrants for their arrest. Though politicians demanded that the MILF turn over these individuals, the MILF has steadfastly refused, in the hopes that the charges will be dropped should the peace process regain momentum. Many politicians have demanded that the suspects be turned in as a precondition to resume congressional deliberation on the BBL.

Thailand is an extremely frustrating case, as it so effectively used general amnesties in the defeat of not only prior iterations of southern insurgents but also with the Thai Communist Party. Yet since 2004, the army has steadfastly resisted any general amnesties. The few amnesties that have been proposed have been highly qualified and applicable to people with no outstanding warrants or criminal charges. And most insurgent suspects are charged under both national security statutes and the criminal code. Few insurgents will ever trust the government's offer, especially because the government's use of extrajudicial killings has increased so much. The military has wholeheartedly bought into the post-9/11 narrative employed by security forces around the world that these are terrorists without any legitimate political grievances. Many civilian politicians and administrators have raised the concern that the current legal strategy of keeping people locked up on multiple charges, in both security and criminal courts as well as legal jeopardy, has only fueled the insurgency. In every round of peace talks, the insurgents have made the release of insurgent suspects a key demand or precondition. The government has steadfastly refused, cognizant that the army will never support it. And if the insurgents cannot secure the release of their comrades at the very least, then what's the point of sitting down for a more comprehensive peace process?

11. INTERNATIONAL SUPPORT IS KEY, BUT IT SHOULD NOT BE OVERWHELMING

A successful peace process requires an adequate degree of international support, including postconflict rehabilitation and development. The role of the international community is immense: it can serve as facilitators, host back-channel meetings, deploy peacekeepers or monitors, engage in training, and coordinate postconflict aid and human capital development. External partners can turn off the supply of arms, funding, and diplomatic support, or they can compel or encourage clients to the negotiating table. Most importantly, the presence of the international community is a type of guarantor that makes reneging, backsliding, and other violations more costly. This is particularly true for insurgents.

At one extreme we can point to East Timor, which could not have become independent without the active involvement of the international community. From a UN-led referendum to ASEAN and Australian peacekeepers and a surge in international donors and UN administrators, the international community played a major role at every stage of the process from 1998 to 2000. But this was and should be the exception and not the rule. Likewise, the civil war in Cambodia could not have been resolved without the massive involvement of UNTAC, a massive operation that included peacekeepers, civil administrators, election monitors, development personnel, and people involved in a host of refugee resettlement, at a two-billion-dollar price tag.

But we should not overstate the power and influence of external actors. A peace process can be facilitated or supported by the international community. The process, however, cannot be imposed, no matter how much leverage, political, financial, or economic, the international community might wield over its clients. No external actor was able to compel the Indonesian, Philippine, or Thai government to the table, nor their respective insurgents, none of which had significant enough state sponsorship.

States, especially in the developing world, are enormously insecure and guarded of their sovereignty. Relatively newly independent, they fear any challenge to their sovereignty at the hands of the international community.

But after years of conflict and mistrust, even a small presence of neutral outsiders with a limited mandate can do a lot to instill a degree of confidence and raise the costs of cheating.

In the case of Indonesia, the government was enormously reluctant to give any outside party, whether a state or an NGO, a role in the Acehnese peace process. For one thing, it did not want to allow any outsiders to see what was happening on the ground, especially the military's egregious human rights abuses. Foreign journalists and NGO workers did not get access to the province until the December 2004 tsunami. The government only began to allow the HDC limited access in 2004. But the reality is that even with the tsunami, which served as a catalyst, neither the government nor the insurgents would have attempted a peace process without the active role of former Finnish president Ahtisaari. His good offices were absolutely instrumental in bringing the parties together and hammering out the MoU. After the MoU was signed, the EU funded the Aceh Monitoring Mission (AMM), which oversaw the implementation of the agreement, demobilization of combatants, surrender of weapons, and release of all political prisoners but also served as an arbiter, a dispute resolution mechanism whose decisions were binding on all the parties. The AMM had a very short mandate, indeed, too short, and even despite Indonesian misgivings about a violation of its sovereignty, the AMM realized that the peace process was too fragile and that it needed to be renewed. I think its mandate was still far too short and could have been renewed. But overall, the AMM was nothing short of a success. And, of course, the post-tsunami relief efforts gave a host of bilateral and multilateral donors a long-term presence within Aceh.

The Philippines was much less guarded of its sovereignty. Unlike Indonesia, which had to fight for its independence, the Philippines negotiated its independence from the United States. It was also due to its history of dealing with the Libyan government and the OIC since the mid-1970s. The MNLF had significant amounts of state sponsorship from Libya, which was also able to use its influence within OPEC to put pressure on the Philippines. With the 1996 accord, Philippine president Fidel Ramos saw no threat to involving Indonesia. Indonesia, as *primus inter pares* within ASEAN, was an important guarantor. It put ASEAN's imprimatur on the agreement, which gave the MNLF further confidence. Ramos was happy to jettison concerns over sovereignty for pragmatic ends. The Philippines was the regional economic laggard, and the war was a drain on national coffers.

President Arroyo, too, was not adverse to the international commune having a role. Obviously the United States, through its counterterrorism efforts, which also included a stepped-up USAID program, was involved. But so too were other international donors, such as Japan, the EU, and multilateral institutions such as the World Bank or the Asian Development Bank. Starting in 2004, the US Institute of Peace was invited in to conduct workshops and explain alternative models of resource sharing, autonomy, and governance that would satisfy the MILF's aspirations. Though these ended, it was not because of the Philippines but because the US ambassador at the time, Kristy Kenny, didn't have any control over the workshops.

The most sensitive international role was played by Malaysia. The Malaysian External Intelligence Organization (MEIO), which reports to the prime minister's office, was the lead facilitator in all of the talks between the government and the MILF. In 2003, Malaysia led the establishment of the International Monitoring Team. Though the IMT was small and at first included only some Malaysians and Bruneians, it would grow to include some

Japanese civilians, Libyans, and Norwegians. It was not large enough to keep peace, but it was large enough to build some confidence to maintain peace when the two sides were trying to make progress in the peace process.

To be fair, the Malaysian role was not without controversy, and in one key way it undermined the peace process. This has to do with the territorial dispute between Malaysia and the Philippines over Sabah. Though the Philippine claim is currently dormant, the MNLF, which is dominated by ethnic Tausigs and is the dominant organization throughout the Sulu archipelago, continues to harbor claims. Indeed, in 2013 followers of the Sultanate of Sulu made a quixotic—some would call it asinine—armed incursion into Sabah. But this played into the MNLF's rivalry with the MILF. As the MILF relied so heavily on the Malaysians for support and mediation and as a guarantor of the peace process, the MNLF could try to accuse it of selling out sovereign claims.

During the peace process, the Asia Foundation played a key role in the talks, serving as a witness, mediator, and scribe. The FAB and CAB established the third-party international monitoring team to oversee implementation of the agreement, while another entity that included foreign representation was established to store the MILF weaponry and put it beyond use.

Thailand has staunchly refused to allow in any third party. The Malaysian government has been allowed a limited role in facilitating talks, but nothing beyond that and certainly not in mediating. The Malaysians could play a more constructive role if given a chance. Quietly and behind the scenes, they have tried to bring the various insurgent factions together. In 2015 they announced the establishment of MARA Pattani, which included the BRN, BIPP, and some factions of PULO.

But successive Thai governments have not allowed anyone in to assist the insurgent groups and provide workshops or training sessions, unlike the cases in Aceh and Mindanao. And it's a shame, because they really need it. At the height of talks in 2013, the insurgents proved to be very provincial and unprofessional.

Should a peace process ever resume in Thailand, some type of third-party monitoring and dispute resolution will be necessary. Without it, the insurgents and the Thai government will never develop trust with each other.

12. THE PEACE PROCESS HAS TO BE PART OF SOMETHING BIGGER

The peace process is unlikely to be successful on its own. It has to be part of a broader political transformation, including the devolution of political and economic powers. For example, in Cambodia, peace wasn't only the end of a Cold War proxy conflict but the end of one-party communist rule. Now

Cambodia remains a one-party-dominated state, yet it has opposition parties and a relatively free press, and the ruling party jettisoned socialist policies in favor of market reforms. Myanmar's ongoing insurgencies with ethnic militias would have had little chance of being resolved under military rule. But the political reforms put in place since 2010, including gradual democratization, space for opposition parties, press liberalization, a constitution that enshrined regional assemblies, and a landslide electoral victory by Aung San Suu Kyi's National League for Democracy make any negotiated settlement far more likely and durable.

In Indonesia, the peace process would not have been possible without the "big bang" decentralization and democratization seen in the seven years since the fall of Suharto's New Order regime. Indonesia had been an overly centralized state, with all political and economic power concentrated in Jakarta. But under Gus Dur, radical decentralization occurred, and at the same time, democracy began to be consolidated. This had two critical impacts. First, it made what the Acehnese were asking for within the realm of the possible; it was now within the political context. But on the other side, it created a national consensus because provinces around the country were also seeking further political, economic, fiscal, and social autonomy. Indonesian legislators, by and large, endorsed the agreement as they were encouraged by the legal precedent. They wanted similar terms. But very simply, had there been no "big bang", no peace process in Aceh would have been possible.

In the Philippines it is less clear cut, as there was no overall political transformation. Democracy had been thoroughly consolidated, and there were no longer fears of democratic reversals. Some critics of the agreement sought political federalism through a constitutional amendment. They argued that it was unconstitutional to give one group or region special rights, privileges, and autonomy. Moreover, federalism would create a national consensus to push the legislation through Congress. Yet proponents of charter change have never garnered sufficient support for their proposal. The fundamental political transformation in my eyes was simply the maturity to reach an agreement that devolved such significant powers. Aquino seemed to have a genuine desire to forge a durable and equitable peace that addressed past wrongs. In a sense, the peace process was part of his quest to enshrine social justice, one of the key platforms of his administration. It is to be seen whether President Duterte will be able and willing to push through his campaign pledge of federalism, but as stated, the MILF is unlikely to accept that alone, without passage of the BBL.

In Thailand, there is not only a lack of political reform or devolution but exactly the opposite. Since the May 2014 coup, the junta has worked to undermine electoral democracy and weaken political parties while strengthening the power of appointed bodies. The junta is increasingly centralizing power, and any thought of political or economic decentralization is far off base. The Thai political system will not undergo a significant overhaul for at least ten years following the imminent passing of the king.[3] It's going to take at least that long for the institution of the monarchy to be weakened. Until that happens, democracy simply cannot withstand two powerful antidemocratic and centralizing forces, the monarchy and the military. Until the monarchy weakens, Thai politics will continue moving backward, becoming more regressive, overly centralized, and less democratic. At the same time, Thai chauvinism is skyrocketing, with the junta's inculcation of twelve core Thai values and slavish obeisance to the monarchy, enforced through the draconian *lèse majesté* provisions (Article 112 of the penal code). In that context, it is impossible for me to see how a lasting peace process that addresses the needs and aspirations of the Malay community could take root.

13. IT'S ABOUT THE PRINCIPLES, BUT THAT DOESN'T MEAN IT'S NOT ALSO ABOUT THE MONEY

No insurgent group will say that its cause is anything about the restoration of lands lost to neocolonialism, the righting of historical wrongs, and the defense of its national identity. For insurgents, great principles are at stake. Insurgents are always indignant when anyone insinuates that they can be bought off with promises of revenue sharing.

However, both the agreements in Aceh and Mindanao were able to gain traction because they had very generous wealth-sharing agreements between the central government and the postconflict region. While most conflicts are never completely about resources or inequitable distributions of wealth, they are often a major contributor to the conflict and one that feeds the narrative of resistance. So a peace process must include mechanisms to allow for greater wealth sharing and/or control over natural resources. This could be in the form of keeping more tax revenue local, receiving larger block grants from the central government, or the collection of rents from subterranean resources, including minerals and hydrocarbons. This is more than what is often described as a "peace dividend."

The regions need a large degree of fiscal and economic autonomy to right the wrongs of internal colonialism that so often fueled the conflict. These civil wars take place in the poorest and most economically marginalized regions of the country, and the insurgents always have a strong sense of internal colonialism, where economic policies have created vast socioeconomic disparities and grievances. In both Aceh and Mindanao, the governments of Indonesia and the Philippines understood this and were exceptionally generous with wealth-sharing provisions. Indeed, that generosity was part of the quid pro quo in getting the insurgents to give up their ultimate demands for independence.

Historically, GAM was always able to capitalize on resentment that 80–90 percent of the natural resource wealth from the province—including from one of ExxonMobil's most profitable fields—went to Jakarta, and only a fraction of that returned through transfer payments to the province. The 2005 MoU gave the autonomous government in Aceh considerable economic autonomy, including the right to set and raise taxes, set its own interest rates, and borrow money, including from abroad. Aceh had the authority over all natural resource (including offshore) exploitation and got to keep 70 percent of revenue from all current and future natural resources. Taxes and revenue shared with the central government will be independently monitored and audited.

The Philippine government, in a way, had a much harder challenge due to its failed implementation of the 1996 accord with the MNLF. The government had a track record of nonimplementation. Despite pledges of fiscal autonomy, the ARMM still remitted over 60 percent of its revenue to the central government and in turn received only 10 percent back through transfer payments.

The MILF is desperate to get its hands on the mineral resources that began coming out of the ground and more importantly from under the seabed. In particular, the MILF had its eyes on several offshore service contracts in the Sulu Sea, near the Malaysian state of Sabah, which all have tested and proven reserves and where drilling was about to begin in 2013. And unlike the Catholic Church or communist New People's Army (NPA), which have both been vociferous in their criticism of mining, the MILF was always eager as long as an equitable wealth-sharing agreement was reached.

In the Revenue Generation and Wealth Sharing Annex (July 14, 2013), the government generously gave the MILF 75 percent of tax revenues and mineral wealth. That includes any potential hydrocarbons. In addition, the two sides concluded a separate agreement, the "Addendum on Bangsamoro Waters," that demarcated the waters that surround the future Bangsamoro territories. In addition, the MILF will receive 100 percent of revenue from surface resources (sand, gravel, etc.). Although the MILF was to relinquish some wealth to the central government, it was supposed to get it back through block grants. The block grants provision of the BBL came under particular scrutiny from Philippine legislators and, at the time of writing, seemed to be in doubt.

In Thailand, no wealth sharing has ever been on the table. The offshore oil fields are codeveloped with Malaysia, and no one has ever proposed that any of the offshore hydrocarbon wealth remain in the Deep South. And under the current regime, not one proposal about local fiscal autonomy, tax revenue, or any other local devolution of economic or development planning has been countenanced. In a sense, the revenue sharing is seen as a type of reparation for a past wrong, and it's that aspect that makes the Thai government so intractable.

14. CIVIL SOCIETY PLAYS AN ESSENTIAL ROLE AND MUST BE DEVELOPED AND ENGAGED

Independent civil society is often weak, especially in conflict zones. Civil organizations are routinely targeted by security forces, which often view them as fronts for the insurgents rather than genuine independent organizations.

But civil society plays a key role in any peace process. Civil society is essential in pushing the warring parties to the table, keeping them honest through investigations and reporting, and mobilizing popular support for the peace process. Women's groups, trade unions, clergy, youth and student organizations, environmental groups, human rights organizations, and the legal establishment or bar association, as well as business groups or chambers of commerce, must be behind the peace process. If a peace process is simply negotiated by political elites without mass buy-in, it will never have traction. The process must have a broad societal buy in, and it is civil society, not the government or substate combatants, that is best able to mobilize popular support before, during, and after the peace process. But most importantly, at its core, an insurgency is about social justice, and the best guarantors and groups committed to expending social justice are noncombatant civil society organizations.

Civil society plays one other critical role. By their nature, insurgencies are violent. And one of the most important things in a peace process is a broad societal rejection of violence as a means to settle disputes. After protracted conflicts, violence is so ingrained in the social fabric that this is arguably the greatest challenge. People have become inured to the violence, while many have no trust in nonviolent mechanisms for dispute resolution. It is the responsibility of civil society to alter the thinking, create moral pressure to sanction offenders, socialize people in nonviolent dispute resolution, and establish effective mechanisms to make that possible.

Insurgencies feed off of zero-sum perceptions and Manichean worldviews. Peace processes moderate those views, but they do not eliminate them. As long as a zero-sum perception pervades the thinking of the combatants as well as society, it prevents the rise of thoughtful deal making and compromise. That is why civil society is so important and must be cultivated for the peace process to be durable.

Indonesian authorities severely curtailed the development of civil society during the New Order era. The fall of Suharto in 1998 opened up space for civil society, with the exception of Aceh, which was still under the control of security forces. The 2004 tsunami and concurrent peace process opened the door for civil society groups to emerge. And while they did play a role in the peace process and rehabilitation, civil society was clearly nascent.

Since the fall of dictator Ferdinand Marcos in the 1986 People Power Revolution, Philippine civil society organizations have played key roles in socioeconomic and political development. It is hard to overstate the role that civil society has played during the entire peace process. The Bishops-Ulamas Conference in Mindanao was an essential organization to bridge the sectarian divide and prevent broader communal violence. It gave religious cover to the peacemakers and served to fill humanitarian needs. Importantly, it served as an important back channel. But most importantly, the respective clergy made sure that people understood that peace was a religious calling. Once the MILF made the decision to seek a negotiated autonomy, it relied on several CSOs. The MILF established the Bangsamoro People's Consultative Assembly to mobilize its constituency and get people on board the peace process. Though its rallies never garnered as many people as it claimed, the BPCA became the MILF's primary nonmilitary instrument. Professor Abhoud Syed Lingga's Institute of Bangsamoro Studies (IBS) was in many ways the MILF's "think tank." Though many in the intelligence services and AFP saw it as part and parcel of the MILF and raided its offices frequently, the IBS had a firewall. What people fail to recognize is how influential Lingga and the IBS were over the MILF's thinking. They were the ones who pushed for an East Timor–style referendum and later designed much of the political framework adopted in the FAB and CAB. The MILF, as an Islamist organization, was not democratic. Those democratic seeds were planted and nurtured by the IBS, which itself went through a fundamental transformation and ideological moderation as the MILF's military fortunes turned. Another critical CSO was Bantay Ceasefire. This was not established to supplant the responsibilities and mission of the CCCH but to independently investigate and verify cease-fire violations. Its reporting was first rate, and it was a model of transparency and inclusivity. Finally, the Institute for Autonomy and Governance at the University of Notre Dame provided needed legal expertise on the peace agreement and the political parameters of autonomy. It ran workshops for the MILF on developing a political party, and it was a tireless advocate for the passage of the Bangsamoro Basic Law. At every step of the way, civil society organizations pushed and prodded their respective governments along.

In southern Thailand, civil society has been greatly restricted, and not just since the 2014 coup. The 2005 Emergency Decree gave authorities significant powers to regulate freedom of association. The south has a number of civil society organizations, including those for students, ex-detainees, women, orphans, and human rights. The Muslim Attorney Centre has played an essential role in preventing the Deep South from becoming a complete black hole in terms of human rights. The MAC has offices across the south that have represented suspected insurgents on a pro bono or subsidized basis. Its leader was disappeared by Thai security forces in 2004. But security forces view the Muslim CSOs as fronts for the insurgents. Though some may have sympathies with insurgents, I've done extensive interviewing with these NGOs and see no formal connection. Indeed, they are often running afoul of the insurgents as they do have to work with the government. And more to the point, the insurgents do not want any CSO to gain political momentum that could serve as a threat to their attempt to consolidate power within the Malay community. Yet security forces regularly harass, detain, or intimidate members of these organizations. Security forces attend NGO events, which has a chilling effect on free speech. As EJKs remain one of the Thai security forces' key tactics, and as their intelligence about the insurgency is so weak, the CSO activists are easy targets. Very prominent NGO activists have been disappeared by security forces in the Deep South, who have failed in terms of their intelligence to identify the insurgent organizations and thus look for low-dangling fruit instead.

15. A THOROUGH AND WELL-FUNDED DISARMAMENT, DEMOBILIZATION, AND REHABILITATION PROGRAM

A core requisite is a well-thought-out and well-funded disarmament, demobilization, and rehabilitation (DDR) program for former combatants. The postconflict zone cannot be awash in both weapons and young men with no livelihoods or career prospects. A portion of—though not all—weapons have to be guarded or put beyond use. This is a highly emotional issue for insurgents, who often went through enormous hurdles to acquire their weaponry, which they see as the manifestation of their struggle and without which they never could have advanced the cause of their population. In regions with endemic crime, which often went hand in hand with or under the cover of insurgency, with weak rule of law, and with a culture of violence, getting people to relinquish their weapons is very difficult. As Mao Zedong quipped, "Power grows out of the barrel of a gun," and in postconflict environments, weapons remain an insurance policy. As mentioned above, conflicts create zero-sum worldviews and cultures that have known only violence as a conflict resolution mechanism.

Something should be in place for the insurgents to return to, that is, job or vocational training, land allocation, livelihood projects, integration into the security forces, or new government jobs. This has to be handled well. Not every former guerrilla will be given a job or be integrated into the security forces, so managing expectations is a serious challenge. The failure to manage expectations with FRETILIN rebels in East Timor led to a mutiny and an attempted coup when the former combatants were not hired as local police. In the Philippines following the 1996 accord, the MNLF demanded that its entire rank and file be integrated into the PNP and AFP, but the government refused. Indeed, after the screening was done, only two thousand were integrated. Many could not pass basic health or fitness tests or were too old.

And another problem with integrations into military forces is that they tend to be exceptionally top heavy. So positions—and usually generalships— are given so that former rebels have a title and status, though often without a portfolio, or men, or a budget. No clearer example of this exists than postconflict Cambodia. In addition to the Cambodian government's already topheavy armed forces, the government bought off officers from three separate insurgent groups, giving them ranks without any real position. Today, the Cambodian military and security forces have some two thousand general officers, which has been highly detrimental to the rule of law and security. They used those titles for predatory behavior, particularly for land grabbing.

So while integration is important, it cannot be top heavy or become a vehicle for predatory behavior.

As most former combatants will not be integrated into the security forces, the peace plan must provide for more effort in helping former insurgents transition back into civilian life. They must see a peace dividend, something more appealing than continued combat or abject criminality. This is an inherently difficult task, not only logistically but also socially. As the World Bank sums up:

> Violent conflict alters the skills that are valued in an economy: during the conflict these skills are related to fighting, but they become irrelevant in the post-conflict economy. Conversely, in the post-conflict environment much needed skills may be in short supply, as often the best-educated and the richest were the first to migrate and escape the conflict.[4]

In Aceh, DDR was sufficient, though not great. GAM pledged to surrender 840 weapons, and after four rounds—and considerable pressure from the third-party monitoring mission—its former guerrillas turned in some 1,080 weapons as well as ammunition and explosives. Many of these were rejected by Indonesian authorities for being too old or out of service, leaving lingering doubts that GAM had fully disarmed. GAM's refusal to turn over all weapons was understandable: progovernment militias were never forced to disarm, and GAM had a lingering mistrust of the security forces. Yet eruptions of violence were very sporadic, concentrated, and low level. Moreover, the former combatants did not cascade significant quantities of weapons to criminal enterprise.

GAM demobilized some three thousand fighters, and many became members of the organic security forces. But as discussed in the case study, one of the greatest failings of the peace process was the mechanism created to financially support the former combatants. While the government pledged to support reintegration of former combatants and either provide farmland or financial assistance to all GAM members, the system for doing so had significant shortcomings. The Aceh Reintegration Board (BRA) was poorly planned and administered. It did not know how to disburse funds for development funds, constantly shifting among community-designated projects, individual applications, and World Bank–led projects.

The government and donor community provided funding to the BRA, but the amount was insufficient, while the fund itself faced issues of corruption and managerial incompetence. The government later broadened the program and allocated some farmland to former detainees and political prisoners as well as civilians who could prove "demonstrable loss" from the war. The two parties established a joint Claims Settlement Commission "for the rehabilitation of public and private property destroyed or damaged as a consequence of the conflict," also administered by the autonomous government.

In Mindanao, the process of DDR has been stalled by the failure of Congress to pass the BBL. The FAB's Annex on Normalization laid out a clear timeline that pegged decommissioning and demobilization to the passage and implementation of the agreement. After the Mamasapano clash, the MILF put fifty-five crew-serviced weapons beyond use and demobilized some 145 combatants. Yet legislators were so incensed by Mamasapano and unconvinced of the MILF's sincerity that they tried to make immediate decommissioning and demobilization a precondition for the passage of the BBL. The MILF refused.

The FAB's Normalization Annex outlined that the weaponry would be put beyond use, not surrendered. The weaponry is under the control of a monitoring team comprising MILF, government monitors, and international monitors and is physically stored in a secured area in an MILF camp, a *modus vivendi* based on the Good Friday Accords in Northern Ireland. The agreement calls for the surrender of some, in particular the heavy, crew-serviced weapons, but not all small arms. This was an issue for the government, as the 1996 accord with the MNLF did not have a formal provision for disarmament, so the weaponry has cascaded down to the Abu Sayyaf, black markets, or other criminal enterprises, contributing to the continued instability across the Sulu Archipelago. Yet total disarmament in such a gun culture was simply unfeasible and a nonstarter with the MILF. I'm not convinced that the MILF leaders thought it was achievable or that they could compel their members to surrender their weapons.

The FAB established the Sajahatra Bangsamoro as a government-funded mechanism to fund rehabilitation of combatants.[5] It also supported the education of the children of MILF members, which seems like a very progressive idea. Like everything else in the Philippines, Sajahatra Bangsamoro was woefully underfunded. But most of all, it became the victim of politics. After the Mamasapano incident, senators attacked its funding, arguing that the block grants were going to support MILF terrorism. Senator Nancy Binay, the daughter of a presidential candidate, as well as senators Ferdinand Marcos Jr. (a vice presidential candidate), Alan Peter Cayetano (a vice presidential candidate), and presidential candidate Grace Poe all called for the ending of block grants to Sajahatra Bangsamoro. Nonetheless, the Sajahatra Bangsamoro Foundation, established to oversee DDR efforts, remains active and has provided assistance to those first-demobilized fighters and their families. At the time of this writing, further demobilization and disarmament have completely ceased.

Thailand has a long history of demobilization and disengagement. As discussed above, in the past, the Thai government effectively used amnesties and offers of land to buy off insurgents, from the Thai Communist Party to the Malay rebels. Right now, such discussion is woefully premature. To date, the government has put nothing on the table to suggest that it is willing to offer anything in return for the surrender of weaponry or demobilization.

16. FROM BULLETS TO BALLOTS

Insurgents must find a way to transform themselves into effective political parties that are capable of governing. This, again, is not an easy task. Retail politics requires a very different skill set from guerrilla warfare. Insurgents have to develop platforms, establish party organizations, mobilize the electorate, appeal to the population without threat of coercion, and compete in an open process. They must reach new constituencies.

They have to accept loss and understand that postconflict governance is not an entitlement but something that they have to earn. That was one of the greatest problems with the MNLF. It acted as if the reins of the ARMM government belonged to it, that governing was an entitlement. And when Nur Misuari proved inept and lost elections to more competent members, he picked up arms two more times.

Most importantly, insurgents have to effectively administer and provide social services, with which they have very little experience. All insurgent groups claim to have shadow governments and provide basic social services, but these are actually quite rudimentary. No group provides the degree of social services that it claims to, as most resources are marshaled into the war effort. Even the Tamil Tigers, who were the most effective, still relied on the government to provide electricity and other utilities in their "liberated zone."

But more than developing a political organization and administrative capabilities, former insurgents have to change their leadership styles. Insurgencies are not as top down or disciplined as the government militaries that they aspire to, yet they are disciplined enough to have command mentalities. They are not democratic, they are not used to compromise, and they are not given to building up popular support or mobilizing the community over low political issues.

Insurgents are romantics and often poorly suited for the task of day-to-day administration. Yet most guerrilla leaders see themselves as the inheritors of political power born of their military leadership. In only a few cases have insurgent leaders stepped aside and handed over power to technocrats and administrators who did not struggle in the *maquis*—or "underground."

GAM managed the political transition fairly well, but not without significant issues arising. GAM has always been beset by intragroup rivalry as to who would become its political leader, in particular, rivalry between the old, exiled leadership and younger, more dynamic candidates. But then again, that's what democracy is about. On the one hand, GAM, and later Partai Aceh, which it morphed into in May 2008, has dominated politics in the province. But intraorganizational rivalry has been compounded by contested provisions within the LoGA, which banned independent candidates. The Supreme Court ruled this unconstitutional, but the provincial legislature saw this as a usurpation of its sovereignty, and Partai Aceh threatened to boycott the elections in 2012. This issue has not completely worked itself out. But there has been one orderly transition of power from an independent—though former—GAM commander to the formal, GAM-linked Partai Aceh. The next gubernatorial election is scheduled for 2017. More importantly, political violence has been at quite low levels, and at the same time GAM and the five other local political parties have made a general commitment to the democratic process. GAM continues to dominate politics because of its more effective network throughout the countryside coupled with its decades of experience in mass mobilization, as well as a public perception that it is the most likely to safeguard the autonomy gained in the Helsinki process. It faces plenty of challenges, not least of all poor administrative capacity, but GAM has transformed itself from an armed insurgency into a functioning political party.

The MILF began to transform itself into a political party in mid-2014. It legally established the Unified Bangsamoro Justice Party (UBJP) and was in the process of setting up a network of party chapters and leadership when the Mamasapano incident occurred. Since the peace process has been put on hold, the UBJP has continued to do some party-building exercises, though at a much less robust rate than in 2014. Though the UBJP pledges to be open to anyone, all MILF members will automatically be considered party members, and top MILF members will assume party leadership positions. The UBJP still has a long way to go. It still has not defined a core party platform or policy agenda, and with the stalled peace process, it is hard to imagine the party taking the steps to develop these without the passage of the BBL in sight.

Malay civil society activists in southern Thailand are frustrated with the insurgency's undeveloped political arm. There is broad concern that other than engaging in violence, the insurgents really had no political program or infrastructure, let alone any media or outreach arm. Though the BRN has a "political wing," most of its work is considering the implications of a particular hit or attack, that is, its political wing is tactical, not thinking in terms of long-term political strategy. There is a strange disconnect between the insurgents and community. Many in the CSO community see themselves as being part of a nascent political movement that would ultimately include the insurgents, meaning the insurgents would be joining them, not the other way around. As one CSO leader told me, "There is a need for force. It is not the main tool. It is just part of the equation. I believe the BRN have in their mind a plan to establish a political wing. But they do not know how to bring it into the public space. I can sense that. They are poking their head up a bit, testing the waters, but to surface as a recognizable political entity, we have not seen that yet." And many sought to remind the insurgents that at the end of the day, war is politics by other means: they need a political strategy, and they need a political exit plan: "What we do is remind the combatants that an exit strategy exists. If they want to exit out from violence they can do so through us." Yet the insurgency was fearful of losing control of the movement. But at the same time, the state tends to view the Muslim CSOs as fronts for the insurgents. So any movement toward developing a legal political body to articulate the interests of the Malay is constrained from both sides.

17. IN A PEACE PROCESS? BETTER CALL SAUL!

Insurgents need to have good independent and external counsel. While they may have proved themselves adept (or at least sufficiently adequate) guerrillas, complex legal negotiations are a completely different skill set. Throughout the protracted peace process, they are facing off with skilled negotiators and legal teams with years of training and practice. Governments do not send their B teams to these negotiations. They have teams of technical experts and legal counsel on issues ranging from mineral rights to the constitution, transitional justice, DDR, amnesties, and tax collection. No rebel group can come close to matching that experience. It needs expert advice on the law and other technical issues. The rebels may reject the constitution in principle, but the reality is that a peace process has to be bound by the constitutional order, which insurgents will likely know very little about.

Moreover, having spent years in the jungle, they are insular and secretive by nature. They need to trust their legal advisers and outside counsel, which is simply not in their DNA. Sometimes they need advice on global politics or simply what type of assistance or support they can call on from key states. It takes a long time for that trust and rapport to develop.

And governments, if they are serious about the durability of a peace process, should encourage rebel groups to seek outside counsel and not interfere with that process. Significant costs can accrue to the government and the peace process if the rebels are not adequately represented with both legal and political counsel.

GAM's team included not only external legal advisers but also included Australian academic and Indonesia specialist Edward Aspinall, who provided significant counsel on the scope of Indonesia's political reforms and the parameters for concessions within the current political context and climate.

The MILF had a team of external legal advisers and negotiators. They were all Muslim with deep ties to the community. One, Musib Buat, was a former MNLF combatant. Datu Michael Mastura, the MILF's top adviser, comes from one of the most influential clans in the south, and as a former congressman, he knew the Philippine political and legal system. In addition to the legal advisers, the negotiating team included outsiders who provided some expertise on political systems and models that could be used to enhance political and economic autonomy. The MILF relied on foreign NGOs and technical experts to provide models, frameworks, and other tools that they employed in negotiations.

In Thailand, what we saw in the four rounds of talks in 2013 was that the insurgents were highly insular and unsophisticated. Clearly they were not all on the same page, which added to the disarray. But their maximalist demands were out of touch with the Thai political situation, and they had no legal expertise. Their demands were broad, general, and constantly changing.

18. A FORMAL MECHANISM, NOT AN AD HOC OR INFORMAL PROCESS

While this might sound like a truism, it is very important that the peace process have a strong sense of formality, legality, and finality. In part this is because the state needs to make the insurgents feel like they are equal partners. Of course, it is an asymmetric relationship, but the agreement is based on the principle of sovereign equality. Insurgents have to be able to prove to their constituents that they—and in turn the community—are respected. Any government that thinks it can simply cut side deals or buy off some of the insurgent leaders without making meaningful concessions or addressing core grievances and forging a durable political peace process is sowing the seeds of future conflicts. But in a region that is plagued with endemic corruption, especially within the security forces, the sense is that anyone or anything has a price and can be bought off. At best, that is a very short-term fix that will not end the conflict. And simply quelling the violence is not enough. The absence of war is not peace.

In Aceh, the Helsinki Accord process was overseen by third parties, including the Finnish government, the EU, and ASEAN. Not only was it a formal, public, and legally binding peace process, it had the international community's imprimatur. That said, the Helsinki MoU is still a very vague document that left much to be interpreted during the implementation stage.

In the case of the MILF, the enormous concern was that the 1996 accord with the MNLF, though a formal process brokered by Libya, was built on a foundation of side payments, on backroom deals with the corrupt MNLF leadership. The 1996 accord was very vague, which made the metrics of implementation harder to judge. The MILF wanted a precise and detailed agreement that it could hold the government to; it wanted nothing left to interpretation. And its negotiators were irate when the government would go back and revisit or renegotiate terms that had already been agreed to. This was even worse following the Mamasapano incident, when Congress called for scrapping key provisions of the BBL, which violated the provisions of the FAB and CAB, and in any event, the BBL had already been negotiated. The agreement has to be inviolable.

In Thailand, the insurgency died out in the 1990s after a series of informal negotiations with liberal amnesty policies and the offer of land and other benefits. But there was never a formal peace process, and the government failed to address core grievances. The hard-liners in the BRN simply went underground until they were ready to restart the insurgency and were joined by other groups who may have been bought off in the past but who had become frustrated with the government's abusive and racist policies and its continued unwillingness to address the concerns of the Malay community. The informal process bought a period of peace, but it did not end the conflict. Indeed, the current iteration of the conflict is far more violent than it ever was in the past, both quantitatively and qualitatively.

19. IT AIN'T OVER 'TIL THE LEGISLATURE SAYS IT'S OVER

The best and most equitable agreements can be negotiated, but they have to be ratified by legislatures, which must also pass implementing legislation. It's more than simply a ratification process whereby the legislature transforms a treaty into national law. The implementing legislation takes a vague peace agreement (Aceh) or even a very detailed agreement (Mindanao) and ensures that it lines up and becomes integrated with existing national legislation and the constitution on everything from taxes to health care, civil service rules, policing, environmental protections, and voting. This is truly the weak link in any peace process because at this point there are hundreds, if not thousands, of provisions that can start to dilute the peace agreement negotiated between executives.

Understanding the role of the legislature is key. Once a deal is reached between the negotiating teams representing the country's executive branch and the insurgent movement, all parties might make a dangerous assumption about the prospects for peace.

Legislatures invariably water down peace agreements that they see as affecting their purview and power or as setting dangerous precedents in other parts of the country. Some members will support the peace process. Many will not. Most will be somewhere in the middle, swayed by political expediency: whether future vote trading is possible, whether support for the agreement impacts their own chances at reelection, or whether a stance, one way or another, can be exploited for political gain or as a springboard to higher office.

What I have found is that a legislator may be in favor of the peace process in general, agnostic on the implementing legislation on the whole, but very concerned due to personal interest, the oversight committee he or she sits on, or key constituent interest on a certain issue. Legislators might push for a small change in the implementing legislation, but when this happens several hundred times, the effects are cumulative, and the implementing legislation looks very different from what had been originally agreed to.

The legislature cannot be expected to work for the common good but instead will be pulled as many ways as there are legislators. Invariably, a lot of political grandstanding and self-interest will be on display.

This is a very hard concept for rebels to grasp, as the leaders who negotiate for them and/or sign off on the agreements don't have large and disparate legislatures to contend with. That they are even at that stage in the peace process does suggest that they already have broad consensus within the movement.

The executive branch of the government must work assiduously to build up a solid coalition in parliament and be willing to use all political capital and cudgels at its disposal to prevent the peace process from being watered down to the point where dissatisfaction is sufficient enough that the rebels quit the peace process *en masse* or *in toto*. The greatest threat to a peace process invariably comes from politicians. Once the agreement is signed, it becomes a political tussle that is very hard for the government to control.

In Aceh, the parliament did pass the implementing legislation, the Law on the Governance of Aceh (LoGA), in July 2006, but that was four months after the deadline set in the MoU—and after several contentious redrafts. The LoGA was an enormously complex piece of legislation that encompassed almost all quarters of government and public policy. And, as such, it meant that a huge number of stakeholders and vested interests within the government and parliament tried to influence the LoGA at every stage. While the Helsinki MoU was very vague, the LoGA was overly detailed. The irony is that the minutiae that the law went into in order to reconcile it with national laws actually undermined Acehnese autonomy and the promises of the four principles negotiated in the Helsinki MoU. While the peace process has been a success, it has not been an unqualified one. In many places, Jakarta has been able to chip away at the province's autonomy, largely because of the way the implementing legislation was drafted to reconcile the vague principles with domestic law.

But SBY, the first directly elected president, enjoyed popular legitimacy, while his vice president was the head of Golkar, the largest single party in parliament, which held 128 of 545 seat (24.5 percent). The president's Democrat Party held a mere fifty-seven seats (10.5 percent), so together they easily commanded over one-third of parliament. And while they were able to easily cobble together enough votes from other parties to pass the LoGA, they did so not without important concessions that further watered down the bill.

In the Philippines, the situation is even worse following Mamasapano. While the agreement had broad-based support within Congress when President Aquino submitted the implementing legislation in September 2014, and although the president himself was enjoying high levels of public satisfaction that he hoped to wield in the passage of the bill, that vanished in January 2015. Congress has significantly watered down key provisions of the BBL, which itself had already been significantly weakened by the president's office. Senator Marcos submitted an alternative bill altogether, one that diminished the autonomy provisions even more. Caught up in an election year, the Philippine Congress stalled on a vote for the BBL. While there remains broad public support for a peace process, in principle, few congressmen or senators saw any political price for delaying the vote. The peace process has become a total hostage to national politics. And it is yet to be seen whether President Duterte will push for passage of the BBL through Congress. He may calculate that he needs that political capital to push through a constitutional amendment on federalism, which is his signature political issue.

20. A FORMAL PROCESS TO RESOLVE POSTAGREEMENT DISPUTES OVER IMPLEMENTATION

Any good law professor will tell you that a contract is a living document. You might think that the peace agreement is signed and ratified, but the implementation stage will always have problems, both sins of omission and sins of commission. What works on paper may be very difficult to implement on the ground. The capabilities of states and insurgent groups to actually deliver and implement agreements can vastly differ. And political will, once the champagne glasses have been put away, has a habit of dissipating.

So a key component of a successful peace process is some sort of redress mechanism. If disputes arise, whether they be questions of interpretation, noncompliance, or nonimplementation, some legitimate body must be able to investigate and redress the dispute before the situation devolves and former combatants quit the peace process.

Having an external third party in control is the most helpful mechanism in cases of such disputes, for three reasons. First, it is more likely to be trusted as a neutral arbiter. Second, either party can pin the blame for having to do something or make a concession on outsiders. It takes off some of the political heat coming from their constituents. Third, an external arbiter usually has some way—diplomatic or otherwise—to exact a sanction for noncompliance.

In the Helsinki MoU, it was the international Aceh Monitoring Mission that had authority to adjudicate disputes and interpret the agreement. Section 4 of the MoU was very clear: until its mandate expired, the AMM had the authority to "investigate and rule on complaints and alleged violations of the MoU." No new mechanism or panel was necessary. But a weakness of the agreement was that it did not include any form of dispute resolution process following the expiration of its mandate. Fortunately, no dispute has unwoven the peace process, though there have been a few crises that came close.

In the Philippines, the MILF has tried to learn from the mistakes of the MNLF. When the government failed to implement key components of the agreement, the MNLF had no recourse. It lobbied the OIC but never received satisfaction. It pushed for "tripartite talks" with the OIC and the government, but the government postposed them for years and then was noncommittal. The MILF has not had a postconflict adjudication mechanism as part of its peace process, but it has relied on the Third-Party Monitoring Team as a sort of body to help work through differences of interpretation and disputes over implementation. It is to be seen what will happen when or if the BBL is ever passed and the agreement can be implemented.

NOTES

1. Office of the Presidential Adviser on the Peace Process, "Terms of Reference for Sajahatra Bangsamoro," April 11, 2013, http://www.opapp.gov.ph/resources/terms-reference-sajahatra-bangsamoro .

2. "Jokowi Rules Out Apology to Defunct Communist Party for 1965," *Jakarta Globe*, June 27, 2016, http://jakartaglobe.beritasatu.com/news/jokowi-rules-apology-defunct-communist-party-1965/ .

3. Llewellyn McCann, "Political Implications of Thailand's Royal Succession," *New Mandala*, July 23, 2015, http://asiapacific.anu.edu.au/newmandala/2015/07/23/political-implications-of-thailands-royal-succession/ .

4. World Bank, *Aceh Growth Diagnostic* (Washington, DC: World Bank, 2009), 18–23.

    5. Leila B. Salaverria, "Nancy Binay Seeks Probe of Aquino Dole-Out to MILF," *Philippine Daily Inquirer*, March 31, 2015, http://newsinfo.inquirer.net/682619/nancy-binay-seeks-probe-of-welfare-program-limited-to-milf .

Index

About the Author

Dr. Zachary Abuza is a professor at the National War College in Washington, DC, where he focuses on Southeast Asian politics and security issues, including governance, insurgencies, democratization and human rights, and maritime security.

He is the author of four books, including *Conspiracy of Silence: The Insurgency in Southern Thailand* (2008), *Political Islam and Violence in Indonesia* (2006), *Militant Islam in Southeast Asia* (2003), and *Renovating Politics in Contemporary Vietnam* (2001). He authored the Southeast Asian chapter in the acclaimed study *Leaving Terrorism Behind*. In addition, he has authored four monographs on security issues in Southeast Asia and has recently completed a major survey on the media and civil society in Vietnam for the National Endowment for Democracy. He is currently completing projects for the National Defense University's Project in Irregular Warfare, the Naval Postgraduate School, and the University of St. Andrews.

Dr. Abuza has lectured at the Foreign Service Institute, the Joint Special Operations University, and other government entities. He has consulted widely to the US government and corporations with interests in Southeast Asia. He has twice served as a congressional witness. In 2004–2005, he was a Senior Fellow at the US Institute of Peace and a recipient of a Fulbright Fellowship.

He received his BA from Trinity College (1991) and MALD (1994) and PhD (1998) from the Fletcher School of Law and Diplomacy, Tufts University. He is a frequent commentator in the press and has lived and traveled extensively throughout the region.